**Indochina
in Conflict**

CHINA

NORTH VIETNAM

DIEN BIEN PHU

HANOI

MUONG SAI

PAK BENG

LUANG PRABANG

MUONG SOUI

LAOS

MEKONG RIVER

VIENTIANE

VINH

OIL PIPE-LINES

MU GIA PASS

HO CHI MINH TRAIL

NORTH VIETNAMESE TROOP STRENGTH:
CAMBODIA: 50,000 – 55,000
LAOS: 70,000
SOUTH VIETNAM: 100,000

■ COMMUNIST CONTROLLED AREAS

■ MAJOR COMMUNIST MILITARY UNIT HEADQUARTERS

◎ MAJOR SUPPLY BASE AREAS

DMZ

KHE SANH

HUE

A SHAU

TCHEPONE

SAVANNAKHET

THAILAND

0   50   100
MILES

SARAVANE

ATTOPEU

KONTUM

BINH DINH

CENTRAL HIGHLANDS

BANGKOK

NORTH VIETNAMESE HEADQUARTERS

CAMBODIA

OLD LINE KHMER ROUGE

SIEM REAP

PHUM ROVIENG

BATTAMBANG

KOMPONG THOM

KRATIE

SOUTH

VIETNAM

5,000 TO 10,000 ARMED KHMER ROUGE

KOMPONG CHAM

PHNOM PENH

WAR ZONE C

ELEPHANT MOUNTAINS

ANGTASSOM

TAKEO

SEVEN MTS.

KOMPONG SOM (SIHANOUKVILLE)

PLAIN OF REEDS

TAY NINH

PARROT'S BEAK

SAIGON

WAR ZONE D

U MINH FOREST

SOUTH CHINA SEA

INDOCHINA IN CONFLICT

CUCL

Indochina in Conflict

A Political Assessment

Joseph J. Zasloff
University of Pittsburgh

Allan E. Goodman
Clark University

Lexington Books
D.C. Heath and Company
Lexington, Massachusetts
Toronto   London

For Tela and Collette

Table of Contents

Introduction

Joseph J. Zasloff and Allan Goodman

The conflict in Indochina has assumed immense proportions. More than 1.5 million combat casualties have been estimated for both sides (of which 60 percent were fatalities) and the number of civilian casualties has probably been even larger. At least a third of the population of Indochina have been refugees. On the United States side, from 1965 to 1971, the estimated cost of the war to each American reached $1,000. United States involvement in the war, it is now widely believed, has been a disaster. In view of the costs, the complexity of the war, and the inadequacy of former policy assumptions, fresh analyses are clearly required.

This book examines, within an Indochina context, the politics of the current conflict. Three themes are pursued: the Communist challenge to the incumbent regimes; the character of these regimes; and the international dimensions of the conflict. The following introductory discussion of these themes draws heavily upon the contributions in the book.

The Communist Challenge

The Communist challenge in Indochina is represented first and foremost by North Vietnam. Most of the current leaders in Hanoi served in the ranks of the Indochinese Communist Party of the 1930s and then in the Viet Minh movement which succeeded in expelling the French from Indochina. As skilled political leaders and organizational craftsmen, they also worked at building Communist-dominated nationalist movements in Laos and Cambodia.

* Having achieved power in North Vietnam in 1954, the Viet Minh leaders committed themselves to the twin goals of establishing socialism in the North and liberating the South. In pursuing these goals, the North Vietnamese have shown impressive strengths. They developed a cohesive leadership early in their struggle against the French, and, following the death of Ho Chi Minh in 1969, power was transferred to successors without apparent cleavages or major alterations of policy. The leaders have adapted their Marxist-Leninist ideology to the conditions of Vietnam and have found their theories to be both a useful guide to policy and a source of confidence in their ultimate victory. They have created a Party which recruits and inculcates a revolutionary spirit in new cadres, and serves as the primary instrument of rule, mobilizing the population in what seems an unending war and simultaneous reconstruction effort. They have developed an Army which has fought courageously against formidable odds, sustaining effective morale throughout.

ix

With partition in 1954, most Southern Viet Minh military personnel, an estimated 90,000, were regrouped to the North, but many political cadres stayed behind. The style of rule employed by Diem in consolidating his power and social conditions in South Vietnam created widespread discontent among many groups besides former Viet Minh. A new Communist insurgent organization was created in this revolutionary environment made up principally, at the outset, of the Viet Minh "stay-behinds" who had been special targets of Diem's repression. Hanoi's 1959 decision to launch a full-scale insurgency in South Vietnam was the Communists' response to Diem. Southern regroupees were sent from the North to help build the insurgent organization and new elements were recruited in the South, particularly from among discontented elements of the peasantry.

The insurgents grew in strength as the Diem government weakened. In the latter part of 1964, the Communists sensed that victory was near and sent ethnic Northerners to the South to reinforce the insurgent organization, probably in the expectation of achieving a "general uprising," the final stage of the rebellion, in 1965. Rather than provoke the collapse of the Saigon regime, however, they were confronted by massive United States escalation. The consequences of the United States intervention are well known: The American troop commitment rose to more than one-half million; air bombardment of the North was launched on a regular basis and bombing in the South was increased; allied troops from Korea, Australia, New Zealand and Thailand joined the hostilities; and a major conventional war was begun.

The Communists have had an especially difficult task in South Vietnam since 1965. In addition to their formidable foreign adversaries, they faced a strengthened and well-armed Vietnamese foe, whose men in arms grew to more than a million. The attempt at launching a general uprising and offensive via the Tet attack of 1968, although a severe psychological blow to the American war effort, was also costly to the Communists. Heavy losses were suffered, and the devastation of the attacks led to an aggressive GVN response. Communist recruits have been more difficult to acquire in the South, and supplies from the local population have been less accessible. As the struggle to maintain their own organization in the South increased with added pressure from their adversaries, the Southern Communists drew increasingly upon ethnic Northern soldiers, and even political cadres. Thus the insurgent organization whose personnel had been largely from the South at the beginning has increasingly been dominated by Northerners.

The Lao Communists have developed in the past two decades into a counter-government with attributes resembling those of their North Vietnamese mentors. Like the North Vietnamese, they possess a cohesive leadership that has served together without apparent major cleavages since their beginning years in the 1950s. They have embraced a Marxist-Leninist ideology which provides the basis for their revolutionary doctrine. The growth and function of their party represents an unusual achievement within the Lao context, and their popular associations and administrative organs show signs of durability not matched by their non-Communist opponents. Joined with their more powerful North Vietnamese allies, the Lao Communists have extended their control to about two-thirds of the land area and more than one-third of the population, and represent a fundamental challenge to the non-Communist regime in Vientiane.

The most powerful participants in the Lao conflict, however, have been—and seem likely to remain—external nations. On the Communist side, the North Vietnamese have played a predominant role, while the United States contribution to the non-Communists has been massive. The United States has conducted bombing campaigns in Laos since 1964, although this was unacknowledged until 1969. Major assistance has been provided to the Royal Lao Army, and additional support administered by CIA personnel has been invested in a special military force led by General Vang Pao and consisting of some 30,000 highlanders. In 1971, a force of 4,200 Thai soldiers, paid for by United States funds, was introduced into combat in Laos, according to the Senate Committee on Foreign Relations. Perhaps even more than in the case of its neighbors in Indochina, the future of the conflict in Laos will depend upon the actions of outside powers.

In Cambodia the indigenous Communist movement is considerably weaker than its counterparts in South Vietnam and Laos. Viet Minh attempts to build a Communist-led nationalist movement prior to 1954 met with only modest success. The Viet Minh effort in Cambodia was not as active as in either Vietnam or Laos, largely for reasons of military strategy. Moreover, Prince Sihanouk served both as a nationalist and traditional symbol, and provided stable, popular leadership, which neither the Communists nor other opposition elements could successfully challenge until recent years. During the past four years, discontent with Sihanouk's rule had been growing among elements of the elite, but the Communists had still made little advance until his overthrow.

Following the ouster of Sihanouk, the Vietnamese Communists faced severe difficulties from the new Lon Nol government. Supplies coming through the port of Sihanoukville that were important to their war effort in South Vietnam were threatened and their sanctuary adjacent to South Vietnam was endangered by the new government's willingness to have South Vietnam and the United States move against their forces. Thus, the Vietnamese Communists began a vigorous effort of harassment against the government in Phnom Penh. Further, they have been building a Communist-led Cambodian counter-government and using it as the public agent of their military campaign. As in Laos, most observers agree that the Vietnamese Communists, if they wished to invest sufficient military effort, could probably take any objective, including the capital. However, there is doubt that the Vietnamese would see their interests served by such an overt seizure in the near future.

The Non-Communist Regimes

The incumbent regimes of South Vietnam, Laos and Cambodia are based less upon political movements than upon uncertain alliances of elites. In sharp contrast to the regime in North Vietnam, the non-Communist governments of Indochina have been plagued by elite fragmentation and the alienation of social and political forces. Fundamentally, these regimes lack both the power to govern effectively and the institutional base to mobilize the population to support their administrations.

For the better part of the last decade, non-Communist governments in South Vietnam have found themselves at odds with Buddhists and students in the cities and ethnic and religious groups in the countryside. Cliques of military officers have displaced each other in rapid succession. The establishment of a constitutional republic in 1967 had little effect upon military domination of the political process. Both opposition movements and pro-government organizations have remained weak and peripheral to the process of government. Ironically for the South Vietnamese regimes, "Indochina in conflict" has meant conflict among non-Communist elements almost as much as between non-Communists and Communists.

The current Thieu government in South Vietnam, by means of a divide-and-rule policy, has achieved a dominant position over the conflicting elites and political forces stimulated to seek power during a decade of internal war and economic change. Though its tenure in office since 1967 lends a certain image of stability, the Thieu regime has not developed effective political institutions and its ability to compete successfully with the Communists, without massive United States support, is still in doubt.

Laos has similar, perhaps more severe, problems. While Souvanna Phouma's uninterrupted tenure as Prime Minister since 1962 gives an impression of government stability, the aging premier presides precariously over constantly feuding civilian and military elites. No permanent political institutions have been developed (in contrast with their PL competitor's achievement) to mobilize and sustain popular energies in support of the regime. Little has been achieved in the task of integrating the lowland Lao peasantry, divided along regional lines, and the varieties of hill tribes, ethnically diverse, into a national political and economic system. There is equal, perhaps more, doubt than in the case of South Vietnam about a non-Communist regime's ability to survive United States withdrawal from Indochina.

Cambodia suffers from many of the same frailties. The overthrow of Prince Sihanouk, whose long tenure also gave the appearance of government stability, laid bare divisions within the elite, as well as the lack of effective institutions of government and politics. While it may have stimulated nationalism and mobilized untapped popular emotions, the relatively recent introduction of war into Cambodia is likely to increase discontent and fractiousness, both among the elites and the masses. Unlike the Vientiane and Saigon regimes, the incumbent leaders in Phnom Penh do not face a strong Cambodian Communist movement, but the Vietnamese Communist threat in their country is substantial, and the availability of Prince Sihanouk to lead an alternative government makes their position more precarious. Withdrawal of United States economic, logistic and air support, and a diminution of South Vietnam's military role in Cambodia, especially if the North Vietnamese were to increase their pressure, would leave the survival of a non-Communist regime in serious doubt.

Each of the regimes analyzed here, however, has increased in scope and function over the past decade. In South Vietnam, government expenditures as a percent of GNP, for example, increased from 18% in South Vietnam in 1960 to more than 33% by 1969. Increases, although on a much smaller scale, are also estimated for Laos and Cambodia. The military establishments in each of these countries have more than tripled over the decade, as have their civil services.

While the above changes have been notable in all three countries, Laos and Cambodia still remain relatively underdeveloped when compared to South Vietnam. Here there has been an enormous increase in roads, airports and harbors; communications have been rapidly expanded; vehicles used not only in the military effort, but in economic activities, have increased substantially. The numbers of Vietnamese living in cities over 20,000 have increased from 15% in 1960 to 55% in 1970. In short, South Vietnam has undergone rapid change in the past decade. While the political cohesion of non-Communist forces does not appear to have increased greatly, some analysts argue that these changes have been fundamentally a modernization process for South Vietnam which makes it much more difficult for the Communists to seize power, short of invasion by the North. While a small, cohesive and therefore powerful Communist minority under the guidance of the North Vietnamese may be able to operate successfully in Laos and Cambodia, the argument goes, time may have passed them by in Vietnam. Modernization has created a set of conditions, particularly a public mood, in which Communists have little appeal to the bulk of the population. Even though the masses may be unenthusiastic about the non-Communist regimes under which they live, new social conditions such as the pull of the market place, have made the Communist alternative appear inappropriate. Proponents of this point of view do not believe the Communist threat will therefore disappear. Rather, they recognize that the Communist cohesion, strength of will, and organization will make likely a persistent conflict.

International Dimensions and Future Prospects

The drama of internal change and reform for the non-Communist regimes of Indochina is taking place against the backdrop of the conflict between the United States and North Vietnam. What Hanoi's Indochina strategy is designed to achieve, United States policy has been designed to prevent.

DRV aims have been constant for some four decades. The leaders in Hanoi have been committed to liberating Indochina from imperialism, first of the French and more recently of the United States, and establishing a new society—a Communist one—throughout Vietnam. They have practiced from the outset of their struggle an "Indochina strategy," coordinating their actions in the three

Indochinese states in pursuit of their goal. While it is certain that their first priority has been the establishment of DRV rule in a united, independent Vietnam, their goals for Laos and Cambodia have not been so clear. It is logical to assume that they wish to have friendly regimes in the countries on their borders, so that one of their principal objectives in Laos and Cambodia is to erode American presence and influence.

In looking towards the future, it is important to assess how a decade of war has affected the will and capacities of Hanoi and its Communist allies in Vietnam, Laos and Cambodia. Certainly the intensity of the war since 1965, with massive United States escalation of troops and airpower, has seriously affected the capacities of the Communist movements. Yet the analysts in this volume point out that the will of the Vietnamese Communists has not been destroyed. Moreover, despite heavy personnel losses, they retain an impressive organizational capacity.

Another critical consideration in assessing the political future of Indochina is United States policy. The United States has had a consistent (if negative) aim in Indochina for some two decades—to prevent the spread of Communism. In pursuit of this objective, the United States supported the French in Indochina from 1950 to 1954. When the French withdrew, the United States sought consistently but ineffectively to shore up anti-Communist governments. The American effort did prevent a Communist take-over in Vietnam, but, as our discussion has suggested, failed to produce a non-Communist alternative which would with certainty survive a complete American withdrawal. Though antagonists, Washington and Hanoi share the doubt—though one in hope and the other in fear—that the present non-Communist regimes can sustain the war independently of the United States. Official rhetoric notwithstanding, United States policy-makers understand that the Thieu government and its counterparts do not possess the qualities of endurance, cohesion and dedication that are characteristic of Hanoi and the Viet Cong.

The papers in this volume were written within the context of a diminishing American presence in Vietnam. By December 1, 1971, according to President Nixon's announcement, American troops were to be at 184,000 or lower, and continued withdrawal seemed likely. It was not clear, however, whether a residual American military force would be retained after 1972, or what role United States airpower would play in the continuing conflict. Robert Johnson's paper, in its analysis of the Nixon doctrine in East Asia, points out that "a policy based wholly upon Vietnamization leaves the central political issues of the war unresolved"; with a continuing American presence in Vietnam, which Vietnamization requires, there is a continued prospect of United States involvement in future disasters. This prospect must be of particular concern to Hanoi. The Communist leadership has noted the determination of both Presidents Johnson and Nixon to block their victory, despite heavy domestic opposition to the Indochina war, and they must assume that their struggle with the United States is far from successfully concluded.

MacAlister Brown's exploration of the impact of the Indochina conflict on American political institutions leaves no doubt of the resulting high political cost of continual involvement in Indochina. The demand of most leading Democratic candidates for the Presidency for rapid and total United States withdrawal from the war is a reflection of the widespread dissatisfaction of the American public with the continued American presence in Vietnam. Public disillusionment was increased with the release of the Pentagon papers and the accompanying charges of deception against policy-makers. Further, President Nixon's moves toward a "normalization" of relations with Communist China would seem to add to the difficulty of continuing an important United States involvement in the Vietnam war. If Chinese Communist expansion—cited by successive administrations as the reason for the United States commitment in Vietnam—were less feared by the American public, an important prop for United States commitment would be removed. Still, all of these factors notwithstanding, if United States casualties continue downward, and if draftees need not be sent to Vietnam, President Nixon may believe that the political costs, even in an election year, would be sufficiently low to maintain a United States military presence in Vietnam until North Vietnam is willing to make a compromise acceptable to the United States at the bargaining table, (an unlikely prospect) or until, as the President states it, South Vietnam demonstrates a "reasonable chance" to defend itself.

The threat to the future stability of the non-Communist regimes, as the following pages will show, emanates both from Hanoi and from within. It is likely that the North Vietnamese and their Communist allies throughout Indochina will continue the struggle for their objectives. The non-Communist groups will continue their opposition to Communist domination, but they are unlikely to develop cohesion. The United States role in the Indochina war will diminish, although the extent and timing of that diminution is not yet clear. Thus, although there will be changes in the dimensions and intensity of the struggle, there is not yet a clear end in sight.

Acknowledgments

The map in this volume was prepared by Nancy Fischman and Norman Carpenter, both of the Clark University Cartography Laboratory. Roslyn Mason of Clark University shepherded the manuscripts through the copyediting stage and provided consistently valuable support in a tight production schedule.

Earlier versions of the papers in this volume were presented at a seminar of the Vietnam, Laos and Cambodia panel of the Southeast Asia Development Advisory Group (SEADAG) of the Asia Society at Asia House in New York on May 7-8, 1971.

Indochina
in Conflict

1

South Vietnamese Politics and the American Withdrawal

Elizabeth Pond

President Nguyen Van Thieu has stayed at the top longer than any other post-Diem politician. How much longer can he last? This is what any question of political stability or change in South Vietnam boils down to for the period of American withdrawal.

In this paper I shall attempt an approximate answer by exploring the sources of Thieu's present supremacy; the relationship between social forces, institutions, and politics in South Vietnam; and the developments supporting and undermining Thieu's control. If this is a highly personal approach, it is so only because politics in South Vietnam *is* highly personal.

In essence, I shall argue that Thieu is probably at his political zenith in the current period; that American withdrawal is sapping his primacy among the generals as well as the primacy of the military oligarchy itself in South Vietnam; that the absence of any strong political organization behind Thieu will probably prove critical; that a deterioration of South Vietnamese political coherence under the surface is more likely than a coup in the next year or so; and that in this contest of exhaustion the National Liberation Front, though very weak at the present time, is the most likely ultimate gainer from the situation.[a]

Prologue: Thieu's Base

In the fluid years just after the coup against President Ngo Dinh Diem, Thieu seemed an improbable sort to rise to the top. He was reserved, something of a loner, hypercautious, suspicious of others to a degree that seemed to block him from decisive action or any durable alliance. School friends recalled him as the boy who played a totally defensive game of table tennis and the one who hid treats from home and nibbled on them secretly rather than sharing them around with the other boys. As an adult, he still seemed the kind who would zealously guard his current position rather than risk losing everything in the scramble for

---

[a]I owe a major caveat to the reader. I have not been in Vietnam since spring of 1970, and I cannot vouch for my comprehension of politics since then. In substance, this paper reflects conclusions I had reached at that time; no subsequent developments I have read or heard about at a distance have caused me to change my opinions. However, I may be badly out of touch.

1

the top. His caution kept him from being among the prominent plotters in any of the series of coups from 1963 through 1965. He did not have the obvious drive for power of the flashy Air Vice Marshal Nguyen Cao Ky or the quasi-warlords who were the various corps commanders. He gave and attracted loyalty sparingly and built no visible clique of supporters in the way Ky did. He did not show any marked knack for politics. He had, according to one of his arms-length supporters, "complexes you could touch." As late as 1965, the background, ceremonial role of chief of state seemed to suit Thieu's temperament and ambition perfectly.

Yet within the three years from 1965 to 1968, Thieu rose out of obscurity to outmaneuver his more flamboyant fellow officers. He made an asset of his quietness and distaste for showdowns, allowing them to disarm his rivals. All the while, however, he went ahead with a network of intricate maneuvers that neutralized competitors and advanced himself while never committing him definitely to any one person, group, or course. And he proved himself willing to take the final risk once he had prepared the ground meticulously.

In 1967, Thieu accepted a direct confrontation for one of the few times in his career. When the Americans decreed that there would be only one military candidate for the new constitutional presidency (thereby assuring election of that candidate over the split civilian field), Thieu forced the powerful military committee to choose between him and Prime Minister Ky. From all accounts, the decision was a stormy and emotional one, but Thieu had calculated correctly. He received the nomination; it was Ky who got eased into the vice-presidential slot.

It was still moot, however, whether Thieu or Ky would prove to be the real master. Ky's allies held such controlling positions as chief of police and commander of the marines; Thieu agreed to let Ky name the new prime minister as part of their nomination deal; Ky was chairman of the military committee, which fully expected to be the power behind the throne.

Once elected, Thieu returned to a more oblique strategy. He avoided any open battles with Ky (to the exasperation of the Americans, who liked clear-cut authority and responsibility). Behind the scenes, however, he continued to move methodically and thoroughly, minimizing Ky, countering other potential rivals in complex preemptive moves, waiting for events to break up Ky's accumulation of power.

Events did, especially the all-out North Vietnamese/NLF Tet offensive of 1968. At first, Ky's position was enhanced by the action. As Thieu was out of Saigon at the beginning of the Tet holiday, Ky coordinated the initial defense against the attack. And after the attack was repulsed, Ky became—briefly—chairman of the Central Recovery Committee.

But then Thieu, in a logical move to unite the nation after the shock of Tet, replaced Ky's lackluster prime minister with Tran Van Huong. Huong, the most highly respected civilian candidate in the 1967 presidential election, had won Saigon's plurality in that election. He was an elder statesman and the acknowledged leader of the Southerners; he had a reputation for personal integrity.

In addition, in a logical effort to correct the poor response of South Vietnamese forces to the Tet offensive, Thieu fired three of the four corps commanders—and therefore, three members ex officio of the military committee. In their place, he appointed new commanders, who would owe their promotions to him. (The only corps commander to retain his post was I Corps' General Hoang Xuan Lam, who had reportedly stuck firmly with Thieu in the military committee showdown over the presidential nomination.) At the same time, Thieu quietly arrogated to himself the power of the corps commanders to appoint province and district chiefs. In his military changes, of course, Thieu prudently kept as generals of the three "coup divisions" near Saigon, men who were more noted for political docility than for military brilliance.

Some of the military committee pressed Ky to object to Thieu's assumption of authority and to hold Thieu accountable to the committee. Ky decided to bide his time, however, and wait for better issues to argue on.

The better issues never materialized. Within a few months, the *coup de grace* was administered to Ky, still not by any hostile action of Thieu's, but by fortuitous events. When the North Vietnamese and the NLF mounted another attack on Saigon in the spring, General Nguyen Ngoc Loan, the police czar and Ky's sidekick, was seriously wounded in street fighting, and several other important pro-Ky officers were killed by a stray American rocket. Ky was on the skids both as a politician and as a ready-made rallying point for restive army officers.

The military committee too went into a decline from which it never recovered. To be sure, Thieu never instituted a real shakedown in the army command. And he was always careful not to cross important generals directly. In particular, he eschewed cutting into the generals' prerogative of corruption; on this tender issue, he might have stirred up determined resistance. While not threatening the other generals' positions with any one step, however, Thieu did manage to disperse any military groupings unsympathetic to him.

For its part, the United States underwrote Thieu's emerging dominance by making it bluntly clear to the military commanders that it would not tolerate any coup. This was no empty threat; in the aftermath of Tet, American public opinion simply would not assent to the spilling of more American blood for yet another musical-chair junta. The ultimate sanction of United States withdrawal became credible for the first time in American involvement in Vietnam.

With Thieu's position essentially stabilized by fall of 1968, there came a period in which little happened politically. The An Quang Buddhists, shocked by the Communist massacre even of antigovernment Buddhist cadres during the Hue occupation, did recoil from flirtation with the Communists. In 1969, Thieu, without enthusiasm, did launch the National Social Democratic Front, a coalition of six old-time parties, as a gesture to the Nixon administration, which for domestic reasons was eager to have tangible evidence of democracy in South Vietnam. But these shifts did not change the basic political landscape.

In the area of policy, on the contrary, there was considerable action. Thieu kept the government functioning after Tet and even provided surprisingly strong leadership for his dazed country. Under the impact of the Tet crisis and subsequent American prodding, total mobilization was effected; the Accelerated Pacification Campaign pushed government forces out into the countryside; the whole pacification program was rationalized and brought under the direction of the competent General Tran Thien Khiem; Thieu replaced province and district chiefs wholesale, appreciably improving the quality of the former if not the latter; the local Regional Forces and Popular Forces, which afforded more continuous village security than the regular army, were upgraded and strengthened; a citizens' militia, which sprang up spontaneously in several places during the Tet fighting, was officially approved as the People's Self-Defense Forces and partially armed in virtually every government hamlet throughout the country; and an effort was made to galvanize local leadership and revive villages as viable political entities through local elections, national training of village officials, million-piaster grants to villages for locally selected projects, and subordination of local Popular Forces, People's Self-Defense Forces, and Revolutionary Development cadres to village chiefs. Under American prodding too, South Vietnam agreed to enter peace negotiations. And quite without American pressure, Thieu decided to institute genuine land reform in South Vietnam. In the weakness of the North Vietnamese and the NLF, the Accelerated Pacification Campaign ended by giving Saigon effective and continuing control of a far higher percentage of the population than it had enjoyed before. The Communists, who had drastically overreached themselves, exposing and sacrificing many of their best local troops and political cadres during the Tet drive, were pushed back far beyond their pre-Tet position. Their political cadres in contested areas were deprived of military cover and crippled in their organizing and propaganda activity.

Denied their former population resources and their capacity to mobilize support, the Communists began putting a tighter squeeze for rice, recruits, and porters on the remaining peasants they could control; they resorted more to indiscriminate attacks on civilians they could not control. In much of the countryside, the Communists not only lost their aura of invincibility because of their Tet failure; they also alienated peasants, especially middle peasants, by their increasing brutality.[1] The anti-NLF shift was particularly noticeable in the populous Mekong delta.

By mid-1969, Thieu was ready to make his final move in consolidating his political command: removal of Prime Minister Tran Van Huong. The crotchety Huong, while a useful counter to Ky in the period when Thieu was edging his Vice-President into a subordinate role, got in Thieu's way once Ky was disposed of.

Huong himself posed no significant threat to Thieu's power. For all his experience in politics, he was curiously apolitical. Partly because he partook of the old-fashioned aloof mandarin mentality, partly because he was too rigid for the jostling and compromise of politics, partly because he was ill and aging, Huong never used his position to build a political organization, either for himself or for his Southern supporters. The dedicated team that had rallied to his cause in the presidential campaign of 1967 gradually dispersed because of the dearth of appointments or even encouragement by the Prime Minister, and because of Huong's inability to curb corruption or provide any real civilian check on military rule. Politically active Southerners grew disenchanted with Huong and broke up into disparate groups. By the summer of 1969, Huong was little more than a sentimental symbol.

Even so, Thieu moved cautiously, bringing all his customary indirection to bear in getting rid of Huong. He displayed public contempt for Huong by sometimes deliberately walking at a faster pace on public occasions than the white-haired Prime Minister with the cane could manage. But he was careful not to make a martyr out of Huong and thus risk uniting the divided Southern factions in defense of their one-time champion. He did not fire Huong. Instead, he maneuvered behind the scenes to persuade the old man to retire. First, he got members of the Chamber of Deputies to call for Huong's resignation over the issue of a tariff hike. (Huong had nothing to do with the tax rise, which was instituted by executive decree under American pressure; but it was the most unpopular issue available to berate Huong with at the time.) Next, Thieu got members of his six-party NSDF to call for Huong's resignation on the grounds that they did not have their share of Cabinet posts. (This again was hardly Huong's doing, but the complainants thought they could benefit from such a campaign anyway.) In this latter ploy, Thieu cultivated the impression among the constituent parties of the NSDF that they would inherit some Cabinet ministries, including even the office of prime minister itself.

Eventually, without ever saying directly that he wanted Huong out, Thieu forced Huong's resignation. Then, he appointed as the new Prime Minister the favored head of pacification, General Khiem. This was a step Thieu had reportedly been wanting to take ever since his own accession to the presidency.

Now, the three top posts in South Vietnam were all held by military officers. The generals were civilianized, but they were generals still, with their primary base the armed forces. Thieu's consolidation was complete.

Once again, Thieu had demonstrated his flair for timing and his skill at intricate political juggling. He had not moved prematurely. He succeeded in dumping Huong without bruising the Southerners or any other important group unduly. (One of the six parties in the NSDF did pull out of the alliance, but this was unimportant; the NSDF was only window dressing for the Americans anyway.)

Furthermore, while he was easing Huong out, Thieu was simultaneously coping, successfully, with several other crises. In June 1969, American troop reductions in Vietnam were announced. In July 1969, under American pressure, Thieu made an election proposal to the NLF. Also in July, a spy ring was uncovered that embarrassed Thieu, as it included some 100-odd suspects in government service and reached high into the presidential palace. The combination of all these things might have created turmoil in the army and among right wingers in South Vietnam. But Thieu carried off the beginning of American deescalation and his own government shifts smoothly.

American disengagement did present a fundamental challenge to Thieu's control. Besides threatening to weaken Thieu's hardline support (a bearable prospect, since the right wing had no alternative but to stick with Thieu if it didn't want to hasten American departure), withdrawal threatened to erode Thieu's whole political base. This was more serious.

It would be misleading to say that Thieu stayed in power on the bayonets of the Americans. But the Americans, in the name of stability, did underwrite the supremacy of the military oligarchy in South Vietnam. And once Thieu established his primacy among the generals, American power underwrote Thieu. More specifically, US Ambassador Ellsworth Bunker guaranteed Thieu as much as former US Ambassador Henry Cabot Lodge ever guaranteed Ky.

Thus, American disengagement held the specter of upsetting Thieu's delicate balance within the military in the short run and upsetting military dominance in South Vietnamese politics in the long run.

The first major probe of the changing atmosphere came within months. In the fall, Generals Duong Van Minh and Tran Van Don, heroes of the 1963 coup, demanded a popular referendum on Thieu's leadership and began calling for an undefined reconciliation in the country. Exactly what policy they were recommending was in doubt; their wish to set themselves up as alternatives to Thieu was not.

Saigon politicians did not really take the voluble, overly Frenchified Don seriously. But "Big Minh" was a figure to be reckoned with. An affable general who was not in power long enough after the 1963 coup to lose his popularity, Minh had been banned from running in the 1967 presidential election and exiled to Thailand. The homesick Minh had been allowed to return to South Vietnam in the post-Tet honeymoon of national union in 1968, but had never been offered any important post in the government.

Minh had little enough organization to support him. But he was a true Southerner and a Buddhist, whom Southern regionalists and Buddhists might unite behind as against Thieu, who was from Central Vietnam and a Catholic. As a senior general, Minh also had a considerable potential following in the army and might cut into Thieu's support there. Moreover, Minh was thought to be exploring a softer line on the war than Thieu's. He might easily focus the vast public war weariness, discontent with rising prices, and latent anti-Americanism into a coherent political opposition.

Altogether, a natural contest between Thieu and Minh was shaping up for the 1971 presidential elections. Thieu therefore apparently began to worry about Minh's challenge.

Minh was too prominent to attack directly. Thieu chose instead, as a warning to all rivals, to jail Lower House Deputy Tran Ngoc Chau.

The maverick Chau had been advocating de-Americanization of the war; a more flexible policy of accommodation with non-Communist nationalists; a political settlement to the war through negotiations by the three Vietnamese parties without the United States; and, concretely, a kick-off meeting of parliamentary delegations from both North and South Vietnam. These views Thieu considered dissident. Besides, Chau had publicly accused Nguyen Cao Thang, one of Thieu's prime political advisers and the manager of political and private funds for Thieu, of buying votes in the National Assembly.

All in all, Chau was an ideal target for Thieu. He had clearly committed lèse majesté. He was sufficiently well-known to show that Thieu meant business in his new toughness toward would-be opposition. But he was sufficiently lacking in allies and organization to be vulnerable.

So Thieu, despite Chau's unambivalent anti-Communism and despite Chau's parliamentary immunity to prosecution under the constitution, had the legislator tried and convicted for not informing on his brother, a North Vietnamese spy. In the process, Thieu gave shrill speeches against neutralists (which he implied Chau was), comparing them with barking dogs and calling for the people to beat these dogs to death. Also involved in the campaign were an assault on the Lower House by a mob of 700 or 800 paid rioters; 20 other anti-Chau demonstrations throughout the country (the first clandestinely government-organized demonstrations in a long time); a Lower House committee report condemning Chau that a majority of the committee refused to sign; a Lower House petition calling for prosecution of Chau, the signatures of which reportedly cost 10 million piasters ($80,000) in bribes, plus considerable blackmail and intimidation; and drumhead trial by the politically malleable mobile military field court.

In a decision rendered two months after the conviction, the Supreme Court declared Chau's trial and sentence unconstitutional because his parliamentary immunity was never legally lifted and because the mobile military field court was itself unconstitutional. In a second decision half a year later, the Supreme Court went further and explicitly nullified Chau's sentence

Thieu responded by ignoring the Supreme Court decisions, getting the National Assembly to legislate an effective continuation of the mobile military field court, and seeing to it that at the next shift of Supreme Court offices the presiding chief justice was replaced by a man more amenable to Thieu's wishes.

In the short run, Thieu's tactics worked. The Southerners, with whom Chau was loosely allied, had not united behind one of their own, Tran Van Huong; much less did they rally as a group to Chau, an outsider from Central Vietnam. The An Quang Buddhists, with whom Chau was also loosely allied, had not united in any politically significant way behind Thich Thien Minh at the time of the militant Buddhist leader's arrest in early 1969; much less did they rally to the outsider Chau. Demonstrations by students and wounded veterans over their own issues in the wake of the Chau trial were easily broken up by police in Saigon. In general, opposition groups subsided back to their usual wait-and-see stance pending some favorable nod from the Americans. As for the American Embassy in Saigon, far from seeking to restrain or punish Thieu's bending of the law through any real leverage, it effectively condoned the action by its silence.

Most important from Thieu's vantage point, Minh and Don ceased their public political soundings, at least temporarily. Their quiescence, of course, was not the result solely of Thieu's new toughness. They were perhaps responding primarily to Richard Nixon's continuing and unwavering support of Thieu. The American President endorsed his Vietnamese counterpart unequivocally in his public address on Vietnam in November 1969. And Washington's unwillingness to gamble with anyone else was apparently communicated directly to Don when he visited the United States in early 1970.

There was some unexpected backlash from the Chau trial, however. Uncharacteristically, the usually cool Thieu had made a personal crusade out of getting Chau, and Thieu's vindictiveness and the excesses of the trial (rather more than Thieu's disdain for the Supreme Court) caused many in Saigon to lose confidence in the President's judgment, control, and predictability. This waning of confidence in Thieu was perhaps most damaging among Thieu's supporters by default, the many politicians who didn't like Thieu but didn't see any better alternative for the time being.

In general, though, a political plateau was reached by spring of 1970 that was to continue for a year and a half. The South Vietnamese invasion of Cambodia which began in May 1970 may have raised right wingers' esteem of Thieu somewhat, but it did not seem to affect his position much otherwise. The rise in prestige of General Do Cao Tri, the commander of III Corps and the successful commander of the Cambodian operations, might have come to pose a personal threat to Thieu. But Tri was killed in a helicopter crash before this could happen.

In the course of 1970, Thieu showed himself more ready than he had been in the past to reach a modus vivendi with the Cambodian and montagnard minorities in South Vietnam and with local leaders of the Hoa Hao and Cao Dai sects. The Senate elections gave an antigovernment An Quang slate the top 11% vote and Thieu's preferred slates only second and fourth places, demonstrating that Thieu's influence was not readily transferable to amorphous Senate contests; that the An Quang Buddhists were dabbling a little more with participation in the existing system of government; and that South Vietnamese political groupings were as unorganized as ever. The elections did not touch the locus of power.

By fall of 1971, however, Thieu's carefully constructed political universe began to show public signs of coming apart. Drawn by the lure of scoring a massive vote in the presidential election, Thieu abandoned his previous willingness to settle for small-margin victories. Given his control of the bureaucracy and the army and the pro-Thieu vote they could easily command in rural villages as a matter of tacit understanding, Thieu probably could have beaten his major rival, Duong Van Minh, without too much outright falsification of the vote.

But Thieu opted for a big victory instead and rammed an endorsement law through the legislature that effectively disqualified Vice President Ky from running and kept all other candidates off the ballot as well. When Minh refused to run under such circumstances, Thieu tried to reinstate Ky as a dummy candidate for him to defeat. The Supreme Court dutifully reversed its own earlier decision and declared Ky eligible two days after the registration deadline had passed. Ky, however, declined such an arranged contest, and Thieu's election juggling exhausted the patience even of the ever-understanding American Embassy.

The preceding summary of the history of Thieu's rule is elementary. It does, however, portray graphically the nature of Thieu's control. In particular, it illustrates the degree to which South Vietnamese politics is personalized and uninstitutionalized. It suggests the extent to which Thieu's style of preemptive maneuvering is also the substance of his politics.

Social Forces, Institutions, and Politics

Involute as they are, the personal maneuvers and countermaneuvers of Saigon politics are in some ways easier to trace than the linkage of politics with broader social forces. Evolving institutions can be described, but their strength or their relationship to politics is very difficult to assess.

The American Dream

The official American contention is that Thieu has legitimacy, which stems from the Constitution of 1967. In this view, constitutionality creates its own imperatives; elections and democratic institutions, even if fledgling at first, gather strength in operation, create their own momentum, and become the customary channel for conflict resolution.

At their most optimistic, the Americans hoped that the United States force reductions would instill a sense of urgency in the perennially fragmented non-Communist nationalists in South Vietnam and convince them that they had to pull together against the Communists in order to survive. Under this Damocles' sword, Thieu's doggedness, his penchant for fine-margin calculation, his stubborn ambition, and his demonstrated ability to grow on the job might lead him to an enlarged perception of self-interest; he might reach out politically beyond the elite of the military oligarchy and the Northern Catholics to the broader strata of the country's citizens and surge into semipopularity. The myriad self-centered political and social forces in South Vietnam might come together on the necessity of a unified leader, accept Thieu temporarily, then among themselves hammer out an agreed successor. Elections on all levels, local and national to begin with, then in the provinces in 1971, would make leaders increasingly accountable to the wishes of the people.

A more modest version of this view holds that even without political compression at the top, social forces throughout the country are now working to give Thieu a grudging consensus; and that this consensus can be extended to convert the present military advantage of the South Vietnamese and the Americans into a long-term political superiority over the Communists.

Thus, the war has destroyed old patterns. The extended family and the isolated village are giving way to more modernized, i.e., more individualistic and yet more universal social patterns. Groupings such as the Buddhists and also a few of the political parties are becoming less utopian and more pragmatic in their demands, especially as a younger generation begins to inherit leadership. Radio and television and Thieu's constant trips around the country, as well as Communist politicizing of the peasantry, are moving South Vietnam away from localism to a sense of nationhood.

Urbanization (even if forced), massive population shifts, and a booming economy are tying villagers to the city as never before. Over the past 15 years, the percentage of the South Vietnamese population living in urban areas has jumped from 15 to 40%. And more secure roads, more Hondas to travel them, more water pumps, and miracle rice are making village and city consciously interdependent. The peasant has more of a stake in the status quo now that the Chinese monopoly of rice wholesaling has been broken and the peasant himself is getting to own land, earn a higher price for his rice, and develop a taste for sewing machines and sampan motors.

In the countryside, the villagers may be no more enthusiastic about Thieu than they ever are about any Saigon government. But, given the choice between Saigon and an increasingly harsh NLF, the balance of peasant preferences is at least passively progovernment. Villagers are eager to protect themselves against the NLF. And with the government program expanding local authority and local security forces, villages increasingly have the capacity to defend themselves. All this provides a great opportunity for Thieu in the countryside.

Realizing this perhaps, the South Vietnamese president has made a concerted effort to appeal to peasants and village leaders over the heads of the chronically discontented urban intelligentsia by pushing land reform, addressing training classes of village chiefs at Vung Tau, and letting himself be seen in villages all over the country. Finding loose arrangements with Saigon more beneficial than the manpower and ideological demands of the NLF, villagers are according tolerance if not commitment to the Saigon regime.

These trends of modernization and village revival exist, indisputably. Nonetheless, the burden of proof that these social forces are in fact leading to the hoped for political transformation in South Vietnam must rest with the proponents of this theory of democratization. And a large proof indeed is required. It would be most unusual for a society conditioned to highly personalized authoritarian rule and the mandate of heaven to embrace democratic institutions within a few short years, especially under the strains of social devastation wrought by an interminable guerrilla, civil, and large-unit war.

Certainly, the most optimistic American hopes about the burgeoning of democracy in South Vietnam seem extravagant. To be sure, Thieu has utilized the ground rules of American-imposed legality where it has suited him tactically. In 1967, he gambled, as Ky did not, that the Americans would enforce the supremacy of the installed president over backroom arrangements for the ascendancy of the military committee. And in his gradual assumption of a monopoly of government power in 1968/69, Thieu was willing to cite constitutionality against Ky, the corps commanders, and other possible usurpers, since constitutionality favored his position.

As it turned out, this approach worked. If the balance of generals had not been so close at the beginning, or if the Tet offensive had not occurred, the United States probably would not have had the will or the adeptness to enforce legality. Given these circumstances, however, the United States could guarantee the existing system by making it starkly clear that it would allow no coup. The decisive factor was no force of legality as such, but a balance that gave the United States leverage.

As soon as tactics of legality no longer suited Thieu's purposes, the frailty of constitutionality became apparent. The legal system had no sanctions of its own and no inducements to make powerful groups or persons defend it in the abstract. The Chau affair proved conclusively that neither the legislature, the Buddhists, nor the Southerners felt strong corporate loyalty or saw in violation of legality any particular threat to their collective entities. Chau was perceived as isolated, unrelated; South Vietnam was as atomized politically as ever.

Conspicuously, the National Assembly did not rise in defense of one if its own members. One-third of the Lower House deputies did bring a constitutional challenge to the Supreme Court over the legality of the procedure used against Chau, but a number of the signatories were persuaded to renege after Thieu's agents contacted them. A Senate committee did write a report blaming Thieu for inciting the riot in the Lower House and condemning the arrest of Chau in the legally inviolate Lower House and the manhandling of Chau during the arrest. But the committee prudently wrote its report well after the fact, too late to have any effect on the observance of legality during the trial.

Most significant was the fact that three-fourths of the Lower House (if under various pressures, equivocations, and deceptions) did sign the petition to prosecute Chau outside of the constitutional procedures for removing immunity. And only 7 out of a possible 197 legislators even went to Chau's trial to see the fate of one of their colleagues. This must have confirmed Thieu's low evaluation of the importance of the legislature. His opinion of the National Assembly was clear in his neglect of it: he never even bothered to build a stable progovernment majority in the legislature. Rather than rewarding senators and deputies who supported his programs, he treated them cavalierly; until last fall, he didn't even care enough about internal elections to get government supporters elected to National Assembly offices.

As for the Supreme Court, its ruling on the unconstitutionality of an action sponsored by Thieu was perhaps as much a measure of the loosening of Thieu's political grip in the excesses of the Chau trial as it was of the illegality of the action itself. In any case, Thieu's total disregard of the rulings by the Supreme Court amply demonstrated the court's impotence as an institution.

In the Chau affair, the American Embassy also displayed its weakness when there is no South Vietnamese leader eager to exploit legality as a weapon in intramural fighting. In such a vacuum, the United States clearly has neither the will nor the day-to-day tactical knowledge to enforce legality.

Nor do the mechanics of elections have much meaning by themselves. Local elections have been used in some places to throw out unwanted village chiefs or reduce demands for tea money. But for the most part, local as well as national elections are seen as ratifying existing power rather than selecting leadership or making leadership responsive to public opinion.

Dearth of Organization

Traditional non-Communist groupings do not appear to have been significantly strengthened or unified under the impact of the Communist danger. There was a reflex pulling together immediately after Tet of 1968. But nothing was cemented. And pressures for unity faded from 1969 on under the very success of the Accelerated Pacification Campaign. Even the continued United States pull-out was not seen as enough of a gut threat to compel cooperation.

The various experiments with party confederations—the National Alliance for Social Revolution and the National Salvation Front of 1968 and Thieu's National Social Democratic Front of 1969—remained confederations in which members easily became aggrieved and quit. The political party law of June 1969 (requiring minimum memberships of 2500 or 5000 in an effort to fuse splinter groups together) proved no more effective than previous attempts to change politics by legislation. The old mutual suspicions very swiftly won out. The political cliques that call themselves parties retained their exclusiveness, concentrating more on secret recruiting of government officials and bureaucrats than on creation of any open mass party. Rather than resolving interests or lobbying for policy, the parties continued to serve personal conspiracy.

The one exception to this, the new National Progressive Movement, formed around the old Tan Dai Viet, is more rational and modern than most and has made a start in organizing a public party. But so far, it has operated on sufferance; it has yet to prove much innate strength. In its first test at the polls, the 1970 Senate elections, the National Progressive Movement worked hard but gleaned few votes.

The Nhan Xa, at core the recrudescence of one branch of the Diemist Can Lao party, has grown, at the expense of the now all-but-defunct Greater Solidarity Force. But in its search for power, the Nhan Xa seems to be counting more on friendly relations with Thieu than on mobilizing the population. The Nhan Xa itself is split into factions. And Catholic unity as a whole is diminishing. The Northern Catholics have become much more diffuse in the years since a million refugees fled the Communist North in 1954, while the Southern Catholics never were tightly organized. In 1967, a hierarchy of Catholic political leadership could agree on what candidates to field and parish discipline could then give Catholic slates half the seats in the Senate; in 1970, five Catholic Senate slates scattered the parish vote.

As for the perennially projected workers' party that is always waiting to emerge out of the Vietnam Confederation of Workers, it has yet to manifest itself. Likewise, the veterans' organization that Tran Van Don keeps hoping to turn into a political influence à la Indonesia, has remained inchoate. The majority Southerners are as individualistic as Sun Yat-sen feared his people were in comparing the Chinese with sand.

Nor has Thieu built any new organization of his own. He had toyed with a neo-Can Lao and a military party, with a government cadre organization and with army reorganization. But none of these ever got off the ground, largely because Thieu would never delegate real authority. Creating a strong organization that some rival might then take over seemed too dangerous to him.

All Vietnamese politics is highly personal, of course, but Thieu's is personal to a degree remarkable even for Vietnam. In his caution and suspicion, he has never entrusted subordinates with the same kind of power Diem or Ky did. The omnisuspicious Thieu trusts no one, including his elder brother, who helps him on freelance political missions and Prime Minister Khiem, who has power second only to him (but Thieu watches him carefully and withholds some funds from him). The partial exceptions to the general rule appear to be Thieu's two closest political advisers, Nguyen Cao Thang (now deceased) and General Dang Van Quang. Thang was presumably considered safe because his ambitions were so clearly fiscal rather than political. Quang is presumably considered safe because he has no prestige; in 1966, he was dismissed by Premier Ky from his post as IV Corps commander on grounds of corruption on a scale lavish even by Vietnam's liberal standards.

In any case, Thieu has not constructed a supporting organization, either at the top or at the bottom. The PSDF have never been whipped into anything resembling a combat youth organization, despite the obvious potential. Information cadres, who are spread throughout the country down to district level, have never been used for any intensive political indoctrination campaign. RD cadres have turned out to be useful more or less as service, intelligence, and paramilitary functionaries, but they have not turned out to be cadres in the Communist organizational sense. Nor has Thieu so far made any discoverable political use of the law providing for appointment of well-salaried assistants to village chiefs.

Maximizing Benevolent Neutrality

Thieu appears now to have abandoned any idea of organization and to be relying instead on an urban strategy of dispersing opposition and a rural strategy of maximizing the peasantry's benevolent neutrality.

Thieu's intentions are obscure here. The only overt actions one can judge from are Thieu's enthusiasm for land reform, his support of village development and local security, his frequent meetings with province and district officials, and his constant public appearances in villages around the country. Thieu may view all this as generating strong and direct support for himself among villagers. But how much of a conscious program it adds up to is impossible for any outsider to know.

In any case, in Western terms the possible rationale of this approach might be analyzed as follows: Rural South Vietnam consists of a mass of largely neutral peasants strung between two political authorities—the Saigon government and the National Liberation Front. There are clusters of Catholic, Hoa Hao, Cao Dai, and some other villages that are staunch anti-Communist bastions for ideological reasons of their own; and there are clusters of villages that have been Viet Minh/NLF heartland for 20 years and still retain something of the old revolutionary mystique. The drain of a quarter century of war has sapped commitment, however; the majority of peasants wish in their hearts that both sides would go away and in practice fall in with whichever power is dominant in an area.

Insofar as there is a choice, the peasant basically favors the side that presses him the least. At this stage of a messy war that has exhibited more the characteristics of a battering ram than a rapier, that less oppressive side is the government. By now, the sheer weight of years of American firepower, massive sweeps, and forced population shifts have reduced the population base of the NLF and made the NLF squeeze its remaining peasants ever harder and less discriminatingly. By contrast, government control over its peasants tends to be much less disciplined and therefore "freer" in the not insignificant sense that one can more easily escape obligations, whether by bribe or evasion.

For the average citizen on the government side, there is also more of that intangible that might be termed a sense of possibility. Villagers who five years ago sought to redress their grievances (and had their grievances articulated and sharpened) by joining the NLF have many more channels for change opened up to them now—and use them. These include joining the local militia to escape national military service away from home; using civil defense forces to keep marauding South Vietnamese soldiers as well as NLF tax collectors off villagers' backs; increasing harvest incomes by selling watermelons or vegetables in Saigon, getting technical assistance to grow high-yield miracle rice, or doubling crops with water pumps bought with funds from mutual loan associations; and complaining about inequities to American advisors or even occasionally Lower House representatives and village council members. In the recent past, these channels have included also tapping American commodities and enthusiasm for wells, schools, and bridges, and drifting to the city for relatively well-paying jobs with the Americans.

NLF capacity to redress grievance has correspondingly diminished as government responsiveness has improved somewhat. A major issue, distribution of land, has been taken from the Communists, and they simply cannot compete with Saigon's American resources in giving the villager economic development and a better life.

In this context, if Saigon can just provide an operating, mildly beneficial government in the countryside, it will stay ahead of the NLF. If Thieu can provide this operating, mildly beneficial government, he will stay ahead of his political competitors. At elections or other public times, Thieu can guarantee the support of the countryside by tactical alliances with various leaders of the Hoa Hao, Cao Dai, and the montagnards' FULRO, and by energizing the 1½-million-strong army, police, and bureaucracy to get out necessary votes or other displays of support.

Denouement

Will this vision be realized? How long can Thieu maintain his present ascendancy? The answer depends in large part on Thieu's rivals. For the foreseeable future, the most important of these are Duong Van Minh, Tran Thien Khiem, other generals, the Southerners, the Buddhists, and, ultimately, the NLF. Among the urban disgruntled, Minh has support probably equivalent to that which the civilian Prime Minister Tran Van Huong had in the 1967 election in Saigon. Other supporters of Minh might include the Southerners, the An Quang Buddhists and their followers in Central Vietnam, antiwar voters, and, as an outside possibility, soldiers in units commanded by officers sympathetic to Minh.

It is most unlikely, however, that all of these groups would have backed Minh even in the Presidential election. Not all of the southern factions trust him. There is a reserve between Minh and An Quang. Peace-prone voters would have to take Minh on faith; for all the rumors that he would accept a soft accommodation with the NLF, Minh has offered no solid confirmation that he would do so.

Another, longer-shot rival to Thieu is Prime Minister Khiem. Far from being an overt challenger, Khiem has exercised his considerable power with the utmost circumspection as an apolitical administrator. He has eschewed any independent action or political aggrandizement for himself.

Nonetheless, Thieu does appear to extend his suspicion to Khiem, too. And Khiem's position and background might well inspire wariness. He is shrewd, ambitious, has managed to stay on good terms with quite diverse people and groups (including Minh), is only in his mid-forties, and has seniority as one of

South Vietnam's two four-star generals engaged in public life. (In their active military days, Khiem was Thieu's commander, the one who promoted Thieu to general.) Furthermore, Khiem's loyalties are balanced rather than fixed. He was, in succession, virtually an adopted son of Diem, an anti-Diem coup plotter, and antijunta coup plotter and strongman, an out exiled as ambassador to the United States and then Taiwan and—probably uniquely in Vietnamese politics—a comeback to the No. 2 position in the country.

Despite his suspicion, Thieu probably takes the risk of keeping Khiem as his deputy both because he needs Khiem's administrative abilities and because of a certain indecisiveness in Khiem. Khiem was cautious about committing himself in the earlier stages of coup plotting against Diem, and after the coup, he did not manage to protect his particular group of plotters. Later, despite his initial leading role in the next antijunta coup, he let General Nguyen Khanh take over the tactical direction and the glory from him.

So far, Khiem seems to prefer being a behind-the-scenes kingmaker to being king. Until such time as Thieu starts slipping badly, he will probably stay apolitical.

At present, it is hard to identify any other generals who might supplant Thieu. The vocal Ky might elicit some sympathy from the marines and possibly the air force. As a four-year loser he has little active backing now, however, and it is unlikely that major segments of the bureaucracy, regular army, or police would defect from Thieu to Ky. As for the corps commanders of II, III, and IV corps, they are sufficiently junior and dependent not to pose any threat. The senior corps commander, General Lam in I Corps, poses no threat either; he is tied to Thieu, he is momentarily in a decline after commanding the unsuccessful Laos invasion in early 1971, and over the past five years, he has kept his preserve precisely because he learned the lesson of the 1966 struggle movement and has not dabbled in independent regional politics.

The Southerners and the Buddhists are the chronic discontented, and their numbers would make them forces to be reckoned with if they could be focused politically. There is no hint of either of them coalescing into any coherent movement, however. Like the generals, they still seem exhausted from the chaos and fighting of the 1963-66 interregnum and apparently prefer an unhappy modus vivendi with the government to an even more unhappy return to struggle.

With no very formidable non-Communist challengers, then, the contest for political power in South Vietnam in the immediate future would appear to be polarized between Thieu and the NLF.

Alternatives

Over the next year or two, the primary factors working to Thieu's advantage, as we have seen, are the current weakness of the NLF; the widespread presence of the Saigon government in the populated countryside, especially the delta; basically sound village and land reform programs by the government; the middle peasantry's greater aversion for the NLF than for Saigon; and a war weariness that favors the status quo.

There are also powerful tides running against Thieu, however: inflation, corruption, and the frustration of rising expectations; the ease with which faltering government programs deteriorate into a counterproductive use of force; dislike of Thieu even among his supporters; rising anti-Americanism; the characteristic Southern fragmentation in politics; and the continued life of the Communist infrastructure.

I. The City Bang

After 25 years of conflict, the war's slaughter, devastation, dislocation, and disorientation have left no lives untouched. 125,000 South Vietnamese soldiers have been killed, 270,000 soldiers wounded; 300,000 civilians have been killed, 700,000 wounded; 258,000 children are orphans. One out of every three South Vietnamese, six million out of a population of 17½ million, has been wounded or made homeless at least once in this war. Unacknowledged refugees have drifted to the cities, at least a million of them. Saigon, swelled ten times over, from 300,000 to three million, has become the most densely populated city in the world, its hordes crammed into one- and two-story dwellings along the canals. Almost six million tons of bombs (just about triple the total of all American bombing in World War II) have been dropped on Indochina, with most of this tonnage falling on Vietnam. The equivalent of one-seventh of South Vietnam's land area has been defoliated.[2] The toll of the war is enormous, first in individual tragedy and heartbreak, then in social fracture.

In no place are the social problems engendered by the war more acute than in the city slums, where the dispossessed and uprooted congregate. These slums portend trouble for the government. The migrants may or may not blame Thieu for the war and bombing they fled in the countryside. They certainly blame him for inflation and misery every time prices go up 10% or 15% or 30%. Economic discontent on top of the suffering of war could unseat Thieu.

Actually, up to now, inflation has never reached feverish proportions, largely because of American footing of the South Vietnamese budget deficit, rice imports that have kept domestic food prices down, subsidies for consumer durables imports that have sopped up extra money, and other measures of quite brilliant juggling by American economists. Grumbling over soaring prices has therefore stayed within bounds so far.

Inflation is sure to accelerate, however, as the Americans leave and progressively remove their props of and controls on the economy. At the same time, unemployment will rise as the United States reduces aid from its present level (accounting, with multiplier effects, for 60% of the South Vietnamese gross national product), and as the approximately 150,000 jobs with the United States armed forces and 600,000 incomes dependent on American troops wither away.[3] Urban dwellers will experience a drop in personal income. And their feeling of deprivation will be the greater for the rising expectations stirred by mass exposure of villagers to the Honda-age cities, a lavish war economy, and the promises and politicizing of war rhetoric.

South Vietnam's rampant corruption and privilege, which are perhaps accepted and bearable in prosperous times, will probably fester more and more, especially in the minds of the urban poor. Stability and order, which now seem so desirable, will probably take a lower priority as families have to cut down their rice rations and as corner shakedowns by inflation-pressed MP's and police increase. The ostentatious wealth of the Saigon and Vung Tau rich will rankle more. The memory of Communist brutality will probably fade and mellow as time passes, people get used to relative peace, and the choice comes to seem less of an exclusive one between the Saigon government and the Communists.

The wounded veterans might again erect squatter shacks in Saigon and defy the police to tear them down. Students might again protest police torture of fellow students. Another round or two of inflation in Saigon could start demonstrations for lower prices. Another incident of GIs killing a Vietnamese boy in Qui Nhon could spark anti-American and antigovernment riots.

A challenge to Thieu might start as a demand for a larger share of the status quo and by its own momentum, Communist agitation, and reaction to police suppression escalate to a demand for the overthrow of Thieu. A combination of inflation, unemployment, extravagant corruption, and latent anti-Americanism in a wartorn society with premature, overdeveloped urbanization but underdeveloped political organization is an explosive mixture. The mass society without mass political organization and articulation is ripe for a demagogue. Embittered and alienated people turn easily to charisma and any radicalism that promises importance and relief to them.

Ironically, the new urban proletariat that the United States has built up in the past five years in its construction and service jobs—and in a military strategy which ensured massive shifts of village populations to city slums—might turn into the Communists' strongest supporters. For a quarter of a century, the struggle in Indochina was waged between government strongholds (however porous) in the cities and insurgent bases or transit routes in the countryside. At the present time, however, insurgent freedom of movement has been greatly hampered in Mekong Delta villages by government pacification (and the subsequent Cambodian invasion), while the potential for urban chaos uncontrollable by the government has greatly increased. And the NLF is reportedly better organized in the cities now than it was in the post-Diem days to turn political disorder to its own uses. If so, Thieu, like Diem, might exit with a bang.

II. The Country Bang

Thieu might also, like Diem, exit with a more delayed bang in the countryside. This could happen if the current government programs go awry and Saigon repeats Diem's errors, resorting to a counterproductive use of force against the peasantry at large.

Programs are only as good as the officials implementing them, and poor leadership at the local level has plagued South Vietnam from the country's inception. The vicars of Saigon in the countryside frequently are self-seeking outsiders, city people with a contempt for peasants, military officers whose careers depend on subservience to their superiors rather than service to their civilian populations.

It is wiser for a commander who will be reprimanded for any loss of troops to uproot whole villages (without providing refugee care) than to mount dangerous night patrols around these villages. It is easier for a district chief to shell a hamlet that Front snipers have gotten into than to provide the security that will keep snipers out of the hamlet in the future. It is more profitable for a district chief to keep PF's and RD cadres under his control than to surrender them to village chiefs. It is less grueling for a local police agent to fill his arrest quota of NLF cadres by random peasants (with a sideline business of random bribes) than to ferret out the real Communist infrastructure. It is perhaps more natural for local elders, medium landholders reelected to village councils out of habit, to perpetuate existing tenure than to yield their rents and fields to the village landless.

This kind of antipeasant action was exactly what the Communists prodded the Diem bureaucracy into in the early 1960s. It helped account for that period's groundswell of peasant sympathy for the NLF. Present rural preference for Saigon is only relative, passive, and fragile. Disorganization and loose control are the most favored government qualities. If villagers now see government coercion increasing and a rigid social system and worsening corruption locking them in place as the lowest class; if they see implementation of land reform faltering and district chiefs sabotaging village development, they may once more come to loathe Saigon more than the NLF.

The most dramatic version of such a trend might again see the Saigon government, as in 1964-65, losing one district capital and one battalion per week to rebuilt Communist troops.

III. The Whimper

Probably, however, Thieu's end will not come in cataclysm. Much more likely would be a political disintegration under the surface. Disaffection might start at the top, among the urban politicians and quasi politicians, the floating elite that keeps the economy, the government, and the society functioning no matter who occupies the presidential palace. Fearing chaos, preferring Thieu's suspicious caution to Ky's pyrotechnics, seeing no compelling alternative leader, adjusting to the reality of American support for Thieu, these people have worked with Thieu, however grudgingly.

Their confidence in Thieu's judgment and control waned perceptibly during the Chau affair, and during the 1971 election manipulation, however, and will wane more with every new mistake Thieu makes. This increasing doubt about Thieu, along with the presumed ebbing of American will to guarantee Thieu as United States troop numbers go down, has reopened the question of possible alternatives to Thieu. If the malaise of this elite worsens, Thieu's preventive tactics of diffusing opposition may prove insufficient to keep him on top any longer.

A coup seems unlikely within the next year or so. Thieu will probably still be sufficiently in control—and the United States will probably still be influential enough in Vietnam in money and residual troops—to block any coup in this period. Furthermore, it is unseasonable for a forcible overthrow of the government just now. Hope springs eternal among rivals to Thieu that the United States will still, suddenly, in a search for a political settlement to the war, smile on some fortunate competitor who keeps himself available. If not, politics should change so much anyway as the Americans leave that coups should become easier with time. It would therefore be injudicious for coup aspirants to expose themselves prematurely.

On a more limited scale, however, opponents will be tempted to make political mileage out of the various political quarrels and demonstrations that may be expected from time to time. For a start, the acrimonious one-candidate presidential election of 1971 helped stimulate political decay as surely as it slowed the momentum of government programs. Everyone's suspicions were refueled, and Thieu's isolation from the real state of affairs in the country, like Diem's before him, was no doubt increased.

Nor, in such cases are acrimony and uncertainty confined to the capital. Saigon politics, which may be maddeningly irrelevant to the countryside in good times, becomes maddeningly relevant in bad times. Province chiefs become jittery about what is going on at the center and its implications for themselves and tend to spend more time scouting out Saigon than running their provinces.

Centrifugal political forces have already received a new impulse. Attentism has been increasing in both the cities and the countryside, with more people hedging and seeking personal guarantees from the Communists in return for neutrality or laxness in performance of government work or military operations. The typical accommodations in the delta between local government and Front officials, which were perhaps working in the government's favor up to 1971, are probably now again turning to advantage the Communists.

Typically, this kind of slippage, it is worth noting, takes place without much visible change at first in the military situation or in the percentage of the population apparently remaining under government control.

It is my belief that an under-the-surface decay of the non-Communist political system is the most likely course of events over the next couple of years in South Vietnam. It is the most likely course, I believe further, even if Khiem or Minh succeeds Thieu in this period. Khiem would inherit all the political shortcomings of Thieu and have no broad political appeal of his own to offset them. Minh would have more personal popularity, but, judging from his brief chance at leadership after the overthrow of Diem, he would not be able to turn his amiability into enduring administrative and governing skill.

Once set in motion, such deterioration would be greatly accelerated by the lack of political organization in South Vietnam. Thieu has no strong organization of his own to brake political dissolution. He has no Can Lao; he does not even have the Republican Youth which seemed so sturdy to Ngo Dinh Nhu but evaporated overnight with the coup of 1963.

Nor is there any organized loyal opposition. The polarization of political choice between Thieu and the Communists which Thieu has fostered has strengthened Thieu personally, in a brittle way, in Saigon politics, but it has tended to weaken the non-Communist system by making some opponents of Thieu feel they have no realistic choice other than the NLF.

Perhaps most critical in the dearth of political organization is the lack of dynamic links between the countryside and the central government.

The most easily accomplished tie would be a tacit coalition between Saigon and the ethnic and religious minorities that are already dominant in various regions.[4] Thieu has come to accept FULRO to some degree as a legitimate representative of the montagnards. And apparently, he has mended fences with the Khmer and the Cao Dai since the unhappy days of 1969/70 on the issues of minority representation and province chiefs.

But Thieu's relationships with the various groups still tend to be tactical deals with leaders of particular factions rather than any constructive long-term commitment; Saigon remains wary of autonomy in the cohesive Hoa Hao and Cao Dai regions, even when a cooperative autonomy could strengthen these regions against Communist inroads.

As for the present village programs of the government, these offer administrative and economic rather than political incentives to secure villagers' loyalty to Saigon.

Such incentives are weak. For all the planning to the contrary, South Vietnam is still overcentralized; administration could easily bog down again under its own weight, as it did under Diem. The economic slowdown that will accompany American disengagement may effectively cripple development, leaving the discontent of peasants the greater for the original promises and raised expectations.

Furthermore, even if the programs work, they are lacking in upward mobility or other contingency incentives for peasants. They do not bestow rewards for greater loyalty to Saigon or enforce sanctions on lesser loyalty, since they are uniform programs regardless of local response to them. The proffered advantages such as land reform are not visibly dependent on the survival of the Saigon regime and therefore do not reinforce it.

Thus, the government programs, while encouraging some village political development, have not managed to couple villagism with a larger national polity. Saigon has never generated, as the NLF has, a stratum of local leaders with the motivation to make sacrifices and take high risks for the cause. It has never induced mass political participation at the hamlet level. It has never succeeded in decentralizing as the Communists have, either in placing primary emphasis on local leaders, in giving them wide discretionary authority, or in integrating local military forces with the local communities.[5]

Epilogue: The Communists

Other developing countries have survived over extended years with rigid bureaucracies, little real government in the countryside, and even a chronic political state approaching chaos. South Vietnam has itself displayed considerable resilience, absorbing the 1966 struggle movement and the rebellion of I Corps—as well as the 1968 Tet offensive and month-long occupation of Hue—without collapsing. For all of their flaws Thieu and a non-Communist government are not necessarily doomed to expire.

As the Communists regain their strength, however, an inertia of muddling through may just not be good enough. The small minority of committed Communist cadres in the population may well prove more decisive than the passively anti-Communist majority. An experienced antagonist will do everything within its power to overburden the government system and goad it into repressive actions, to make government violence the overriding issue in peasant minds. Given South Vietnam's record, it seems quite possible that the government will oblige its enemy. The question then arises as to how soon the Communists might be able to rebuild themselves to take advantage of political deterioration on the government side.

As a preliminary answer, I assume the following.

1. That North Vietnam is far from mortally tired, that it can continue to get all the small arms it needs from China, and that it can continue to supply its desired level of troops in the South;
2. That the deprivation of military cover for Communist political cadres that has been achieved in the Mekong delta will slow down but will not prevent the still-healthy infrastructure from rebuilding Communist troops by recruitment

in the new crops of 17- and 18-year-olds in the South, first in such strong-holds as Binh Dinh and Kien Hoa, later over widening areas;

3. That no ceasefire can possibly be agreed upon and observed until some battle-field stability (probably in Cambodia as well as in Vietnam) has been reached and perceived. And that stability will not be attained until the United States reduction has been virtually completed and Communist forces have probed the new balance and recovered some of what they lost in the 1968-1969 pac-ification drive;

4. That neither Washington nor Saigon will negotiate a central coalition that would not reflect current American and South Vietnamese supremacy on the battlefield;

5. That Hanoi adamantly opposes any political settlement to the war, because the Communists got so badly burned whenever they ceased hostilities in the past, first in the 1954-56 period before the scheduled Geneva elections, and then in the 1956-59 period, when Hanoi's strategy was not to fight and Diem destroyed 80-90% of the party organization in many Communist base areas in the South; and that the NLF will never agree to localized representation or a guaranteed bloc of seats in the existing legislature, the settlement that Thieu has implicitly proposed; and

6. That the impasse in negotiations will therefore continue indefinitely.

Just what these assumptions imply as far as timing is concerned is not alto-gether clear. There would appear to be less than a year's breathing space be-fore military pressures on the South Vietnamese government begin mounting up again. When that happens, I would expect the South Vietnamese to be pushed back to some extent, especially in the vulnerable I Corps and in the highlands of II Corps. After an initial fallback, I would expect the South Vietnamese to be able to hold their own militarily. Even a limited military success by the Com-munists would probably erode citizen confidence in the South Vietnamese government disproportionately. Such loss of confidence in Saigon would not automatically translate into a mandate for the Communists, however.

Factors inhibiting or delaying a Communist takeover would include the ab-sence of any leader comparable to the towering Ho Chi Minh; the timespan necessary for rebuilding local forces in South Vietnam and the loss of political momentum during this period; the experience of delta villagers in two or three years of relative security sponsored by the government; greater peasant skepti-cism toward the Communists than existed a decade ago; and the absence of land hunger as a major exploitable grievance (if government land reform gets carried out as planned).

Yet, I should think that with time the superior Communist organization, dis-cipline, intelligence gathering, mass mobilization, and staying power could again bring the government to the verge of collapse and again bring the party, perhaps itself exhausted, to the brink of victory in South Vietnam.

Notes

1. For changes in village attitudes, see Samuel Popkin, "Village Authority Patterns in Vietnam," in *Vietnam: Some Basic Issues & Alternatives*, edited by Walter S. Isard (Cambridge: Harvard University Press, 1969).

2. Official South Vietnamese figures for South Vietnamese military casualties and orphans; official United States figures or estimates for wounded and homeless, unacknowledged refugees, bombing tonnage, and defoliation. For civilian casualties, see U.S., Congress, Senate, Subcommittee to Investigate Problems Connected with Refugees and Escapees of the Committee on the Judiciary, *Refugee and Civilian War Casualty Problems in Indochina: A Staff Report*, (Washington, 1970); and General Accounting Office, *Refugee and Civilian War Casualty Problems in Vietnam* (Washington, 1971).

3. Figures on United States aid and armed forces jobs from Buu Hoan, "The South Vietnamese Economy in the Transition to Peace and After," *Asian Survey* II (April 1971): 305-20; USAID estimate of jobs dependent on American troops.

4. For development of this thesis, see Gerald Hickey, "Accommodation and Coalition in South Vietnam," Rand Corporation Paper, P-4213 (January 1970).

5. See Jeffrey Race, "How They Won," *Asian Survey* 10, no. 8 (August 1970): 628-650; and John Donnell, "Expanding Political Participation—the Long Haul from Villagism to Nationalism," Ibid., pp. 688-704.

2

The DRV since the Death of Ho Chi Minh: The Politics of a Revolution in Transition

William S. Turley

If there are any conventions in the study of the internal politics of the Democratic Republic of Vietnam (DRV), one of them certainly is a concentration on factionalism in the leadership. Such a focus would seem to be especially appropriate for interpreting the DRV's collective leadership and internal political developments since the death of Ho Chi Minh. However, while not denying the intrinsic interest of this approach, the present effort holds that other questions about the DRV also need to be asked. For this reason, the central questions asked here are not only: "Who are the most powerful men since Ho's death and what are they doing?" but also: "What kind of communist system is the DRV becoming and why?"

The DRV Political System

Students of non-Western societies generally strive to rise above culture-bound analytical schemes and perspectives. While this laudable attempt at objectivity has been successful in many studies of Communist China, it has not yet been effectively developed by American observers of Vietnamese Communism. The state of war, of course, is responsible for much bias, giving a highly selective and ideological flavor to our understanding of the North Vietnamese regime. Therefore, prior to an itemization of issues and problems facing the DRV, a note on some important but often overlooked features of DRV political life is essential.

Political participation in the DRV, as in China,[1] is extended to virtually all citizens in accordance with the mass line, not so much as a right as an obligation. Political participation is conceived as a means to secure the people's voluntary and conscious support for Lao Dong Party (Vietnamese Labor Party) policies; it is an organizational technique to mobilize people for Party-defined purposes at a high level of commitment and exertion. In practice, it involves the use of democratic and decentralized decision-making mechanisms designed to create and exploit mass willingness to obey. Within the framework of village government and occupational associations, the people take part in political activities that affect their lives, such as publicly criticizing local Party cadres, electing village leaders, deciding when to move to a higher stage of collectivization, coordinating the use of collectively owned tools, deciding whether to introduce a new local industry or not, and, how to contribute to militia training and recruitment. These activities must produce decisions that fall within the bounds set by Party policy, but

Party cadres take great care to predetermine the outcome without resorting to forcible intervention. Maximum feasible reliance is placed on struggle movements, manipulation of incentives, and propaganda. Ideally, the people, regardless of how guided their decision-making may be, are made to feel that the decision is in some way their own, hence their willingness to support it. Obviously, there is a totalitarian element in such methods,[2] but repeated exercise of a degree of political participation never allowed in the pre-Resistance Vietnamese village is fairly convincing to the poor peasant that the regime is just and its rule good.

In China, perhaps the most important value pursued through mass political participation is the retention of the vitality of Mao's populist revolutionary ethos against the encroachments of bureaucratism. In the DRV, similar importance is attached to preserving the spirit and working style of the Resistance, but mass political participation has come to be valued also as a means to organize society for war. In practice, the Lao Dong Party's conception of political participation is an exchange relationship between the regime and the population: the regime sells social justice, virtuous administration and rural order in return for intense popular commitment to war-related tasks and to production.

It has been easier for the DRV to retain its Resistance ethos than for China to preserve its populism in large part because of the sustained hostilities. Thus, the regime devotes great attention to techniques aimed at securing maximum control over the nation's resources, especially the human ones, in order to compensate for the DRV's material weaknesses. The result has been that the Party has had to make its rule highly pragmatic, flexible, and sensitive to popular opinion and grievances. These characteristics are fervently maintained by Party leaders and deeply embedded in the Party's ideological baggage, including its military science, as recently reemphasized by General Giap:

Our military science has adequate conditions for developing to a high degree the role of subjective endeavor—that is, the role of the revolutionary energy, initiative, and creativeness of the leaders, the masses of cadres and combatants, and the masses of people in winning victory for the war. In a situation where a small strength is used to defeat a bigger strength, subjective endeavor is of particularly important significance.[3]

If extensive American involvement in the war has had any lasting effects on North Vietnamese politics, one of the most important would be the reinforcing of a strong state in Northern Vietnam led by one of the most responsive communist parties in power and certainly the most popular army in the communist world.

It is not surprising that in such a system the military should play a prominent role in the nation's politics, society and economy. This prominence is reflected by the fact that the DRV devotes a larger percentage of its GNP to military expenditures than any state in the world. This figure was 25% in 1967,[4] declining to 21% in 1970.[5] It is possible to maintain such a high level of military expenditure only through the willing as well as demanded sacrifices of the civilian population. The military itself contributes to this effort by participating in mass emulation campaigns, providing technical and administrative skills to industry and local economic formations, and offering the society's major avenue through which the individual can improve his capacities, status, and prestige. The military, which includes the regular People's Army of Vietnam, the regional forces and the village self-defense militia, is probably better integrated with the people than any other institution in the DRV,[6] and the values and work style of the military are hardly distinguishable from those of civilian society.

The DRV's political system, in other words, vividly reflects the demands of prolonged warfare against a more numerous and better equipped force; it is a mass mobilization system that thus far has responded dynamically to the requirements of the competition in which it is engaged. However, the regime's goals and the means it has chosen to pursue them have restricted its freedom to change directions radically and require that certain present priorities be maintained indefinitely.

There are many things the regime cannot do and many it must. First, after thirty years of zealous effort to establish a unified state of Vietnam, the Lao Dong Party cannot abandon the goal of reunification without irreparably dividing its ranks in the North and losing the adherence of all but suicidal Southerners. This is the lesson of the late 1950s, the Party's darkest days, when hope for early reunification collapsed before the efficient counterterror of Diem's Cong An (security force).[7] Second, the DRV cannot take an exclusively one-sided position in the Sino-Soviet dispute without jeopardizing the flow of materiel and technological resources on which it depends heavily. Third, it cannot alter domestic priorities in any way that prohibits pursuing reunification, casts doubt on its commitment to reunification, or which irreparably offends the ideological sensibilities of Moscow, or Peking. And fourth, the Party leadership cannot engage in fractious quarrels over these issues so as to impair the regime's effectiveness. A corollary is that the DRV must tread a consistent path with a single-minded sense of purpose, regardless of changes in the leadership, and major disagreement must be confined primarily to the question of continuing past policies with more or less intensity. Disputes among Party leaders must be viewed against the background recent DRV political developments.

Evolving National Priorities

The DRV's national economic priorities as outlined in the annual State Plans changed significantly, though not dramatically, from 1969 to 1970, the period bracketing Ho's death on 3 September 1969. An article in the Party journal, *Hoc Tap* (Studies), explained that "as the North no longer suffers from the war of destruction, we must reorient our economic activities so that they may be in accordance with the new situation . . . ."[8]

From 1965 to 1969, the yearly State Plans assigned the highest priority to maintenance of communications and transportation facilities in order to link the rear base with the front line while under intensive aerial bombardment, and to development of small, dispersed economic formations to meet basic needs at the local level. But the 1969 State Plan, publicized in January 1969, for the first time included emphatic directives to prepare for long-range economic development beginning in the near future on an improved technical base.

It is necessary to continue making preparations for the coming years and for the restoration and development of the economy after the war . . . . To fulfill this task, we must pursue the tasks of studying long-term plans and conducting basic investigations; we must study the main branches' plans, make preparations for the execution of these plans, and pay attention to improving scientific and technical research and stepping up the training of technical cadres, and technical workers.[9]

Thus, the intention to change priorities from an almost purely resistance economy to a postwar development economy was clearly articulated before 1969, while Ho still lived. The year 1969 was a year of formulation of plans to make this transition, and 1970 was to be the transitional year.

In organizational matters, the 1969 Plan laid greatest stress on the economic managerial task, in which the military had a special responsibility to provide labor and coordinated leadership to dispersed economic production units and an example of austerity in the use of resources.[10] The 1969 Plan reflected the reliance on small production units introduced during the air war and the preponderance of military considerations in economic activity.

According to *Hoc Tap* in January 1970, "*The main objective* of the State Plan for 1970 is to increase agricultural production (essentially foodstuffs) and the production of consumer goods."[11] To support this objective, the Plan stressed the need to accelerate "the production of light industry and the food processing industry." And as a foretaste of the DRV's long-range development plans, it gave third-rank in priority to a project which had been set aside for five years: ". . . to make efforts to restore, and increase the production of a number of the most important heavy industry sectors, such as coal, electricity, wood, machinery, construction materials, etc." The 1970 Plan very clearly laid the groundwork for major industrial expansion, after a period of recovery and improvement in the people's material well-being. In the words of Premier Pham Van Dong, the 1970 emphasis on agricultural and consumer needs was "to eliminate in the shortest time possible the sequels of war" and "prepare the necessary forces for starting large-scale socialist construction whenever conditions permit."[12] The order of priorities in the Plan, therefore, was temporary and did not constitute a radical departure from the general economic principles and goals the Lao Dong Party has been trying to implement since 1954.

With regard to organizational problems, the 1970 Plan replaced 1969's emphasis on the economic managerial task with the labor management task. Essentially, the object of labor management was to rationalize the labor force and reduce supervisory overheads, particularly in the state apparatus.[13] During the air war, dispersal of production units and decentralization of supervision had led to inefficient use of labor and duplication of administrative work, resulting in poorer production. A member of the State Planning Commission gave the following explanation.

The general tendency was to create a new organization with more people for a new job. As a result, the number of workers in the nonmaterial production sector in general, and state administrative machinery in particular, was higher than necessary for many years. The ratio of cadres and officials involved in state administration, as well as cadres not engaged in production in the various groups, increased at a far greater rate than the total number of workers and employees each year.[14]

In another article, the same official asserted that the major organizational aim of the 1970 State Plan was to reconcentrate economic units and streamline the administrative machinery supervising them in order to increase the number and effectiveness of workers engaged in production with the "important political and social" goal of creating "conditions under which to lead the technical revolution ... and to accelerate the building of socialism in North Vietnam."[15] The 1970 Plan was preparatory to a concerted effort to industrialize on a large scale, and it was a natural progression from the 1969 Plan.

The 1971 State Plan is simply a continuation of the 1970 priorities,[16] although prospects for early development of heavy industry are less bright than originally hoped. Eighty percent of the work force is still occupied in food production and one-crop cultivation, therefore agriculture must be made more efficient before labor can be diverted to other pursuits.[17] Obviously, there may be disagreement over how to solve these problems, but there is sufficient continuity to suggest that the general course of change had its origins in elements present long before Ho's death, reflecting a stable working consensus among the leaders.

The theoretical underpinning and authoritative discussion of this transition was presented by Le Duan in a lengthy, very important article published in *Nhan dan* (The People), 14 February 1970.[18] The attention this document has received since its publication indicates both that it is to be taken as the Party line and that Le Duan's position as *primus inter pares* was secure shortly after Ho's death. With regard to the economy, Le Duan was even more emphatic than the State Plans that the DRV must build heavy industry. He pointed out that this has been the basic direction ever since the Third Party Congress and that it has been in practical effect for fifteen years. Perhaps as a rejoinder to those who would be satisfied with building light industry and perfecting agriculture—programs which do not produce the large industrial proletariat on which a mature communist state presumably is predicated—Le Duan approvingly quoted

Lenin: " 'The only possible economic basis of socialism is mechanized heavy industry. Whoever forgets this is not a Communist.' " However, Le Duan fully realized the inability of the DRV to devote its current attention exclusively to heavy industry and the impracticality of a Chinese-style Great Leap Forward, because in order to build heavy industry, he said, ". . . we must have the prerequisite conditions created by agriculture and industry. These prerequisite conditions are labor power, consumer goods, initial capital, and markets." It would be necessary first to make more efficient use of the labor pool, develop some light industry, rapidly advance in the "technical revolution," and to organize large units of agricultural production better integrated with the national requirement to "centralize the people's capital." Given such views and goals, the DRV appears to be deeply committed to the establishment in the long run of larger units of production and greater centralization of control over its economic development.

One of the most important aspects of this program was implemented early in 1969 and continued through 1970: the consolidation of collectivization in agriculture.[19] For years, the regime has been forming high level agricultural cooperatives out of low level ones[20] as the appropriate direction for socialist construction in agriculture. According to DRV statistics, in 1963, there were 30,600 cooperatives of which 35% were high-level ones containing 46% of all farm families.[21] In 1968, there were 22,360 cooperatives of which 79% were high-level ones containing 92% of all farm families; in the same year, 95% of all farm families lived in cooperatives, and the cooperatives covered over 92% of the DRV's farm land.[22] Moreover, in 1964, the average cooperative contained 45 hectares and 83 farm families (rising to an average of 108 farm families per cooperative in the Tonkin delta),[23] in 1968, it had 77 hectares and 136 families (rising to 270 families on 128 hectares in the delta).[24] The growth and expansion of the high-level cooperatives have progressed steadily, although less rapidly than desired because of the need during the air war to encourage local autonomy and self-sufficiency. But the Party insisted on continued cooperativization and overcoming communal isolation because of its orthodox belief that it must socialize agriculture as the first step toward rapid industrialization.[25]

On 28 April 1969, the Standing Committee of the National Assembly promulgated the first, and long overdue, statute on high-level agricultural cooperatives. Described as a "very important document," this statute was designed to hasten the integration of agricultural development with the regime's general economic goals and to clarify some procedures in cooperative management that had been improperly executed or neglected by Party cadres and state officials. As the cooperatives increased in size and complexity, the absence of adequate regulations had encouraged management agencies and cadres to abuse their power, against which cooperative members had little defense, and thus the principles of collective ownership and of "voluntarism, mutual benefit and democratic management" had been attenuated. "This situation," admitted one official, "has caused a lack of enthusiasm among the members for production and has given rise to many other negative features."[26]

In the Party's view, it was not cooperativization itself that was responsible for "lack of enthusiasm," but the imperfect implementation of Party organizational principles intended to counteract elitist and bureaucratic attitudes among cadres. These attitudes had appeared because of the more complex, hierarchical, specialized and impersonal organizational procedures required by the increased size of some cooperatives and by the policy of opposing the tendency of villages, on which cooperatives mainly are based, to drift toward self-sufficient isolation from national demands. The Party, faced with the contradictory needs to bring local units under more effective central command and at the same time to increase the motivation of peasants who resented the attitudes and practices the new organizational requirements induced in cadres, chose to renew emphasis on "voluntarism" and "democratic management," that is, essentially, the mass line. In accordance with this principle, Party cadres were instructed to ". . . actively struggle to overcome administrativist, authoritarian, and coercive methods of economic management which fail to respect the interests of the cooperative and the legitimate interests of the members."[27] At present, the DRV has too little materiel and financial capital to neglect the human factor in increasing production. According to Party doctrine, reinvigoration of the mass line need not thwart other processes of centralization and enlargement of production units. The problem is to keep the cadres sensitive to mass grievances. This sensitivity must be guaranteed by buttressing peasant criticisms of cadres with improved procedures to articulate grievances and to find legal redress. The mass support thus secured, it is hoped, will help accelerate the rate of development on the entire agricultural front.

The Party leadership has found it necessary, in other words, to continue encouraging the self-reliant spirit of Resistance agriculture, while awaiting future improvement in the State's capacity to invest greater amounts of material and technological capital. As long as the DRV has not succeeded in securing the economies of scale the cooperatives are supposed to provide, it must devote a substantial portion of the restoration and expansion of industry to increasing agricultural and consumer goods production. Le Duan gave the following explanation.

At present, the most important task of heavy industry is to create conditions for equipping the nation's labor force—first of all, agricultural and light industrial labor—with all kinds of tools of different technological levels, from rudimentary to modern, appropriate to each branch and each type of work—so as to rapidly raise social labor output to at least twice or three times the current level.[28]

Before it can resume major industrial development, industry must for a time serve agriculture, so that agriculture can be strengthened in order better to serve industry. At present, the regime cannot concentrate as much as some leaders would like on heavy industry. However, many apparently believe that improvements in deployment and motivation of labor constitute a latent source of capital for industrial development without excessive dependence on foreign aid, even while the DRV's agriculture is relatively primitive.

Le Duan shares this favorable orientation toward the Chinese model with most members of the Political Bureau, despite his evident leaning toward Moscow for ideological authority to justify the ultimate goal of development of heavy industry.

Speculation about the leader's future ideological orientation, however, must take into account factors peculiar to the DRV's history and situation. For example, without substantial foreign aid and a termination to hostilities in Indochina, the present course almost certainly will require retention of a vital Resistance ethos and mass line. Should there be a significant diminution of these elements because of the contradictory demands of economic centralization and administrative bureaucratization, pressures within the Party for a Vietnamese Great Proletarian Cultural Revolution might grow irresistible.

The Military Situation

While Ho Chi Minh lived, the Party was firmly dedicated to reunification by all available means, including military. There has been no change in this goal, or in the means, since his death, but disputes over how to organize and strengthen those means continues unabated.[29] As long as the DRV has not won the war, there will be experimentation. A detailed, updated and somewhat revised analysis of the Party's military line appeared in mid-December 1969 in commemoration of the People's Army of Vietnam's (PAVN) twenty-fifth year, in the form of three articles[30] by General Giap; Col. Gen. Van Tien Dung, the PAVN Chief-of-Staff; and Lt. Gen. Song Hao, Director of the PAVN's General Political Department.

The unifying theme of these articles is that the theory of people's war has had to undergo modification in the light of experience with vastly superior American firepower and mobility. Giap's lengthy piece, a major effort superseding his own and others' works on people's war, emphasizes the prolongation of the war and the maximization of the capabilities of small, dispersed forces. Throughout his analysis, grounded firmly in the concept of balance of forces, there runs the tacit admission that the situation had been militarily unfavorable for some time because of the enemy's superiority in weapons and manpower. However, he does not recommend reversion to guerrilla war or argue that the DRV must first make up its material deficiencies in order to win. Nor does he downgrade the traditional Party faith in the efficacy of political struggle and of human factors in war, for these are essential aspects of small-unit warfare. Rather, he stresses the need to strengthen in-place forces, to coordinate guerrilla warfare with regular warfare, and to consolidate national defense in the North. It is, essentially, a strategy of protracted warfare, which requires the entrenchment of existing defense capabilities and expansion of regional and militia forces along with refinement of the regular forces' technical competence.

Articles and speeches subsequent to Giap's essay indicate that the DRV is indeed upgrading the regional and militia forces, partly to improve defense forces-in-being and partly to expand the reserve of trained personnel for instant mobilization.[31] The implication for the Southern command, because of the limited availability of Northern regulars, is that it too will have to improve local forces. Giap's closing exhortation, that ". . . we must be all the more imbued with the idea of using a small force to fight a bigger one in order to defeat him," actually is a summary of the DRV's present formula for maintaining its military commitments throughout Indochina. The DRV is also limiting military manpower requirements in order to increase the labor supply in the North and release technical cadres for development projects. Giap observed the following.

If all our units possess a high quality and are capable of fighting the enemy with high combat efficiency, we can greatly increase the combat strength of our limited armed forces, and, at the same time, reduce the organizational and leadership problems, replenish our forces, meet our armed forces' material requirements, and use our forces economically. This represents a major problem of strategic importance.[32]

Two months later, the newspaper *Hanoi Moi* republished and explained in detail the civilian pay scale for soldiers transferred to nonmilitary jobs.[33] Although these trends in the DRV's military line were present before Ho's death—in fact they came to dominate policy in 1967—they appear to have become more pronounced since then.

Recent military thought increasingly reflects a new tone: despair at the PAVN's numerical and technological weakness, preoccupation with the enemy's superiority in these fields, and a controversial upgrading of the consideration given these factors when assessing the balance of forces. Thus, Giap and Dung stress the need for innovation and flexibility in the following way.

Giap: We should not apply old experiences mechanically or reapply outmoded forms of warfare.

Dung: We have known how to learn from experiences, improve them, and creatively use our fraternal countries' experiences; our procedure for waging war as well as our armed struggle methods have entirely originated in our country's concrete revolutionary struggle in the present era. *We do not bind ourselves to any fixed form or method of struggle.* [Emphasis in original.]

The most explicit statement that innovation must stress the technological and expert aspects came, significantly, from Song Hao who, as Director of the General Political Department, is the ranking Party political officer in the military. Song Hao is a Resistance general who rose from division political officer in 1954 to his present position in 1961, from which he has defended the primacy of men over weapons and of revolutionary awareness over purely military factors against a sizeable group which advocates greater reliance on weaponry and technical expertise. Over the last several years, he has altered his views, to the point where he now emerges as the leading exponent of a position which does not disparage revolutionary awareness and human factors but which admits with uncharacteristic readiness that without sophisticated weaponry and technical expertise ". . . there can be no army . . . with good combat ability."[34] This view amounts to a tacit repudiation of the Maoist belief that revolutionary élan is sufficient to sustain the PAVN in protracted war, and it is a view with which leading military officers, such as Giap and Dung, seem to concur. Defenders of this position are predisposed to favor economic programs which strengthen the DRV's technical and material resources as well as to seek greater aid from the Soviet Union while remaining very willing to accept whatever sophisticated weaponry China is able to provide. In oblique criticism of the parsimony of the DRV's allies, Song Hao noted that the Vietnamese have been waging war while relying "mainly on our own strength, and doing our best to procure international assistance."

Le Duan, in the major article cited earlier, does not address himself directly to these issues, but his analysis of the balance of forces and his criticisms of certain weaknesses are not inconsistent with the views of these military leaders. Noting that the United States forces possess "modern equipment and much greater military and economic potentialities," he says that "we need time to gradually annihilate and weaken the enemy's forces, . . . deepen his weaknesses, while improving and developing our military and political forces, thus creating favorable balance of power."[35] Le Duan agrees here, that for the ultimate goal of reunification, the balance of forces is unfavorable, and that it is material and technological disparities which are primarily responsible. These obstacles must be overcome by long and careful effort on political, economic, and technological fronts. In passages strongly reminiscent of the important 1956 document (which Le Duan may have written) "The Revolutionary Line in the South" (Duong Loi Cach Mang Mien Nam),[36] the unfavorable balance of forces in the South at that time are acknowledged and plans are suggested to reverse it.[37] Le Duan argues that all preceding successes have been based on lengthy, arduous, political groundwork, and that although the international situation may be favorable, it is impossible to take advantage of it without adequate internal revolutionary strength. The implication clearly is that, probably for several years, it will be necessary to strengthen forces-in-being and to refrain from rash adventures. It is obvious that this view is not unanimously held in the Party. Some members hold a more optimistic view of risk-taking, to which Le Duan strenuously objects.

A matter of principle is the fact that in his daily policy as well as in the actualities of struggle, in whatever form and under whatever condition, the revolutionary must never lose sight of the final objective. To consider struggle for small daily victories and for immediate objectives as being 'everything' and 'the final objective to be zero' and to 'sacrifice the future of the movement for the present' are the manifestations of the most disastrous kind of opportunism whose results can only be the keeping of the masses of the people in eternal slavery.[38]

It is not known at whom these criticisms are directed, but it is reasonable to surmise that the target may include some Southern cadres (if the events of 1956-1959 can be taken as precedent) and members of elite, specialized units of the armed forces (antiaircraft, tank corps). The most volatile cleavages of opinion over military strategy, it may be conjectured, would most likely develop between the highest leaders and lower ranks of the Party, between policy-makers and policy-executors, between theorists and practitioners, and not among the highest leaders themselves.[39] This is not to say that harmony reigns in the Political Bureau, but that there is sufficient agreement on military questions of long-range consequence to allow publication of detailed plans and policies.

Despite the prominence now given to technical expertise in the regular army, no vigorous high-level defense of redness has appeared, at least not in public, even though recent discussions of Party military doctrine have presented excellent opportunities for such issues to find expression. While the value of redness is still unquestioned, there is reason to doubt that it may remain so indefinitely. The recognized need to alter the balance-of-forces in large part by technical and expert means contradicts the simultaneous effort to strengthen forces-in-being through mass movements and cultivation of red zeal. Yet it is assumed by the highest military leaders that the military can be kept both red and expert. This may be possible within the context of a war which justifies quasimodern tactics and techniques of the regular army. But if the present programs are made long-term features of DRV military development, especially in a period of lower military activity or a shift to a strictly conventional offensive in the South, it is likely that the regular PAVN would become a more exclusively expert organization and the irregular local and regional forces would remain the home of red virtues. A split in ideology attitude within the ranks of the military thus would occur. The potential for disagreement within the Party over such a situation is considerable, and it is enhanced by recent developments in other areas.

The Condition of the Party

One of the most significant developments in 1970 was Le Duan's announcement that the Party would "purify the ranks" (thanh lọc hàng ngũ) in conjunction with the creation of a "Ho Chi Minh Class" of Party cadres. This two-pronged campaign was begun to reduce excess and inefficient Party members and to forge a younger, leaner, more professional Party organization.

The campaign provides additional evidence regarding the regime's priorities and the kinds of skills those in power now think are most useful to achieve them. It is unclear to what extent, if any, this purification is merely a screen for internal Party rivalry over leadership succession, but it does offer opportunities for some to improve their relative advantage. Perhaps more important, the age, skills, working style and training of Party cadres is being changed, thus affecting how the Party will relate to the masses.

The number of Party members increased from 800,000 or 4.4% of the population in 1965 to 1.1 million or about 5% of the population in 1970. Expansion of the Party in an emergency situation resulted in the admission of many new members who had not served adequate apprenticeships in appropriate organizations which indoctrinate recruits for the Party.[40] Lacking thorough knowledge of the Party's working methods, these members were thought to possess excessive individualism and other characteristics of weak revolutionary ethics. Old Party cadres showed similar deficiencies because heavy workloads had weakened them, and many had failed to keep up with developments in industry, economics, technology which required specialized knowledge as well as political zeal. In addition, Party supervision of the cadres had been slack for too long, and many cadres had become corrupt, abusing their power for private gain.[41]

These instances of deviation from Party norms are probably temporary adaptations to the stress of war, made possible by economic and administrative decentralization. The partial reversion in some regions to communal self-reliance encouraged administrative innovation by Party cadres who were faced with the problem of accommodating the traditional values and practices that reappeared in a time of acute crisis, and the constant pressure for ever greater sacrifice undoubtedly led both citizens and cadres to seek relief in exceptions to the rule. If this view is correct, then the war definitely strained the political fabric of the DRV, and the present effort to reform the Party and weed out members who "lack sufficient character" is an effort to restore the effectiveness of central political institutions. It is, in a sense, a remobilization of the nation's political resources.

It is not, however, a remobilization for precisely the same purposes or projects that have existed before, and the predominant conception of the best means to accomplish the new ends has assumed a form seldom articulated so concretely as it has been in the last year. Throughout the discussion of the Party's purification and the creation of the Ho Chi Minh Class, there is criticism of overreliance on political motivation and a preference for organizational efficiency and technical expertise. In the words of the Hanoi Party Committee Secretary: "The revolution requires that cadres provide leadership not only in party development and mass activities but also in regard to culture, industry, agriculture, finance, and so on."[42] And Le Duan chastised those who would substitute "general ideological and political tasks" for hard organizational work which is necessary to lead "the State machinery and all its specialist, professional and technical organs."[43] According to published statements of Party leaders, redness is not repudiated, there is no decline in faith that the power of ideology and political struggle will surmount material obstacles, and excessive bureaucratization is not tolerated. On the contrary, the Political Bureau's "Resolution . . . on the Campaign to Improve the Quality of Party Members and Recruit the Ho Chi Minh Class of Party Member," signed by Le Duan for the Political Bureau on 6 March 1970, explicitly states that the Party will adhere even more closely to the mass line to motivate the masses to "exert democratic control" and "struggle against manifestations of bureaucracy, authoritarianism, arrogance, abuse of power, or violations of state laws and the people's right to collective ownership."[44] But the principal criteria are consistent with the current economic trend, which places a high value on technical expertise and central control. For the moment, the Party is dominated by men who favor cultivating the productive potential of professional expertise while neither abandoning the Resistance mystique nor relying on it too much. These attitudes set criteria both for weeding out old cadres and for recruiting new ones for the Ho Chi Minh Class.

Recruitment of the Ho Chi Minh Class of Party cadres began intensively on 19 May 1970 and continued on a concentrated basis until 19 May 1971, when it was established as a permanent recruitment procedure.[45] The campaign is explained as the rectification and temporary intensification, under a special label, of a Party practice that had fallen into disuse, i.e., the continual admission of new members and expulsion of old ones in order to improve the overall quality of Party members. This practice, "aimed toward keeping the Party ranks constantly clean, strong, and stable," had not been "stressed and satisfactorily carried out for a long time."[46]

While the accuracy and sincerity of such explanations may be questioned, it is evident that the campaign is a concerted effort to infuse new life into the Party and to strengthen the Party's links with certain key sectors of the population. In a nation with an average age of sixteen, it is not surprising that the Party should have become the victim of a generation gap. The Ho Chi Minh Class, consequently, is being recruited solely from the Lao Dong Youth Group, whose membership is between the ages of eighteen and thirty. This has been the primary procedure in the past, but apparently there had been many deviations in execution and the Party had failed to attract enough of the best young people who have lived their entire lives trained in the realities of production and combat. The present campaign is based on the assumption that the years of war and hardship have imparted great revolutionary consciousness to many, particularly the young. Apparently the Party feels it has not appealed adequately to youth. There is a curious inconsistency in this diagnosis, because presumably the more youth have been awakened to revolutionary values the more they should support the vanguard of the Revolution, i.e., the Party. The Party in effect may be admitting its own staleness and failure to keep up with youth, but it is equally if not more possible that the gap in age and in world views between old Party leaders and the post-Resistance generation has become wide enough to warrant attention for the first time. In any event, the present campaign to recruit the Ho Chi Minh Class should reaffirm the role of the Party and of the Lao Dong Youth Group as the avenues through which ambitious youth can seek status and prestige. By giving high priority to "knowledge about science and techniques, economic and specialized management,"[47] the campaign also guarantees that youth in the DRV will seek status and prestige through the perfection of these skills. It seems to be a foregone conclusion in the Party that these youths already have been charged with "high combat determination and a high revolutionary assault spirit" by their participation in the war effort and that they will not lack revolutionary zeal.

Conclusion

As the leaders of the DRV frequently note, the death of Ho Chi Minh marked the end of an era for the Vietnamese Revolution, an era in which all present and future leaders for perhaps two generations have been raised. It is not perfectly clear that the style and tone of the Vietnamese Revolution will remain the same. There is some uncertainty within the Party over interpretation of its Revolutionary imagery and the psychological sources of the Revolution's vitality; and since Ho's theoretical writings are inexplicit and unsubstantial (where they exist at all), there is considerable leeway in which to conduct an exegetical dispute. Divergent opinions have appeared in the form of a quiet contest for the remains of Ho's authority as expressed in his military ideology.

On the one hand, there is the extravagantly Maoist interpretation rich with assertions that military units have been victorious because they were "armed with President Ho's ideas" and which assumes that Ho's example, (his personal ethics) constitute a major part of his thought. Greatest approval is given to quotations from Ho that stress unending struggle to overcome obstacles, to which the only restraints are fear and lack of perseverance.[48] The tendency in this interpretation is to deify Ho and to elevate his thought to a level equal to that of other major ideologists of the communist movement and to give the Vietnamese Revolution an historical status equal to that of the Soviet Union and China.

On the other hand, there is a view which readily admits that Ho never produced any writings on military affairs of theoretical importance, but which seeks to identify Ho and his military thought with the nationalist content of the revolution and to approve, even stress, the idiosyncratic aspects of Vietnamese Communism. In September 1970, the historical journal *Nghien cuu Lich su* published an article by Tran Huy Lieu who summarized this view succinctly:

Though President Ho did not publish a separate work for our army and our people on military topics, military regulations, or strategy and tactics, his ideology on the people's war and liberation war . . . went into the resolutions of the Party and were put into action by the masses. It may be said that in the history of the people's armed struggle over the past nearly 30 years is a living book on the people's war inspired and led by President Ho. Through his instructions and appeals, the ideology of people's war penetrated deep into the minds of our troops and people. There is nothing strange about this, for his ideology is the crystallization of the national revolutionary spirit and came from the people. Refined by proletarian revolutionary spirit absorbed by Ho, this ideology returned to the people in a more scientific and exact form.[49]

There is less concern in this view to assign a place to the Vietnamese Revolution in the rank order of communist revolutions and considerable anxiety to avoid any implication that the Vietnamese Revolution is a derivative one. The article cited here was presented as a proposal for a major work on this subject and was prefaced by an editor's note that Lieu's ideas "will probably all require further study," indicating that his interpretation currently prevails but that the question of which image of the revolution Ho's ideological legacy will serve is still unsettled. It should be noted, however, that all the leaders have had a sufficiently uniform revolutionary experience to make the appearance of lasting antagonisms over these questions unlikely, and that such debates may signify attempts to legitimize a position on a particular issue.

It should not be assumed that disagreements indicate a power struggle from which radical policy changes or shuffling of personnel necessarily will emerge. The extremely high demands of the international environment and of domestic problems severely circumscribe issue areas and available alternatives. Even if consensus on policy does not exist in fact and is imposed by necessity, among the great achievements of the DRV has been the high degree of subordination of all aspects of political and personal life to the overriding concern for maintaining the regime's effectiveness. Fractious struggles are something the Party leaders may engage in, but not to any extent where they would be significant.

In the DRV, the most complex issues are resolved and the most divergent points of view reconciled not by making a clear-cut decision in favor of one side but by doing more of everything. As in any small, beleaguered state, the DRV must devote more attention to increasing strategic options than to choosing among them. Priorities may be revised, but not displaced. Thus, the Party will strive to improve the technical and professional expertise of its cadres and to strengthen the specialized functions of the State apparatus, but never with neglect to the cultivation of revolutionary élan. The war in the South might be fought by less expensive methods in order to permit more attention to economic and social problems in the North, but the war in the South cannot be abandoned without forsaking the Party's claim to legitimacy as the leader of Vietnamese nationalism. And the war may receive greater increments of resources, but never at the expense of the economic development and social revolutionary change considered necessary to waging it. The regime cannot afford to do one thing to the exclusion of another.

One of the major factors which has allowed the Vietnamese Revolution since the days of the Resistance to mobilize otherwise passive peasants into high-risk revolutionary roles has been the presence of a cumulative distribution of inequalities in Vietnamese society maintained by the regime in Saigon.[50] The Party policies and organizational methods perfected to exploit this condition and to struggle for reunification have been doubly sanctified in the minds of the leaders because of their perception that an analogous situation exists in the international system. In relation to its competitors, the DRV is in a very disadvantageous position in terms of material resources, technological sophistication and manpower. Every compensatory measure the Party implements to overcome this inequality—mass mobilization in accordance with the mass line, protracted war, reliance on local self-sufficiency in agriculture, great emphasis on the human factors in warfare—is absolutely necessary because no alternatives exist, and are therefore justifiable to the Party, army and populace alike, as long as the most striking feature of world society is the cumulative distribution of inequalities between nations. Even the current attempts to narrow the technological gap, the leaders believe, must be accelerated by employing techniques that value zeal and mass participation as highly as expertise. The overwhelmingly technological character of the American role in the war has had the paradoxical effect of accentuating the need to overcome this particular inequality while breathing vitality into the Party and North Vietnamese society's inheritance of Resistance attitudes. Should the gap be closed by successful economic development and American withdrawal, the DRV might experience considerable tension between the vestiges of its guerrilla origins and the growth of bureaucratic modernity.

But present conditions impose consensus on the leadership and give credibility to the Party's description of the world and legitimacy to its methods. They also force the leadership to remain extremely sensitive to the values, grievances and perceptions of the populace, insofar as these factors have a bearing on the Party's capacity to secure active and conscious support for its policies. In a sense, the Lao Dong Party is a party only partly in power because it aspires to govern all of Vietnam and because its entire history has been one of crisis provoked by its efforts to achieve this end. Because of the prolonged intensity of this crisis, the Party has had to be more diligent in cultivating popular support than any other communist party in power. Support, of course, always must be specifically for Party-defined ends, not just general goodwill for the regime. But the effort to secure this support has allowed the regime to preserve the nation's Resistance mentality and its remarkable emphasis on voluntarism in political participation without resorting to the artificiality of a Chinese-style Cultural Revolution. This fact will allow the DRV to commit a large proportion of its resources to the war as long as it still has not been won, and this is its intent. Prolonged peace in unification undoubtedly would require changes in political style and would entail a period of flux from which significant departures from the present structure and style of the Revolution could arise.

Notes

1. See James Townsend, *Political Participation in Communist China* (Berkeley and Los Angeles: University of California Press, 1969).

2. The author recognizes that the word "totalitarian" is so lacking in rigor as an analytical concept that its value for purposes of making comparisons or for describing the DRV is limited. Constraints on the autonomy of popular choice in making political decisions may come from a variety of sources, and it would be misleading to define only organizational constraints as totalitarian. The high value placed on ideological conformity and majoritarianism in American civilization, for example, is also an important constraint on individual political autonomy.

3. Vo Nguyen Giap, "Let Us Step Up the Task of Reviewing, Studying, and Developing Vietnamese Military Science in Order to Actively Contribute to Defeating U.S. Aggression," *Quan doi Nhan dan*, 30-31 October 1970; *Viet-Nam Documents and Research Notes*, no. 87 (Saigon: U.S. Mission, December 1970), p. 21.

4. United States Arms Control and Disarmament Agency, *World Military Expenditures* (Washington, D.C.: Economics Bureau, 1969).

5. According to an estimate provided by Douglas Pike, February 1971.

6. The army's relations with the general population exhibit an interesting combination of leadership by example, public opinion sampling, and interest formation. Throughout the DRV's brief history, the regime has been extremely solicitous of wounded soldiers, "families of heroes," and families of men in uniform; and the military has not been reluctant to remind the Party of the needs and grievances of these groups. In 1955, for example, a PAVN cadre reporting on the unsatisfactory treatment by village Party cadres of a soldier's mother concluded with the threatening admonition: "If these weak points are not repaired in time, they will have a bad influence on the thought of soldiers in the army who have similar family situations." Minh-Chau, "Y kien ban doc: Can bo xa T. C. doi voi gia dinh bo doi." "Readers' Views: Cadres of T. C. Village with Regard to Soldier's Family," *Nhan dan* (12 October 1955), no. 588, p. 3.

In the rectification of errors there was a campaign following land reform in late 1956 in which troops, wounded soldiers, demobilized men and families of war dead were defined as "revolutionary military personnel" and given special privileges regardless of class origin. This had the effect of exempting them from the Population Classification Decree. "Nghi quyet cua hoi dong chinh phu ve may chinh sach cu the de sua chua sai lam ve cai cach ruong dat va chinh don to chuc" ("Resolutions of the Council of Ministers Concerning Various Concrete Policies for the Rectification of Errors in Land Reform and Reorganization"), *Nhan dan* (7 November 1956), no. 977, pp. 1-2.

Similar examples of Party sensitivity to the impact of its social policies on military effectiveness—a sensitivity maintained by periodic prods from the military—appear frequently, especially in periods of intense pressure from outside or of policy and economic development changes internally. In this regard, see "The All-North Local Military Conference Had Great Success," *Quan doi Nhan dan* (15 August 1970); *Viet-Nam Documents . . .* , no. 89 (February 1971), p. 4. Because the military's "constituency" is large, the army's advocacy of its interests casts the military in a role analogous to that of a people's lobby within the elitist Lao Dong Party, even though the military is motivated purely by concern for military morale and popular support for war-related tasks. Military leaders, especially in the first few years after Geneva, but to some extent even now, are the most important voice for the populist strain in Marxist ideology.

7. See Jeffrey Race, "The Origins of the Second Indochina War," *Asian Survey* 10, no. 5 (May 1970): 359-382.

8. "Struggle for the Successful Fulfillment of the 1970 State Plan," *Hoc Tap*, January 1970; *Viet-Nam Documents . . .* , no. 78, p.4.

9. Nguyen Van Dai, Vice Chairman of the State Planning Commission, "Plan for Strengthening the Vast Rear Base and the Vast Front Line," Radio Hanoi domestic service, 17 January 1969, in *Viet-Nam Documents . . .* , no. 53, p. 4.

10. Ibid.

11. "Struggle for the Successful Fulfillment . . . ," p. 5 (emphasis in original). Production of vegetables had declined to 96 percent of the 1968 levels.

12. Speech on the 25th Anniversary of the Founding of the Democratic Republic of Vietnam, Radio Hanoi international service, 1 September 1970, *Viet-Nam Documents . . .* , no. 83, p. 22.

13. "Struggle for the Successful Fulfillment . . . ," p. 9.

14. Che Viet Tan, "Strengthening the Management of Labor in the State Sector in Order to Contribute to the Successful Fulfillment of Current Economic Obligations," *Nhan dan* (2 December 1969): 2; JPRS (Joint Publications Research Service), no. 49,890; MC (Monthly Catalog of U.S. Government Publications), 1970, no. 7,350-20.

15. Che Viet Tan, "Intensify Productive Labor Campaigns to Attain Success in 1970 State Plans," *Quan doi Nhan dan* (8 January 1970): 4; JPRS 50,051; MC 70/7,350-20.

16. Che Viet Tan, "Let Us Successfully Fulfill the 1971 State Plan, Firmly Build and Defend the Vast Rear, and Collaborate with the Front Line to Defeat the U.S. Aggressors," Hanoi domestic service, 1 January 1971; *Principal Reports From Communist Radio Sources* (Saigon: U.S. Mission, 11 January 1971).

17. Editorial, "To Redistribute Labor in Agriculture," *Nhan dan* (18 February 1971); *Principal Reports . . .* (25 January 1971).

18. Le Duan, "Under the Glorious Party Banner, for Independence, Freedom, and Socialism, Let Us Advance and Achieve New Victories," *Viet-Nam Documents . . .* , no. 77.

19. For a more detailed discussion of this subject, see Alexander Woodside, "Decolonization and Agricultural Reform in Northern Vietnam," *Asian Survey* 10, no. 8 (August 1970): 705-723.

20. "In agricultural production, cooperatives of the low (semi-Socialist) type, the peasants do not have the right to ownership over the land or over any other property. However, the lands of the members of the cooperatives are worked together (the peasants retained for their personal use no more than 5 percent of the land allowed per capita). The use of the draft animals and agricultural equipment of the cooperative members is done on a rental or purchase basis. Labor

payments are based not only upon the number of labor-days worked, but also on the basis of the amount of land contributed to the cooperative by each member.

"The agricultural production cooperative (Socialist type), as a superior form of production cooperative, is different from the cooperative of the lower type by the fact that here the entire land and all means of production are publicly owned (joint peasant ownership is achieved by paying adequate compensation to members of the cooperative). The distribution of cooperative income is based upon the labor invested by every cooperative member. Here the rule of auxiliary industries and public funds is more important. There is planning, distribution of labor and specialization of farming." A.G. Mazayev, *State Structure of the Democratic Republic of Vietnam* (Moscow: State Publishing House for Juridical Literature, 1963), p. 18; JPRS 22, 138.

21. Democratic Republic of Vietnam, *1963 Statistical Data* (Hanoi: Su That Publishing House, 1964), p. 30; JPRS 28,726.

22. Le Thanh, "Thoroughly Understand the Spirit of the New Statute on Agricultural Cooperatives," *Hoc Tap*, no. 9 (September 1969): 21-33; JPRS 49,255; MC 70/1,980-25.

23. Vo Nhan Tri, *Croissance economique de la République du Vietnam (1945-1965)* (Hanoi: Éditions en langues étrangères, 1967), p. 418.

24. Le Thanh, "Thoroughly Understand the Spirit . . . ."

25. For example, presaging Le Duan's article of February 1970 in *Hoc Tap* in September 1969 observed: "Our party views agricultural cooperativization as an indispensable prerequisite to the use of agriculture as a foundation for industrial development and to the achievement of socialist industrialization in North Vietnam.

"Because of this outlook, we are resolutely opposed to every tendency to view the agricultural production cooperative as a guild-type collective economic organization which is only concerned with the small narrow interests of individual, small groups of cooperative members, instead of seeing the duty of the cooperative member to the state and to the overall development of the socialist economy." "Properly Implement the New Agricultural Production Cooperative Statute," *Hoc Tap*, no. 9 (September 1969), 5-15; JPRS 59,255; MC 70/1,980-25.

26. Le Thanh, "Thoroughly Understand the Spirit . . . ."

27. Ibid.

28. Le Duan, "Under the Glorious Party Banner . . . ."

29. For discussion of these disputes in the past and other matters related to the military in the DRV, see W.S. Turley "Civil-Military Relations in North Vietnam," *Asian Survey* 9, no. 12 (December 1969), 879-899.

30. Serialized in *Nhan dan* and *Quan doi Nhan dan*; *Viet-Nam Documents. . .* , nos. 70, 71 and 72, respectively.

31. A number of these articles are contained in *Viet-Nam Documents . . .* , no. 89.

32. Giap, "The Party's Military Line is the Ever Victorious Banner of People's War in Our Country," *Viet-Nam Documents . . .* , no. 70, 27-8.

33. *Hanoi Moi* (17 February 1970); JPRS 50,322; MC 70/8,829-17.

34. Song Hao, "Party Leadership in the Cause of the Growth and Victories of Our Army," *Viet-Nam Documents . . .* , no. 72, 28.

35. Le Duan, "Under the Glorious Party Banner . . . ," pp. 39-40.

36. Race Document no. 1002 (Chicago: Center for Research Libraries). For discussion of the significance of this document, see Race, "The Origins of the Second Indochina War . . . ," pp. 363-68.

37. According to the captured notebook of a Party political cadres. *Working Paper on the North Vietnamese Role in the War in South Viet Nam: Captured Documents and Interrogation Reports* (Washington, D.C.: U.S. Department of State, 1968), item 301.

38. Le Duan, "Under the Glorious Party Banner . . . ," pp. 19-20.

39. Le Duan's article is often favorably cited by other members of the Political Bureau. See, for example, Pham Van Dong's Speech of 1 September 1970 in *Viet-Nam Documents* . . . , no. 83. Truong Chinh's statements are more ambiguous, but the policy line described by Le Duan is not unacceptable to Truong Chinh's well-known preference for protracted war. Furthermore, Truong Chinh appears to be in ill health and his public appearances have been few and brief; he may not be able right now to personally lead a vigorous opposition to Le Duan. The most concrete report on Truong Chinh's condition was a brief announcement over East Berlin domestic service radio on 11 January 1971 that he was "taking a cure" in the German Democratic Republic. See *Principal Reports . . .* (13 January 1971). Subsequent reports indicate that Truong Chinh has returned to Hanoi to take an active part in the affairs of the National Assembly in his capacity as Chairman of the Assembly's Standing Committee, but he has not made any major policy or theoretical statements since then.

40. "Resolution of the Political Bureau of the Party Central Committee on the Campaign to Improve the Quality of Party Members and Recruit the Ho Chi Minh Class of Party Members," *Hoc Tap*, no. 3 (March 1970), pp. 9-17; JPRS 50,598; MC 70.10,255-17.

41. Nguyen Van Tran, Secretary of the Hanoi Municipal Lao Dong Party Committee, "Be More Concerned about Party Development," *Hanoi Moi* (1 February 1970), 1, 3. JPRS 50,332; MC 70/8,829-17. Tran writes: "Some cadres do not enforce Party and State policies such as failing to fulfill their obligations and not allowing their children to fulfill their military obligations. Some are bureaucratic and do not keep abreast of the affairs of the installation. Some are not fair in distribution or demand more than their share; some are even corrupt and wasteful and use public property for private use. Some are arrogant, undemocratic, oppressive, and overbearing toward their subordinates and the masses. In short, a number of cadres are individualist, selfish, and lack exemplary ethics in work and daily life."

42. Ibid.

43. Le Duan, "Under the Glorious Party Banner . . . ," no. 77, pp. 94-6.

44. "Resolution . . . ," *Hoc Tap*, no. 3 (March 1970).

45. "Properly Carry out the Campaign to Raise the Quality of Party Members and to Recruit the Ho Chi Minh Class of Party Members," *Hanoi Moi* (25 April 1970), 1, 3; JPRS 50,807; MC 70/11,488-24.

46. "Fully Understand and Satisfactorily Carry Out the Political Bureau Resolution on Party Member Work," *Hanoi Moi* (26, 28, 29 April 1970); JPRS 50,826; MC 70/11,488-24.

47. Ibid.

48. For example, Brigadier General Le Quang Hoa, "Under the Banner of Ho's Military Thought, the Army and People of the Former Region 4 Resolved to Complete Every Task in an Outstanding Manner and to Help to Completely Defeat the U.S. Aggressors," *Hoc Tap*, no. 1 (January 1970), 31-42; JPRS 50,098; MC 70/7,350-20.

49. Tran Huy Lieu, "Some Preliminary Reflections on the Military Ideology of President Ho," *Nghien cuu Lich su* (September 1970), pp. 18-36; JPRS 50,574; MC 70/10,255-17. In the same spirit, Le Duan said: "President Ho was the crystallization of the moral value of our people throughout the 4,000 years of history." Le Duan, "Under the Glorious Party Banner . . . ," p. 4.

Tran Huy Lieu is said by some to be "pro-Peking," and in the sense that he subscribes to Peking's brand of Marxism-Leninism and admires Mao's writings on leadership and "new democracy"—as evident in the passage above—this may be so. But it is important to note that this orientation serves the autonomy of the Vietnamese Revolution and does not necessarily indicate a willingness to invite Chinese influence. "Maoism" in a non-Chinese setting may have the paradoxical effect of encouraging national communism and independent adaptations of Marxism-Leninism.

50. For a brilliant exposition of this process as it applies to South Vietnam, see Jeffrey Race, "How They Won," *Asian Survey* 10, no. 8 (August 1970): 628-650.

3

The Decline of Prince Sihanouk's Regime

Donald Lancaster

The regime set up by Prince Norodom Sihanouk in 1955—the Sangkum Reastr Niyum or People's Socialist Community—presented a glittering shop window to the outside world. Distinguished visitors, foreign journalists and even itinerant groups, such as "Americans Want to Know," were greeted in such courteous fashion and became the object of such attentions that they came away dazzled by the apparent progress, untroubled internal security and the considerable achievements of the regime. Indeed, even Prince Sihanouk, that brilliant showman, may have persuaded himself at times that this impression was correct. Nonetheless, there was evidence that the state of the realm left much to be desired, and that anarchy in the provinces and even in Phnom Penh itself was slowly, but inexorably disrupting the national economy, administration and political affairs.

The deterioration of the political climate of Cambodia under Sihanouk was a slow process culminating in his elimination in March 1970. In 1947, King Norodom Sihanouk had granted his people a constitution, modeled on the French Constitution of 1946, which vested ultimate governing responsibility in the National Assembly. This constitution was both unsuited to the national men-

---

Author's note: I submit this paper with due diffidence, as I am fully aware that the subject deserves to be treated in greater detail and in clearer fashion. But, in my capacity as the only "Anglo-Saxon" at liberty in Cambodia for a number of years, I was under very strict surveillance, while my access to information was restricted. Cambodians show a preference for treating their affairs "en famille," and outsiders are debarred from such discussions. But the atmosphere in Phnom Penh became increasingly oppressive, and the coup d'etat in March of last year was no more than the culmination of attempts made for a number of years past to persuade the Prince to "put water in his wine," and to behave in less autocratic fashion.

H.R.H. himself added to the confusion by his gift for lucid exposition, coupled with a capacity for moral indignation and an extraordinary verbosity. I still feel quite groggy myself as the result of having been exposed for so long to a torrent of Royal eloquence. But H.R.H.'s performance undoubtedly deteriorated—the "Norodoms" tend to deteriorate mentally with advancing years—and the attractive young man who mounted the Khmer Throne in 1941 became a megalomaniac. However, he retained to the end the gift of arousing sympathy, and of charming certain members of the diplomatic corps, who became his most ardent defenders. During the coming months, I shall try to clarify these conceptions, and to produce a book on this complex facet of the Indochina situation.

tality, and was at variance with the Asian conception of the proper exercise of political power. In addition, the Democrat Party, founded and led by Prince Youtevong, who died in 1947, included within its ranks the bulk of the elite, who organized themselves in such a fashion, with the assistance of civil servants and members of the scholastic profession in the provinces, that its control of the National Assembly could not be broken. Following the death of its founder, the Democrat Party, which had no political platform, devoted its energies to factional disputes, to the advancement of special interests, and to the enrichment of individual members. Such activities effectively blocked or frustrated all attempts to govern the country in a positive and constructive fashion.

King Norodom Sihanouk, whose unorthodox tactics had forced a reluctant French government to grant Cambodia complete and untrammelled independence in November 1953, and who had been accorded by popular acclaim the proud title of "Hero of National Independence," was not a monarch to be discouraged by difficulties of this sort. In March 1955, he abdicated, and in the following month his father, Prince Norodom Suramarith, was persuaded to occupy the vacant throne. The ex-Monarch then descended into the political arena and founded a mass movement—the "Sangkum Reastr Niyum" or People's Socialist Community—which all Khmer citizens, irrespective of their previous political affiliations, were invited to join. In September of that year, the Sangkum candidates, with some assistance from constituted authority, swept the polls, capturing all the seats in the National Assembly. Although the Democrat Party's stranglehold had been broken, the National Assembly members, now exclusively made up of deputies adhering to the Sangkum Movement, were reluctant to confine themselves to the modest role assigned them, which was that of voting a government into office, and approving legislation submitted for that purpose. For example, whenever Prince Sihanouk himself was persuaded to accept the office of Prime Minister, the deputies remained quiescent and created no difficulties of any sort. But, as soon as the office of Prime Minister was entrusted to someone else, they were emboldened to bring down the government by raising charges of corrupt practices against individual ministers.

Prince Sihanouk sought to curb this fractious tendency by convening a national congress of Sangkum members, constituting a semidirect emanation of the sovereign power vested in the people, which met twice a year in Phnom Penh. In January 1957, the National Congress attained the status of a constitutional body, the directives of which the Government and the National Assembly were required to implement. The Prince, who was chairman of the Sangkum Movement and had accepted the office of Head of State following the death of his father, King Norodom Suramarith, in 1960, presided over the debates with verve, skill and authority.

However, Cambodia's position on both the national and international levels became increasingly difficult. The economy and administration were crucially affected by two decisions made by Sihanouk in November 1963. The first was to nationalize the import/export trade and banking and the second, announced ten days later, to dispense with further instalments of American military aid and technical and economic assistance.[1] There was a steady worsening in the economic position and rampant corruption among members of the Prince's entourage, the government, the army and the administrative services, which the Head of State seemed either unwilling, or unable to check. In addition, there were recurrent frontier incidents, which were not diminished by Sihanouk's action in breaking off diplomatic relations with Washington in May 1965. These involved American aircraft, troops of the Bangkok and Saigon governments and armed bands of Khmer Serei, who had been recruited from among the Khmer minority (Khmers Krom) in South Vietnam, and probably trained, equipped and paid through the good offices of the American Central Intelligence Agency.

Military aid together with technical and economic assistance, were forthcoming—as might have been anticipated—from the socialist camp represented by the USSR in company with its satellites, and from the People's Republic of China. The French government, presided over by General de Gaulle, was likewise prepared to step into the gap, following the liquidation of its commitment in Algeria. It had apparently decided that conditions were ripe for a forward policy in Asia offering discreet assistance to hasten the dismantling of "Anglo-Saxon" military bases, and the destruction of "Anglo-Saxon" political influence. This would earn France the gratitude of Peking and open the rich China market to her. To implement such a policy, a secure base on the Asian mainland was essential. In Cambodia, where a French military mission was installed, French technicians served the Cambodian government and the French scholastic profession was represented; the required facilities for independent access to China were also present. French support to the Sangkum regime included the provision of some military aid and economic assistance for carrying out specific projects. Also monies held in Paris which were owed Cambodia by virtue of the decision to terminate the Quadripartite Agreements in December 1954, were released without prior notice to Saigon or Vientiane.

Although the country served as a convenient clearing station for business connected with the Vietcong war and an advance post for the intelligence services of many nations, including that of the People's Republic of China, the Soviet Union, France and even that of the Djakarta government, the aid furnished in exchange for these facilities tended to be on the modest side, and was calculated on the basis of the minimum required to maintain the Sangkum regime in power.

Furthermore, recurrent attempts to obtain an official declaration of recognition of Cambodia's neutral status and territorial integrity from the Saigon and Bangkok governments had been persistently rejected. Prince Sihanouk had addressed a message to twelve Heads of State and Prime Ministers in August 1962 requesting that an international conference be convened, and the National Assembly and the Council of the Kingdom had voted a resolution in November of the following year that an approach be made to the cochairman of the Geneva Conference (1954) for the purpose of obtaining international recognition of the country's neutrality and territorial integrity. Yet, neither of these proposals was destined to lead to the desired result.

In October 1964, the Head of State was to profit from a visit to Peking, where he had been invited to attend the Independence Day celebrations. He approached the DRV delegation with a request that Hanoi subscribe to a guarantee of the frontiers. The Hanoi delegates pointed out that they were not empowered to furnish such a guarantee and suggested that since the two countries possessed no common frontier, the request should be addressed to the Central Committee of the National Liberation Front of South Vietnam. When this step had been taken and the guarantee had been given, the Hanoi government, for its part, would be happy to proclaim its own readiness to respect Cambodia's neutrality and territorial integrity.

It was not until May 1967, however, that this procedure was finally adopted. Moreover, there are grounds for supposing that the price exacted was that Cambodia would connive in the clandestine passage of military supplies to the Vietcong through Cambodia's seaport, Sihanoukville. The timely arrival of these supplies probably facilitated the mounting of the Vietcong Tet offensive in early 1968 against the principal towns and military objectives in South Vietnam.

Connivance in arms traffic was accompanied by an official undertaking to supply the National Liberation Front with a stated tonnage of paddy. The officers responsible for organizing the traffic both in arms and foodstuffs were quick to appreciate the profits to be made from such activities, with the result that all manner of goods, in some cases smuggled in from South Vietnam for this purpose, were soon being transported to the frontiers. Trafficking on such a scale contributed to the ruin of national finances and to the downfall of a regime which approved in early 1969, the opening of an immense gambling casino in Phnom Penh. Here, due to the national propensity for gambling, suicides were of daily occurrence, while the currency in circulation tended to disappear. Indeed, the decision to open a casino in Phnom Penh afforded final proof of the bankruptcy of the regime, and the initiative was generally ascribed to one of Sihanouk's wives, Neak Moneang Monique, whose mother enjoyed notoriety as the biggest racketeer in the country.

Change in the Political Climate

It was in the general elections held in September 1966 that a change in the political climate had become apparent. Indeed, Prince Sihanouk must have had his attention drawn to the mounting opposition to his autocratic rule, while rumors were abroad of military unrest. He refrained, therefore, from his usual practice of personally selecting the Sangkum candidates for the 82 parliamentary seats. He confined his intervention to an attempt to prevent the return to the National Assembly of three left-wing deputies, Hou Yuon, Hu Nim and Khieu Samphan, whose subversive activities and critical propensities he had been stigmatizing in speeches in the provinces for some months past. Despite strict surveillance of their activities and personal approaches to the electors in their respective seats by police and agents of the security service, all three candidates were returned to the National Assembly with increased majorities, a rebuff which seems to have left the Head of State in a reflective mood.

In the course of the autumn in 1966, the rumors of military unrest received some confirmation in the decision of the Prince to relieve Lieutenant-General Lon Nol of his post as Chief of the General-Staff, and to entrust him with the task of forming the new government. Hitherto, Prince Sihanouk had confined himself to praising the activities of the Royal Khmer Army, which was engaged in opening up the frontier provinces—activities which included the building of roads, the construction of bridges and the founding of settlements—and had refrained from interfering actively in military affairs. But he had finally been brought to realize that the time had come to reassert his authority over an army which had forgotten his exploits in 1953 when he had taken the war path in person against Khmer/Vietminh bands in Battambang Province (Operation Samakki)—and against Vietminh from the north who had invaded Kratie and Stung Treng Provinces in 1954.

Although he is reported to have been surprised at this decision, General Lon Nol nevertheless formed his government, which was formally invested by the National Assembly on 22 October. But, Prince Sihanouk, who may have been uneasy lest the new Prime Minister should prove reluctant to carry out his directives, set up an extra constitutional body—the Countergovernment—which he staffed with his stalwarts and two of the left-wing deputies whose reelection had caused him such displeasure. This body was provided with a charter to express opinions, to formulate wishes, suggestions and criticism and, on occasion, to praise. Following the opening of the first Asian Games in 1966, in Phnom Penh's magnificent new stadium, (attended by athletes representing 17 countries, in which Cambodia obtained third place with 104 medals to its credit), the Head of State left for France in clandestine fashion as though to convey displeasure at the turn political events were taking.

After the Prince's departure, Prime Minister Lon Nol adopted an energetic approach to his new duties. He toured the country in simple fashion, paying particular attention to those areas where the Vietminh had set up bases during the Franco-Vietminh war. His purpose was to ascertain the nature of the grievances peasant-farmers might have in those areas, and to establish whether they were satisfied with the price they were receiving for their paddy. He instructed his ministers to follow his example. But, although this sensible concern with the bedrock of the national economy contrasted in favorable fashion with the Head of State's royal progresses and distribution of largesse, it came too late to prevent an outbreak of violence in the Samlaut region of Battambang Province. Villagers, enraged by the brutal conduct of a military party charged with collecting paddy, murdered two of its members and then proceeded to assail and destroy an agricultural settlement at Stung Kranhoung, to attack defense posts garrisoned by detachments of the Provincial Guard and to demolish bridges. Following these disturbances, thousands of villagers took to the foothills of the Cardamomes, where they had been preceded by some schoolteachers and students who had had some reason to suppose that they were in imminent danger of arrest.

The pacification of the disturbed region was undertaken with the rude vigor peculiar to soldiery who had been promised a monetary reward for each severed head they might forward to military headquarters in Phnom Penh. Villages were given over to the flames, while the surviving inhabitants fled for their lives to the shelter of the hills. Gentler methods were employed by Buddhist monks to persuade the errant population to return to their abandoned homes and neglected fields. On June 18, the Samlaut region was officially declared to have been pacified, but the troubles spread to the provinces of Pursat, Kompong Chhang, Kompong Thom, Kompong Cham, Kompong Speu and Kampot.

Meanwhile, Prime Minister Lon Nol had met with an accident in Koh Kong Province on March 5, when he had been pinned under a jeep, driven in reckless fashion by his colleague, General Nhiek Tioulong. He was transported to the military hospital in Phnom Penh with a fractured shoulder. Early in April, the Head of State returned to be faced with a sea of troubles. His return was the occasion for a popular demonstration in front of the office of the Counter-government, and demands were made for the dismissal of the Lon Nol government, the dissolution of the National Assembly and for the withdrawal of the troops operating in the Pailin region of Battambang Province. Inquiries in the disaffected villages had revealed the existence of communist cells, which had been dormant since the Franco-Vietminh war. This discovery enabled the Prince to deny, in his usual vigorous fashion, that the disturbances were a symptom of rural discontent, and to ascribe the rising to the machinations of Khmer "reds."

In view of the state of emergency which had arisen, the National Assembly decided to vote the Head of State special powers to deal with the situation. On April 29, Lon Nol resigned on the grounds that he was physically incapacitated from discharging his duties. Thus, the Head of State was able to prove to his own satisfaction that his presence at the helm was still essential to national progress. However, the disappearance in 1967 of the three left-wing deputies, Hou Yuon, Hu Nim and Khieu Samphan whose return to the National Assembly the Head of State had done his best to prevent, casts a lurid light on the methods used to govern the country. Khieu Samphan—"the only honest minister Cambodia had ever had"—was the first to disappear on April 24. His disappearance was followed five days later by that of Hou Yuon; and, on October 9, Hu Nim joined his colleagues "in the maquis." Despite the Prince's frequent assurances that he had done everything within his power to ensure that these three young men were not troubled or harmed by the military, or the police, the rumor spread, and was widely believed in Phnom Penh, that the three deputies had been arrested, tortured and executed, and that such a crime could only have been perpetrated with Prince Sihanouk's tacit approval.

Meanwhile, Prince Sihanouk had agreed that the circumstances warranted his assumption of special powers for a period of three months, and the formation of a government under his personal direction. This was formed on April 30, 1967, and was destined to remain until January of the following year, when the acting Prime Minister, Son Sann, Governor of the National Bank, resigned on the grounds of ill health. He was succeeded in office by the elder statesman, Samdech Penn Nouth. In August 1969, the Head of State was compelled to ask General Lon Nol to form a government in conformity with the wishes of the National Assembly. On this occasion, the portfolio of Deputy Prime Minister was given to Prince Sirik Matak, who was made of sterner stuff than General Lon Nol, and was charged with the task of ensuring that the Head of State renounced autocratic rule, and confined himself henceforth to his duties.

Relations between the Head of State and the National Assembly became so tense and even stormy that orders were issued at one time that no deputies were to be admitted to Damnak Chamcar Mon, which was Prince Sihanouk's official residence in Phnom Penh. However, the National Assembly proceeded nonetheless to repeal the measures nationalizing the import/export trade and banking, which had been passed in 1963 and, although Prince Sihanouk was to make an ultimate attempt to reverse this decision by recourse to the National Congress in December 1969, it was apparent that the Deputy Prime Minister, Prince Sirik Matak, was prepared to stand firm. The Head of State left for France the next month, confident that the anarchic state to which Cambodia had been reduced, and factional disputes would assure him of an enthusiastic reception on his return. But opposition to Prince Sihanouk's autocratic rule had now become so universal that this hope was destined to be disappointed.[2]

Sihanouk's Character

The explanation of Prince Sihanouk's character is probably to be found in its schizophrenic nature: he can be both a prince charming and a prince of darkness. He has always tacitly connived in the corrupt practices of his entourage, his family, the armed services and the administrative services in general, and presumably considers corruption to be a method of government. He can be ruthless, and even ferocious to his enemies, including those whom he senses are latently critical of his rule. Hypersensitive to criticism of any sort, egocentric and extremely aggressive, he has a capacity for enthusiasm of so incandescent a nature that its duration is perforce brief. He is endowed with phenomenal energy, childlike lucidity, and some talent for the arts. Histrionic and indiscreet, he is nonetheless an attentive host and a kind master, and was perhaps secretly convinced that he had been personally entrusted by the Lord Buddha himself with the dual task of equipping his country and leading his people into the modern world and, also, of taking Cambodia at some propitious juncture into the "socialist camp."

Prince Sihanouk, like his predecessors, has many children. But, as it was his custom to declare on many occasions, he is an indifferent father, and has never shown much interest in the education or general welfare of his progeny: a task assumed by his mother, Queen Kossamak.

On his accession, Sihanouk's attention was first attracted by his mother's half-sister, Princess Pongsamoni, by whom he had five children. His mother was reported to have tolerated this arrangement on the assumption that she could always dominate her fiery and lovely half-sister. But, when Princess Pongsamoni lost her figure, she forfeited Sihanouk's favor. The Monarch's attention was then momentarily diverted to a dancer in the Royal Ballet, Neang Moneak Kanh tol, who bore him two children: Prince Ranariddh and Princess Bupha Devi, who was until recently the premiere ballerina in the Royal troupe. Meanwhile, he had occasion to note the charms of a young Eurasian girl, who had won a beauty competition while she was still attending the French secondary school in Phnom Penh. It became the destiny of this shy girl, Monique, to gain a permanent place in the Royal affections: she studied his whims, encouraged his fancies, joined in his enthusiams, surrounded him with her supporters and accompanied him on trips abroad with the result that she came to be accepted in the eyes of the outside world as his official wife.

Sihanouk is extremely superstitious and, on travels abroad, was always accompanied by the ashes of an infant daughter, Princess Kantha Bopha, who had died in 1952. These ashes were contained in a small jewel case, which was generally entrusted to an aide-de-camp, and were deposited—beflowered—by his bedside on arriving at his destination. Although he pretended to make light of such things, he was attentive to the predictions of the Palace horae, and to the predictions obtained through this channel of the spirit of a young princess, devoured by a crocodile more than a century ago, whose ashes are interred in a stupa at Sambor-on-the-Mekong (this stupa was restored and regilded on the instructions and at the expense of the Head of State).

These characteristics were displayed in Prince Sihanouk's oriental conception of power, which was based on the divide-and-rule principle. He was always extremely well-informed about the activities—particularly if these should be of a reprehensible nature—of those who served him. Such information would probably be furnished either by the ladies of his entourage, or reach him in the form of reports furnished by an ubiquitous security service, or by the police. He seemed incapable of divesting himself of any particle of his authority, or of forming a team from among the young men, who had completed their studies abroad, and were then returning in increasing numbers, capable and eager to serve their country to the best of their ability. Finally, the Head of State was personally persuaded of his ability to outwit all comers, and to perform brilliantly upon the international stage—the latter conviction being perhaps well-founded.

Notes

1. Departing Americans, employed either by the Military Assistance Advisory Group (MAAG) or the Agency for International Development (USAID), professed their personal conviction, based on their knowledge of the country and its resources, and on their estimate of the capacity of Khmer technicians to replace them, that they "would be back in six months' time." However, due to the agricultural nature of the national economy in an underpopulated country, and to aid and assistance furnished by governments, which stood to profit from the absence of the United States, the Americans did not return.

2. Foreign residents in Phnom Penh were in most cases unaware of the extent of this opposition to Sihanouk. It was only when the decision had been taken to open a casino in the Capital that indubitable proof was afforded of the extent to which the moral climate had deteriorated. Indeed, a proper appreciation of the situation was only to be found among members of the French colony, which had a military mission installed in Phnom Penh, and advisers and experts in the provinces. But the French colony was animated by such lively resentment of the American presence in Vietnam, and was so attracted by the prospects opened up by General de Gaulle's grand design in the Far East that it tended to trim its sails to the prevailing wind, and to conceal its belief that the days of the Sangkum regime were numbered.

4

Effacing the "God-King" — Internal Developments in Cambodia Since March 1970

Milton Osborne[1]

The ubiquitous portrait photographs and the plaster busts of Prince Norodom Sihanouk have gone, as has the prefix "royal" which was so much a part of the old regime's style. Yet, the man whose residual presence the new Phnom Penh leadership has worked so hard to efface is seldom far distant from the thoughts of those who discuss developments within Cambodia. Whether execrated, regretted or remembered wistfully, Prince Sihanouk and the legacy of his fifteen years of virtually unchallenged rule remain very much a part of the new, republican Cambodia. It would be strange if it were otherwise. For Sihanouk was deposed by those who, in large part, had been his close associates over the years. General Lon Nol—as he was until his designation as Marshal of the Cambodian Army in late April 1971—had been one of Sihanouk's closest colleagues throughout the 1960s. Former Prince Sirik Matak had never hidden his dislike for Sihanouk's style of government, yet he, too, had served Sihanouk's state as a diplomat and cabinet minister. Despite the many, and on occasion dramatic, changes which have followed the March 1970 *coup d'état*, much of the old Cambodia survives, providing part of the explanation for the tensions and paradoxes which are a significant aspect of the new regime.[2]

The existence of paradox in contemporary Cambodia is, perhaps, more immediately apparent than the existence of tensions among the relatively restricted leadership circles. Under Sihanouk's regime criticism of the Chief of State, and of the policies which he pursued was muted, particularly until the closing years of the sixties. While criticism did come from both the left and right of the Cambodian political spectrum, it was restrained by the continuing power which Sihanouk was able to exercise over his mass political movement, the Sangkum Reastr Niyum (People's Socialist Community), even with its increasing politicization which was apparent after 1965. Reports of Sihanouk's charisma at the height of his powers generally needed qualification. There is no doubt that in the final years of his rule over Cambodia, he could no longer rely on a simple appeal to his personality and position to force through a policy. Yet when recognition is taken of this fact, the leaders of the new regime are generally men who were associated with the government of Cambodia before Sihanouk's deposition; the character and the administrative leadership of the various ministries remain little changed more than a year after the *coup*; and the problems of privilege and position, which were of such importance for the discontented youth who rallied behind Lon Nol and Sirik Matak, are unresolved.[3]

57

To note these continuities is not, however, to qualify the magnitude of change. The existence of war throughout Cambodia's territory is a change of the most fundamental sort, and one which dominates the political judgment of Cambodians when they come to consider their own individual political position. And beside the war, or because of it, other notable changes have taken place which have ensured that there will be no easy return to the policies of the Sihanouk period. After years in which a close political relationship with the Chinese People's Republic was a cornerstone of Sihanouk's foreign policy, diplomatic relations with that country have ended and official contacts have once more been established with the Taiwan Government. Relations no longer exist with North Vietnamese and the Provisional Revolutionary Government of South Vietnam (the NLF), but, after years in which the exchange of vitriolic insults appeared to be the only level of contact, relations have now been reestablished with both South Vietnam and Thailand. Possibly most significant, in terms of Cambodia's foreign relations, has been the readiness of the new regime to accept the massive military and economic aid supplied by the United States government. Without this aid, and the military assistance given by the South Vietnamese Army operating in Cambodia, there is little doubt that the new regime would be unable to survive.

Internally, a republic has replaced the curious monarchial system which, from 1960 onwards, existed without a reigning monarch, while the titles and privileges of the large and factious Cambodian royal family have been ended in theory if not completely in fact. The economic policies of Sihanouk's regime with their emphasis on state enterprise and the nationalization of the import-export trade have been renounced. And assurances have been given that an opportunity will be available for all to take part in the business of the state, free from the restrictions on personal freedom of expression which the new leaders denounced as so characteristic of Sihanouk's rule.[4]

Stated in the most succinct fashion, the dominant paradox of post-Sihanouk Cambodia is that with a major, if not total, reversal of the country's external policies and the announced intention of a total break with the internal past, the direction of government policy remains in the hands of men who, with some notable exceptions, were closely identified with the previous regime. This provides an explanation for the still largely muted discontent which has received little attention in newspaper reporting on Cambodia, and it also goes far in explaining the alignment of factions or interest groups within the new regime. Just as was the case under Sihanouk, the absence of parties in the new, republican Cambodia has not meant the absence of factions. What is notable, indeed, is that the identifiable interest groups and political factions under the new regime are so little changed from the time before March 1970. Awareness of this situation, and an understanding of the developments leading up to Sihanouk's overthrow are important for any analysis of the balance of forces within Cambodia in mid-1971.

The Coup d'État

Commentary on the planning and execution of the *coup d'état* which deposed Norodom Sihanouk in March 1970 has been highly speculative and frequently more reflective of the ideological position of the commentators than of the actual developments. In his own description of Cambodia's problems, Prince Sihanouk highlighted the external dangers and minimized the difficulties which existed internally. So it was that his sudden overthrow, at a time of continuing uncertainty for the whole Indochinese region, was seen by many as the malevolent work of those governments which had opposed Sihanouk's policies over the years. Many regarded the Thai and South Vietnamese governments, with the United States as at least an interested observer from the wings, as responsible for the planning, if not the execution of the *coup d'état*.

Such a perspective paid little attention to the decline of Sihanouk's popularity among his most important constituents, the urban elite. Cambodia in the second half of the sixties was no longer the untroubled oasis of peace which Prince Sihanouk's propaganda machine proclaimed it to be with such assiduity. The Prince's efforts to find a *modus vivendi* with the Vietnamese Communists which would spare Cambodia from the ravages of the war in Vietnam were less and less successful as the use of Cambodia by the Communists became progressively more important. Although it may be possible to exaggerate the degree of damage involved, the strains placed upon Cambodia's relations with the Chinese People's Republic during the Cultural Revolution in 1967 suggested the existence of problems in Cambodian-Chinese relations which had previously not been so clearly apparent. Internally, the existence of dissident groups in widely separated areas of Cambodia could no longer be ignored and led to army operations against those described variously as Khmer Rouges and rebels particularly in the northeastern and northwestern regions of the country. Moreover, despite the efforts which were made to minimize the fact, the Sangkum Reastr Niyum's capacity to act as an umbrella institution which sheltered all political outlooks within the kingdom was increasingly strained as Sihanouk's policies pleased neither the right nor the left.[5]

With an awareness of external problems very firmly in mind, the Cambodian political elite in the late 1960s became concerned with a series of internal problems for which they increasingly felt it was appropriate to blame the Chief of State, Prince Sihanouk.[6] Among a relatively limited power elite which had come, particularly before the severance of economic and diplomatic ties with the United States, to expect an unrealistically high standard of living, the failure of Sihanouk's economic policies was a matter for sharp criticism. Contrary to Sihanouk's own expectations, his programs for nationalization and austerity had a far wider impact than their planned effect upon the foreign business interests, mostly French and Chinese, which had dominated the economy in the past. As the urban-based elite pondered their reduced opportunities for additional income in the years after 1964, they looked with increasing discontent at the efforts of Sihanouk's consort, Madame Monique, to promote her own aggrandizement beyond even the tolerant standards which existed in the kingdom. Prince Sihanouk was not, generally, believed to be involved in such bald-faced corruption himself, but he was criticized for permitting, if not condoning, Monique's actions.[7] When, in late 1969 and early 1970 the urban elite came to believe that Monique was actively seeking political power, this was seen as a further reason for action against her husband.

Prince Sihanouk's own apparent inclination to ignore the problems of government in favor of such interests as film-making, while the economy declined and external threats became more serious, represented a further reason for deepening discontent among the elite. Not only was Sihanouk's apparent preoccupation with the production of films regarded as undignified and frivolous by many in the elite, it was also seen as symbolic of his unreadiness either to deal with emerging problems or to make some effort to solve the already apparent problems which had resulted from policies which he had instituted. Not the least of these latter problems was the existence of a group of discontented and under- or unemployed youth who, having passed through secondary and tertiary institutions, could not find satisfactory opportunities for employment.[8] With the accumulation of these difficulties, the presence of many thousands of Vietnamese Communists on Cambodian territory during 1969 and in early 1970 acted as a catalyst for the various groups who now came to the conclusion that there had to be, at least, a confrontation with Prince Sihanouk which would lead to his making substantial changes in policy. While probably seen as a last resort by the men who decided that some action had to be taken against Sihanouk, the possibility that confrontation could lead to the Prince's overthrow was clearly in the minds of some of those who chose to act against him.[9]

Not surprisingly, many of the details of the planning for the confrontation and subsequent *coup d'état* remain unknown. The following account of some of the developments associated with the plotting, and those who participated in it, is tentative and incomplete. But within the uncertainties which surround it, this commentary takes into account the complexities of the affair and provides essential background to an understanding of the political alignments in contemporary Cambodia.

There is now considerable evidence to suggest that there was more than one plot in preparation in the final months of Sihanouk's rule as Chief of State of Cambodia. When General Lon Nol accepted the appointment as Prime Minister in August 1969, with the then Prince Sirik Matak as his Deputy Prime Minister, many well-placed observers in Phnom Penh were of the opinion that united though these two men might be in disapproving of certain policies pursued by Prince Sihanouk, they were, by personal inclination and background, unlikely to work easily together. Despite his lengthy tenure of senior military rank, General Lon Nol was regarded by many associated with the royal family as, essentially, an uneducated *parvenu* who had risen to power through dogged devotion to Prince Sihanouk, even to the point of being regarded by some of his more bitterly critical detractors as Sihanouk's executioner, the man who had gladly acted on the Prince's behalf in the rigorous suppression of domestic dissidence during 1967. However accurate, or inaccurate, such estimations were, it now seems that shortly after assuming the office of Prime Minister, and quite independently of Sirik Matak, General Lon Nol embarked on his first, possibly quite hesitant, preparations for a possible plot against Sihanouk. In the period between assuming office in August 1969 and leaving for France for medical treatment in late October 1969, General Lon Nol, during September, entered into negotiations with Son Ngoc Thanh, the leader of the anti-Sihanouk Khmer Serei (Free Khmers), who had long sought to overthrow the Prince while exiled in Thailand and South Vietnam.[10] During these September 1969 negotiations, General Lon Nol, according to the account given by Son Ngoc Thanh's brother, Son Thai Nguyen, remained uncertain as to the wisdom and possibility of either confronting Sihanouk or overthrowing him. While Lon Nol's meeting with Son Ngoc Thanh was an effort to ensure that he could gain material assistance from the dissident leader's rebel troops, he was not yet convinced of the necessity for action against Sihanouk. With the issue unresolved, Lon Nol departed for France leaving the impression, at least among some Phnom Penh observers, that he had given some thought to the possibility of remaining abroad indefinitely.

In Lon Nol's absence, Sirik Matak became acting Prime Minister and embarked upon an active and overt campaign to solve his country's ills. Despite Sihanouk's presence in Cambodia until early January 1970, Sirik Matak set in motion a program which in many ways represented a direct challenge to many of the political and economic policies which Sihanouk had long pursued. Whether the difficulties which he had in achieving any substantial success for these policies was instrumental in his own decision to consider the possibility of working for a confrontation with Sihanouk is not clear. By the end of January 1970, however, it was apparent that Sirik Matak was seeking to consolidate his position even if this did mean a head-on confrontation with the Prince. The major difficulty facing Sirik Matak in his efforts to move beyond minor reforms of the situation in Cambodia was his lack of any material force with which to bolster his political program. Despite his very public efforts to associate himself with the operations being undertaken by the army in the northeastern provinces,[11] and his discreet and frequent discussions with army leaders in the privacy of his Phnom Penh residence, it does not appear that by the middle of February 1970 Sirik Matak had successfully established any workable base for movement against Sihanouk.

In a situation of growing concern on the part of the Phnom Penh elite at the implications of the continued presence of Vietnamese Communist troops within

Cambodia's borders, General Lon Nol returned to Cambodia in the latter half of February, apparently determined that some action now had to be taken against Sihanouk.[12] Once again, Son Ngoc Thanh's brother asserts, Lon Nol entered into discussions with the Khmer Serei leader, seeking an assurance that those ethnic Cambodian troops under Thanh's control, then fighting with Vietnamese Special Forces units in South Vietnam would, if necessary, be available to aid those who acted against Sihanouk in meeting either the possible danger of attack from elements of the Cambodian army which might remain loyal to the Prince, or some form of intervention from the Vietnamese Communist forces in Cambodia. With a firm proposal before him, Son Ngoc Thanh is said to have given Lon Nol his assurance that material aid would be forthcoming.[13] Whether Lon Nol consulted with Sirik Matak before, or after, reopening negotiations with Son Ngoc Thanh is not clear. Thanh's brother tends to diminish Sirik Matak's role in the final planning of the confrontation which began on 11 March. Whether this version is correct, or not, Lon Nol would have been aware of the efforts which Sirik Matak had undertaken, in his absence, to gain the support of army officers for some effort to change the policies, if not the leadership, of the existing regime. By the time that confrontation did take place, to be followed by Sihanouk's ouster on 18 March, Lon Nol and Sirik Matak were ready to stand together publicly as Sihanouk's sworn opponents. Son Ngoc Thanh remained very much in the background, in these early stages, but he too emerged fully into public association with the new leadership, assuming an appointment as a Special Counsellor to General Lon Nol in August 1970, a position which carried with it the rank of a deputy Prime Minister in the Cambodian cabinet. The delay in announcing this appointment, and the terms in which it was announced, did little to dispel the view that the new leadership in Phnom Penh had far from resolved the issue of where power is to lie in the era following Sihanouk's physical removal from the Cambodian scene.[14]

The Political Personalities

Before Lon Nol's resignation of 20 April 1971, a decision which carried with it some clear indications of army discontent with the composition of the existing Cambodian cabinet, there had been little sign of government instability following the new regime's accession to power in March 1970. To a considerable degree, the apparent stability of the cabinet which Lon Nol directed in the months immediately following upon Sihanouk's disappearance was a reflection of an almost desperate effort to maintain the show of solidarity in the face of increasing pressures from the expanded Indochinese war. But in part, also, the stability of the cabinet was the direct result of the quite genuinely felt, if possibly misplaced, air of euphoria which hung about Phnom Penh for the first six months of the post-Sihanouk period. Despite the grave dangers posed by the loss of control over large areas of the country, many in Phnom Penh, and in particular the students in secondary and tertiary institutions, believed that Cambodia's problems, whether political or military, would soon be solved, and that the deposition of Sihanouk would in some manner usher in a golden age of freedom and prosperity. The reshuffling of various posts within the cabinet which has taken place from time to time, and the promotion of various secretaries of state to the rank of minister in July 1970, gave little real indication of the more important tensions and factional groupings which are present among the political elite. The key to any understanding of these factions, and of the political positions which they hold is found through a consideration of the principal personalities within the new regime.

Until the end of April 1971, at least, Lon Nol and Sirik Matak were clearly the two dominant figures on the transformed Cambodian political stage. On the one hand, Lon Nol could provide the material force of the army to back the new government. On the other hand, Sirik Matak's undoubted intelligence and energy, which had so often been regarded with deep suspicion by Prince Sihanouk, provided the administrative drive necessary for the survival of the state. Before his emergence as the leader of the new regime, Lon Nol was widely regarded throughout Cambodia as one of the most loyal of the Prince's men. As the economic policies which Sihanouk had instituted in 1963 and 1964 bit deeply into the army's budget, there were clear indications of army discontent with a situation which sometimes left them with insufficient gasoline to fuel their vehicles and armed them with an ill-assorted inventory of weapons rapidly growing obsolete. Sihanouk himself made frequent reference to the pro-Western tendencies of many of his army officers. Yet, in this situation of scarcely hidden discontent, Lon Nol led the army in maintaining loyalty to the Prince. These estimations which argue that Lon Nol possesses something of the common touch are probably valid. His family origins, unlike so many other members of the Phnom Penh elite, are neither royal nor of the hereditary official class. His apparent capacity to inspire loyalty from his troops and officers did not, however, lead to his ready acceptance by many within the elite. While Sirik Matak has clearly found it desirable, and even essential, to work with Lon Nol, there remains an important group of the deputy Prime Minister's supporters whose attitudes towards Lon Nol range from the derisory to the sharply condemnatory. Lon Nol's past association with Sihanouk is remembered. The allegation of his immensely large financial gains as the result of that association are given frequent if discreet airing. The part which Lon Nol and the army played in bloodily suppressing challenges to the regime in the closing years of the sixties are spoken of in horror. Or the man is denounced as something of a buffoon whose speeches are delivered in "the voice of an advocate"–a derisory French description suggesting dullness of delivery. He is, for his critics, the "Khmau," the Cambodian term meaning "black," made as a reference to his peasant origins.

Frequent though these criticisms of Lon Nol may be, in the conversations of the Phnom Penh elite, and despite the presence of some opposition to him in the army itself,[15] his control of the army and the image which he has projected of being above politics made his leadership vital after March 1970. Whether the decline in his health after he suffered a stroke in February 1971 will finally remove him from the political scene is unclear. There is no doubting his importance, and it is interesting to find that Prince Sihanouk grudgingly shares this estimation. In his Nineteenth Message to the Khmer Nation released through the New China News Agency, Sihanouk said the following of the General:

Lon Nol is the least stupid among them and less unpopular than they, though as much a corrupted fellow, a thief, a pirate, a murderer as they are. Without Lon Nol their difficulties would have multiplied a hundred fold or a thousand fold.[16]

Where Lon Nol's apparent lack of personal dynamism seems to have aided him in maintaining some degree of popular support, and not least the continued loyalty of the army, former Prince Sisowath Sirik Matak's drive and energy appear as something of a handicap. In a country which has frequently seen ministers who have preferred to approach their duties more with an eye to the preservation of their personal comfort than a conviction of the necessity for action, Sirik Matak's energy and organizational ability have sometimes provoked antipathy. Even before Lon Nol's departure for medical treatment in Honolulu following his stroke, Sirik Matak had assumed the role of dealing with the major administrative and political questions facing the Phnom Penh government, while Lon Nol attended to military matters. By the end of 1970, this style of government was provoking the criticism that the direction of affairs was, once again, taking on a highly personal character, just as it had done under Sihanouk. Such a criticism was probably unfairly directed towards Sirik Matak whose personal involvement in so many major decisions since March 1970 is probably much more correctly seen as a reflection of the continuing low level of competence among so many of his colleagues. But more significant, for Sirik Matak, than these allegations of excessive personalization of power has been the continued existence of suggestions that he remains a "royal" whatever formal steps he may have taken to end the importance of the royal family within Cambodia. One of the earliest advocates of a republic to replace the existing monarchy, and a leader in the movement to abolish royal titles, the suspicion remains, particularly among Phnom Penh intellectuals, that Sirik Matak has not completely shed his royal affiliations. In one sense, this suspicion does have some basis of fact. Whatever efforts Sirik Matak may have made, and however genuine those efforts, to end the importance of the royal family in Cambodian political life, it would be difficult, indeed, for him to end completely his *family*, as opposed to his *royal*, associations. It is possible, as some Cambodian observers have suggested, that Sirik Matak has played a discreet role in preventing Prince Sihanouk's mother, Queen Kossamak, from suffering too great indignity in the period since March 1970. But such intervention should, most correctly, be viewed as protection of a member of his family, rather than as an effort to protect the prerogatives of royalty. Moreover, some of the criticism which has been directed towards Sirik Matak has stemmed not from his own attitudes on royalty and privilege, as much as from the apparent unreadiness of other former princes to forego the deference which they had previously received.[17]

A man who projects the image of both efficiency and cold ambition, Sirik Matak seems unlikely to be able to escape tarring with the royal brush for a considerable period, and in particular, by the more radical elements in the capital's youth. While his efficiency may be sufficient in itself to preserve him in power for the moment, Sirik Matak does not have any clearly defined constituency beyond certain sections of the civilian elite in Phnom Penh. What such a situation should mean for the future, if Lon Nol were no longer able to play any significant role at the head of the army, must remain in the realm of speculation. While Sirik Matak has, both under Sihanouk and in the more recent past, acted as Lon Nol's replacement at the head of the cabinet for lengthy periods, this has always been in circumstances where there was some expectation that Lon Nol would eventually return to take up his post. Clearly, the army's own attitude will be important here. Sirik Matak's assumption of general rank within the army has not pleased some of the officer corps who regard it as presumptuous, on Sirik Matak's part, and denigratory of the rank held by career officers.

The problem of playing a role as the representative of a significant constituency is an important factor in the positions occupied by other important figures within the new regime. Men of considerable ability, such as Yem Sambaur and Douc Rasy, have been of real importance in serving the post-Sihanouk Government, but the question remains as to the extent to which they are able to rally any substantial constituency about them in addition to their contributions as technocrats.[18] Both men had solid reasons for disliking the Prince's regime. Yem Sambaur was some years in the political discard, and Douc Rasy, particularly as the editor of the newspaper *Phnom Penh Presse* in the middle sixties, found himself frequently under bitter attack from Sihanouk. There is no reason to discount Douc Rasy's account of the denunciation which Sihanouk made of him in June 1968 when, speaking in Takeo province, the Prince angered by Douc Rasy and Sim Var, another long-time Cambodian political figure, threatened to "send them to another world, without asking for the removal of their parliamentary privilege."[19] But the memory of past wrongs and the vigorous desire of both Douc Rasy and Yem Sambaur to serve their country does not, particularly in a time of stress and fragmentation, guarantee the attraction or preservation of support.[20] In considerable contrast, however, one of the more shadowy figures of Cambodia history since the middle fifties, Son Ngoc Thanh, does in his association with the new regime represent a political figure with an important constituency appeal.

Few accounts of Son Ngoc Thanh's life exist, and those which do are generally affected by the ideological overtones of a particular period or the personal ideological position of a particular author.[21] In contemporary Cambodia, Son Ngoc Thanh does represent a rallying point for one important group of supporters of the changes which followed upon Sihanouk's overthrow. From the early twentieth century onwards, but particularly in the nineteen twenties and thirties, many young ethnic Cambodians who had been born in what was then Cochinchina—the area known in modern Cambodia as Kampuchea Krom or Lower Cambodia—came to Phnom Penh to complete their studies. Son Ngoc Thanh was, indeed, one of these. The tradition continued after the second world war, and many of these Khmer Krom found their careers in government service, particularly as government school teachers. Although often disregarded in accounts of recent developments in Cambodia in the nineteen fifties and sixties, the Khmer Krom who had been resident in Phnom Penh for a considerable period, preserved some sense of their particular regional origin, in part as a defense mechanism against the subtle discrimination to which some of them felt they were subjected.[22] For some of these men, at least, Son Ngoc Thanh remained an appealing figure, even during the 1960s when he was bitterly and frequently denounced by Sihanouk. Now that Thanh is, once again, associated with the direction of affairs in Cambodia, he is seen by a significant number of Khmer Krom as a man who, under conditions of considerable adversity, remained loyal to his long-held goal of bringing down Prince Sihanouk.[23] More than this, Son Ngoc Thanh has been able to supply material aid to the new regime in Phnom Penh through the provision of trained troops formerly fighting under his direction as members of the Khmer Serei, and through recruiting ethnic Cambodians to fight on the side of the Phnom Penh Government among these minority populations in both South Vietnam and Thailand.[24] Although Son Ngoc Thanh's importance is thus immediately apparent, his association with the new regime involves certain difficulties. While some of the most highly placed Cambodians in Sihanouk's regime preserved private admiration for Thanh through the 1960s, this was far from the case for many others. Men such as the current Cambodian Ambassador to the United Nations, Khim Tit, have, in the past, committed themselves to bitter personal attacks on Thanh, and one would be naive to imagine that personal antagonisms of this sort have disappeared just because of the change of regime in Phnom Penh, no matter how significant and substantial the changes associated with Sihanouk's overthrow may be.[25] For the foreign observer, part of the explanation for Thanh's long and often difficult period of dissidence would take account of his deeply held ambition to return to real power in the Cambodian state. The existence of such an ambition, and the possible problems which it might pose for other members of the governing elite in contemporary Cambodia, have not escaped the attention and consideration of other members of the Phnom Penh leadership.

Political Attitudes of Youth, Buddhist
Clergy and Peasantry

For all who now govern in Phnom Penh, whatever the extent of their constituencies, the support, or lack of it, from three groups within the country is of signal importance. The groups in question are the youth, most particularly the capital-based youth of some education, the Buddhist clergy and the peasantry. Commentary on the political attitudes held by members of these three important groups cannot be other than highly speculative, for no sustained research in depth has been carried out in relation to any of them. Such research was not possible in the sensitive atmosphere of Sihanouk's Cambodia in which the expression of scholarly interest in the internal affairs of contemporary Cambodia was treated with considerable suspicion. In the conditions of war and threat which have faced the new regime, restraints exist to make it difficult for dissident or disenchanted members of these three groups to make known their feelings to foreign observers. Demonstration of dissent through active association with those who are fighting against the Phnom Penh leadership does, indeed, provide one alternative and clear indication of position, but as will be argued later, great difficulty attaches to any attempt to analyze the composition and motivation of all but a few well-known members of those aligned against the Phnom Penh Government.

Because it so often went unreported by external observers, the degree of discontent with the Sihanouk regime among Cambodia's intellectual youth was widely unrecognized.[26] This lack of awareness made the manner in which the youth in Phnom Penh, and to a lesser extent in provincial regions, rallied to the new leadership in March and April 1970 surprising, and even unconvincing to outside observers. Yet, the rallying did take place and, at least initially, the youth in Phnom Penh was among the warmest of the new regime's supporters. More than a year after the *coup d'état*, the attachment of the youth to the Phnom Penh leadership is less certain. Some, though probably a very limited number, have chosen to associate themselves with the forces which fight against the Phnom Penh Government. A substantial proportion of those who have not chosen this option have, however little they may wish to see the return of Sihanouk, come to be bitterly critical of the failure of Lon Nol and Sirik Matak to make any inroads upon the problems of corruption and nepotism which were so much a part of Sihanouk's Cambodia, and which remain an important part of the government and social structure today. Belief that Sirik Matak still favors members of the royal family, a recognition that despite the change of leadership, the composition and character of government departments has scarcely changed, and a growing awareness of the real costs of the war in terms of numbers killed and refugees forced into Phnom Penh troubles the youth of Phnom Penh deeply.

The Government has made some effort to placate its youthful critics by incorporating young people in the discussion of government policy, and it has, on occasion, made very clear that criticism has clear limits in a state at war. There is little, if any sign, however, that the Phnom Penh leadership which itself must operate with the weight of past association with Sihanouk as part of the personal political burden of most of its members, has taken positive steps to move beyond placating and warning to confront the issues which draw criticism from the educated youth. In this respect, the defection from the Phnom Penh regime of some highly regarded older intellectuals could be of importance in further accentuating the doubts of the youth.[27]

Even less readily gauged than the attitudes of the youth are the feelings held towards the new regime by the Cambodian Buddhist clergy. Just as was the case with Prince Sihanouk's regime, the new government in Phnom Penh has sought to align the clergy closely with their policies. Very shortly after the *coup* took place, senior monks were brought to Phnom Penh from throughout the country so that the new leaders might explain the basis of their actions and their intentions for the future. Subsequently, a special effort has been made to emphasize the Phnom Penh Government's concern with Buddhist affairs and to contrast this concern with the claimed disrespect shown towards Buddhism by those Vietnamese Communist troops fighting within Cambodia.[28]

The effect of these efforts to bind the Buddhist clergy to the new Cambodian Government is uncertain. As with so many other institutions in post-Sihanouk Cambodia, the Buddhist church was closely identified with the now deposed Chief of State in the years which preceded his overthrow. The Venerable Chuon Nath who, until his death in 1969, had long been the chief of the larger of the country's two Buddhist sects, the Mohanikay, had not hesitated to align himself publicly with Prince Sihanouk's regime, to the point of making critical comments about those whom were regarded as the Prince's domestic opponents. Less elevated members of the Mohanikay order used addresses to the faithful in their village pagodas to counsel support and admiration of the Prince, a practice which led to criticism among adherents, both monks and laity, of the stricter Thommayut order.[29] Whether in this overt form, or as a result of Prince Sihanouk's own efforts to ensure that the clergy were seen as an integral part of his regime, the Buddhist *sangha* with its formal links to the Cambodian monarchy was ill prepared for the sudden changes which were brought about in March 1970. If the Phnom Penh leaders frequently proclaim the total loyalty of the Buddhist clergy to the new regime, less clearly interested parties in Cambodia are somewhat skeptical of the ease with which long-established patterns of behavior and loyalty can be disrupted and destroyed. A more cautious estimation of the attitudes held by the monks would probably take account of the manner in which many senior clergy have been ready, in the light of recent events in Cambodia, to be Buddhist Vicars of Bray. Among the less elevated, moreover, it appears that there is still very real confusion as the result of Sihanouk's sudden ouster. One senior monk offered the following commentary on developments which suggested that a degree of *attentisme* was to be found in the clergy's ranks.

We supported Sihanouk because he looked after the monks and the Buddhist church. We did not know that he had allowed the Vietnamese Communists to take over large areas of Cambodia. But this does not mean that we have automatically become supporters of the new government. I do not believe that it should be part of a Buddhist monk's task to make political speeches on the Government's behalf.[30]

The position adopted by the Buddhist clergy towards the regime in Phnom Penh will be important in determining the nature and extent of its support. While detailed knowledge of the Buddhist clergy's pastoral role is not available, there is sufficient awareness of the part played by monks historically in preserving, through their very presence in the villages of Cambodia, an awareness, however dim and ill-defined, of the existence of a Cambodian state in which Buddhism played a vital part. While nothing in developments since March 1970 suggests that the Buddhist clergy in Cambodia are likely to play a political role similar to that of the Mahayana monks of Vietnam, the negative proposition that a failure on the part of the new regime to maintain substantial support among the clergy would be damaging to its interests certainly appears correct.

A similar negative proposition has obvious validity when there is any discussion of the Cambodian peasantry In a country which is so heavily peasant in composition, the extent to which the peasantry choose or are coerced to align themselves is of fundamental importance.[31] Commentary on the Cambodian peasantry during Sihanouk's tenure usually laid heavy stress on the manner in which the Prince had successfully brought them within the political structure of the state (adding to the prestige which he enjoyed among the peasantry through once having been king) and imported a newly important sense of association with, if not actual participation in, the business of government. Such an estimation was deceptively attractive and excessively simple in its characterization of the modalities of Sihanouk's state. Although there is some evidence of peasant reaction in support of Prince Sihanouk immediately after his deposition, and while it is also clear that some Cambodian peasants are fighting in the forces which oppose the new regime, the relative ease with which Sihanouk was removed from his position as Chief of State, and the relatively limited spontaneous peasant reaction to that development gives point to the contention that the support given the Prince by the peasantry before his deposition was, essentially, passive in nature. This has, historically, been the case for the royal leaders of Cambodia. Able through their special position to rally the peasantry about them, Cambodian kings have, nevertheless, always had to contend with the threat that others, particularly other princes, frequently were able to pose a challenge to their authority through claiming to possess the same rights and powers as the ruler. While the support, at best, and acquiescence, at worst, of the peasantry have always been necessary for the survival of a particular regime in Cambodia, the truly vital support for each ruler has been that which came from the urban-based elite; the men whose hands rested on the levers of power. Dramatically, in Sihanouk's case, when these men chose to act his position became untenable.

Passive though support for Sihanouk was, the memory of the Prince has clearly not disappeared overnight from the peasantry's minds. While the frenetic nature of Sihanouk's rule, with its repeated radio appeals to the people often lasting several hours and broadcast night after night, may well have had an exhausting effect upon the peasantry, to dismiss the existence of a deeply felt bond between the peasantry and their "god-king"—even if one now realizes the passive nature of that bond—would be a foolish misestimation. Cambodian peasants have joined the Vietnamese forces fighting against the Phnom Penh regime willingly, as well as because of coercion. There is no doubt that Prince Sihanouk's name is being used as a symbol to attract peasants to their side by those who fight against the Phnom Penh Government. What is far from clear for the moment is whether there are, in fact, peasants fighting against Phnom Penh within an organization which is clearly separate from that controlled by the Vietnamese Communists.[32]

Although accurate numerical estimations of the nature and disposition of peasant support for either Prince Sihanouk or the new Phnom Penh regime would be of the greatest interest for an analysis of developments in Cambodia since March 1970, none of those estimates which have so far been advanced appear reliable.[33] Probably more important in the volatile and fluid situation which obtains in Cambodia is some attempt to estimate the effect of the war on peasant attitudes. Here, the estimates of a number of well-placed and capable Cambodians seems worthy of attention. Their argument is that the greatest single feeling to be found among the Cambodian peasantry is that of confusion. Regret for the end to Prince Sihanouk's rule, and for the tragic harvest of death which has followed upon it, has led some members of the Cambodian elite to formulate, privately, the obvious proposition that Sihanouk's rule, despite its manifold mistakes and difficulties, was preferable to the state of war in which the country now finds itself. For the peasantry, however, it was suggested, the formulation is less complex, even if the factors which lie behind that formulation are complex indeed. After years in which the peasant's political life related to Prince Sihanouk, the former king who had lost little of his regal aura through abdicating, and in which governmental decisions were promulgated in terms of the Prince's wishes, this truly important figure was suddenly removed from the scene. And with his removal came war and devastation such as Cambodia has not known since the terrible years of the Vietnamese occupation in the early nineteenth century. If confusion had not accompanied these developments, that would be the surprising thing. In seeking to overcome the prevalent confusion among the peasantry, the new regime has made its appeal in terms of invoking the nationalism of Khmer ethnicity. Although, within the capital and for the benefit of the outside world, heavy weight of argument has been placed upon the claimed constitutionality of Sihanouk's deposition, appeals for peasant loyalty have been much more fundamental, portraying all those who fight against the Phnom Penh Government as Vietnamese, or the tools of the Vietnamese, who seek to colonize Cambodia and have blasphemed the national religion of Buddhism. The one major difficulty associated with this approach is the fact that for Phnom Penh, no less than for those Cambodians who oppose Phnom Penh's control, the support of Vietnamese troops is vital. Indeed, it is part of Cambodia's continuing tragedy that on occasion, the country seems little more than a marching ground for contending Vietnamese forces with little, if any, regard paid to the Cambodian population.

Opposition to the Regime

An attempt to describe the nature of developments in Cambodia since March 1970 would not be complete without some reference to those Cambodian forces which oppose the Phnom Penh Government. Possibly the most interesting commentary which may be supplied relates to the estimations which are held of Prince Sihanouk, his government in exile and the political front associated with it, among elite Cambodians who continue to live within the Phnom Penh Government's control. Such estimations, which frequently differ substantially from the public positions adopted by the Phnom Penh regime, are an almost constant part of private conversation among the Cambodian elite and show a preoccupation with the position of Prince Sihanouk himself.

Any future close analysis of the March 1970 *coup d'état* will, of necessity, give considerable attention to why it was that Sihanouk should have chosen, before his actual deposition took place, to continue his planned travels to Moscow and Peking.[34] Whatever the reasons for his action, the Prince's decision to establish his government in exile in Peking has been seen by many members of the Cambodian elite as a reason for discounting any future role for the Prince in Cambodian affairs. Even among those Cambodians who are prepared, in private, to express their regret at Sihanouk's passing from the Cambodian political scene, the feeling has grown that the Prince is a political prisoner in Peking, however much respect is accorded to him by the Chinese. Fundamental to this judgment is the belief that it could only have been as the result of Chinese restraint that Prince Sihanouk did not attend the funeral of President de Gaulle, the man whom Prince Sihanouk so much admired and whom he regarded as his political mentor.

Private commentary on those who have chosen to associate themselves with Prince Sihanouk in Peking is notably less marked by the rancor which is the stuff of public denunciation of Sihanouk's "lackeys" and "accomplices." Men such as Huot Sambath and Ngo Hou may be dismissed as mere creatures of Sihanouk's will who could not have faced any future under the changed regime and so might have been expected to align themselves with the Prince. But there is a degree of understanding, and even on occasion respect, for the decisions made by such men as former Prime Minister Penn Nouth and Ambassador Sarin Chhak to remain loyal to Prince Sihanouk. Venal reasons are easily conjured up to explain such men's decisions. Penn Nouth is alleged to be in the pay of the Chinese, while Sarin Chhak's rise to prominence in the Cambodian Foreign Service is attributed to his subservience to Sihanouk. The knowledgeable Cambodian elite, however, is aware that such characterizations are excessively simple. Penn Nouth's decision to remain with the Prince is seen by many of the elite as, at least in part, reflecting a genuine and deep loyalty to Sihanouk. Sarin Chhak, although he may have advanced rapidly because of the Prince's patronage, is also known to have privately endeavored to persuade the Prince, in years gone by, that his policy towards the Vietnamese Communists was dangerous in its future implications.

Apart from discussion of Prince Sihanouk himself, however, the most actively discussed topic in Phnom Penh elite circles is the extent to which the National United Cambodian Front (more usually known by its unfortunate acronym from its French title, FUNK), has succeeded in establishing itself as a viable entity within the country, directed by men with some loyalty to Sihanouk. It is in this regard that so much attention is paid to the three Cambodian left-wing deputies, Khieu Samphan, Hou Youn and Hu Nim, who disappeared in mysterious circumstances in 1967. Prince Sihanouk's messages to the contrary, there was little inclination among elite circles in Cambodia at the end of 1970 to believe that Prince Sihanouk had succeeded in implanting a functioning alternative government within the "liberated areas" of Cambodia which had passed out of Phnom Penh's control. The most common estimation was that there were, indeed, Cambodians associated with the Vietnamese Communist forces in northern and northeastern Cambodia, but these men were not regarded as having any role that was independent of their Vietnamese allies. In the Battambang region of northwestern Cambodia, the estimation was slightly different. Here, in an area which had experienced left-wing opposition to Prince Sihanouk's Government, the judgment was that the continuing opposition to the new Phnom Penh regime was, essentially, Cambodian, but by political sympathy little inclined to associate itself with the former ruler.

Whether or not these estimations are correct, their skeptical tone in part reflects the unreadiness of members of the Cambodian elite to believe that the three deputies who disappeared in 1967, and whom Sihanouk now claims as his most important representatives in the field, are still alive. The elite believes, in fact, that they met their deaths at Sihanouk's orders in 1967 and that their current resurrection is a measure of both Sihanouk's desperation and the extent to which his own freedom of action has been eliminated through his association with the Chinese.[35] Statements from Sihanouk which have candidly admitted the extent to which his government in exile is dominated by those whom he describes as Khmers Rouges are a further reason for the elite's unreadiness to concede to Sihanouk any real control over whatever Cambodians are associated with the forces in the country which seek the overthrow of the Phnom Penh Government.[36] Cambodian observers are well aware of developments in Vietnam and Laos and this leads them to be wary of any easy dismissal of a continuing future role by antigovernment forces in which Cambodians play a part. At the same time, they point with accuracy to the very different circumstances of Cambodia when it is compared with its northern and eastern neighbors. In considerable contrast to both Laos and Vietnam, the history of the past twenty-five years in Cambodia has never seen the development of a major indigenous political movement of the left similar to the Pathet Lao or the Viet-Minh. Without the background of such a movement, the task of the living opponents of the Phnom Penh regime is believed to be that much more difficult. Yet because they are aware of developments in Laos and Vietnam, the fear is also expressed that the longer the war continues, the greater is the possibility that an indigenous, left-wing movement will take hold in the Cambodian countryside.

Political Prospects

The flurry of activity and the concurrent generation of rumors which accompanied Lon Nol's resignation of 20 April 1971 brought briefly to the surface some of the tensions which are so much a part of contemporary Cambodia. The suggestion that the group of army colonels associated with Lon Nol's brother, Colonel Lon Non, had sought a complete change in the Cambodian cabinet is not surprising in a period during which the army has even more than under Sihanouk come to regard itself as the preserver of the regime. Dissatisfaction with the performance of the existing cabinet and a feeling that military men are being excluded from some of the personal benefits which stem from the ministries has played a part in developing Army criticism of the cabinet which has led Cambodia since March 1970.

The considerable length of time required for a resolution of the crisis touched off by Lon Nol's resignation was a reflection of the underlying lack of consensus among Cambodian political, military and parliamentary leaders. Although necessarily muted by the existence of the war, this lack of consensus was sufficient for the Phnom Penh regime to take some six weeks before a new cabinet could be assembled and sworn in on 6 June.[37] That many of the issues raised at the time of Lon Nol's resignation, in April 1971, were still not resolved was indicated by the fact that Lon Nol returned to be Prime Minister, with executive powers delegated to Sirik Matak. The interests of those in the Army who had aligned themselves with Colonel Lon Non did not appear to have been met in any notable fashion. The divide between the cabinet and the members of the

National Assembly equally seemed no less. Possibly the most notable aspect of the six weeks' *malaise* was the suggestion that Son Ngoc Thanh was ready in the wings to assume a more active role within Cambodian internal affairs than has, apparently, been the case to date. If the selection of a prime minister was left entirely in the hands of the members of the National Assembly, it might well be that their choice would fall on Thanh. The role played by Colonel Lon Non in the period of *malaise* may well be interesting less for the fact of his personal efforts to gain stature in political as well as military matters, as for the indication which it provides of the way in which any regime in Phnom Penh could in the future become hostage of a popular military commander. Should Lon Nol's health once again take a major turn for the worse, the temptation to act to institute a military-led regime may be too great for a member of the armed forces to resist.

The formidable catalogue of problems which face the Phnom Penh leadership both encourage and inhibit speculation on the future. Without suggesting the likely outcome of attempts to overcome these difficulties, even a brief listing of the more obvious among them casts a somber, if not totally black hue over the prospects of the Phnom Penh Government. Short of a general settlement in the Indochinese region, there seems little prospect that the fighting which has now spread to Cambodia will readily come to an end. The human cost of that fighting in Cambodia has already been high. For the economy of the country, the spread of the war has represented a disaster. The mending of political bridges with the South Vietnamese Government has played a substantial part in preserving the Phnom Penh regime in power, but this has been gained at substantial cost. Fear and distrust of the South Vietnamese has not been dissipated because it is known that Vietnamese fight as the principal enemy on the other side. Hope of important military aid from Thailand has not followed upon the renewal of relations with that country, and there are private expressions of surprise and dissatisfaction that the United States does not seem ready to intervene with troops in Cambodia in order better to protect the Cambodian Government.

Within the areas controlled by the new regime, and particularly in Phnom Penh, varying degrees of discontent and disillusionment exist. For the young intellectuals, the extent to which the new regime appears to have inherited the corrupt and nepotistic ills of the old is a matter for bitter commentary. For the older members of the elite, many of whom have always been conservative by political inclination, the apparent inability of the new regime to make substantial progress in any of the tasks which it undertakes, be these economic, military or political, is a reason for deepening concern. This concern appears to have been part of the explanation for the consideration given by some sections of the elite, in early 1971, to the possibility of reinstituting the Cambodian monarchy with Prince Sisowath Monireth, Sihanouk's uncle, leading the country from the throne.

With continuing South Vietnamese and United States support, the Cambodian army is unlikely to be defeated in any dramatic fashion, but despite its expansion to a figure of perhaps 150,000 men, it still is not capable of assuring the security of the main road system throughout the country, or of preventing psychologically damaging attacks of the sort so dramatically carried out against Pochentong airport in the early hours of 22 January 1971.

It is a measure of the all-embracing nature of Prince Sihanouk's rule over Cambodia in the past that so much of what exists today, in terms of institutions and the persons who direct them, is a legacy of his rule. The formal symbols of that rule have been effaced, but much of its presence remains. Possibly the final paradox is that Prince Sihanouk should maintain such a residual presence in Cambodia at a time when, on his own admission, political developments have made it unlikely that, even were troops fighting under his name to win, he would be unlikely to have any role in the government which would later be established.[38]

Notes

1. This paper takes account of developments in Cambodia up to the end of May 1971. Given the extreme fluidity of the situation in Cambodia, it is possible that events since that date could qualify a number of the author's judgments.

2. The new Cambodian regime rejects the term *coup d'état*, arguing that such a description implies that Sihanouk's overthrow was unconstitutional. See the article by Douc Rasy in *Réalités Cambodgiennes*, 4 April 1970; and the "Mise au point du Gouvernement de Sauvetage," *Agence Khmère de Presse*, 5 April 1970. In the present writer's view, however, the overthrow of Sihanouk involved plotting and a sudden change in policy and the disposition of power which fully justifies the more conventional description.

3. These general observations, and much of the commentary in the paper dealing with leading personalities in the new regime, reflect recent personal investigation of developments in Cambodia as well as the analysis of published materials. The author's most recent visit to Cambodia was in December 1970. He also carried out research in Phnom Penh in February 1970, one month before the *coup*.

4. A number of statements of the new regime's policies exist. One of the more interesting is Sirik Matak's refutation of the article by Prince Sihanouk in *Foreign Affairs* (October 1970), which was published by the official Cambodian news agency in *Agence Khmère de Presse*, 29 January 1971, and republished in translation in the *Far Eastern Economic Review* (6 March 1971).

5. The author's own analysis of the immediate period leading up to Sihanouk's deposition may be found in "Cambodia's Choices," *Current Affairs Bulletin* 47, no. 1 (30 November 1970). Since the publication of an early analysis, information suggesting important external knowledge, and possibly involvement in the coup has come to light and has been taken into account in this paper.

6. For a discussion of these developments, see R.M. Smith, "Cambodia:

Between Scylla and Charybdis," *Asian Survey* 8, no. 1 (January 1968): 72-79; M. Leifer, "The Failure of Political Institutionalisation in Cambodia," *Modern Asian Studies* 2, no. 2 (1968): 125-140; M.E. Osborne, "Regional Disunity in Cambodia," *Australian Outlook* 22, no. 3 (December 1968): 317-333.

7. No easy definition exists for the Cambodian elite. Made up of members of the former royal family, legislators, senior officials, members of the officer corps and rich Cambodian businessmen, often of mixed Sino-Cambodian descent, its members are certainly aware of their own elite status and perpetuate or reinforce their position through intermarriage within the elite group.

8. Allegations of personal corruption have now been levelled at Prince Sihanouk and formed part of the formal charges against him at his trial *in absentia* held in July 1970. The author's own research in Cambodia, as close to the *coup d'état* as February 1970, suggests that there was then little belief in Sihanouk's own personal involvement in grand, as opposed to functional, corruption.

9. For an account of the trial at which Sihanouk was sentenced to death, see *Réalités Cambodgiennes*, 10 July 1970. The coolness of the Phnom Penh elite towards the Prince's films was noticeable as early as the *première* of his first feature length film, "Aspara," which the author attended in Phnom Penh in 1966. Some commentators have suggested that Sihanouk spent his nights poring over government dossiers after involvement with film-making during the day. See, for instance, Daniel Roy in *Le Monde Diplomatique*, April 1970. While there may be room for some argument on this point, such an impression was not widespread among the Phnom Penh elite shortly before the Prince's overthrow.

10. Again, controversy surrounds the discussion of how many North Vietnamese and National Liberation Front troops were using Cambodian territory. The widely believed figure among members of the Phnom Penh elite in February 1970 was 50,000. The new Phnom Penh Government has cited a figure of 55,000 Vietnamese Communist troops present in Cambodia. Prince Sihanouk, himself, stated in March 1970 that at the end of 1969 there had been 40,000 Vietnamese Communist troops in Cambodia, but that their numbers had diminished since then. See *Le Monde*, 12 March 1970. Very importantly, concern on the part of those in Phnom Penh was heightened by the fact that Vietnamese Communist troops had now heavily infiltrated areas relatively close to the capital.

11. The information presented of Son Ngoc Thanh's association with Lon Nol, and of Son Ngoc Thanh's involvement in Sihanouk's eventual overthrow must still be treated with some reserve. The author obtained his information in the course of an extended interview with Thanh's brother, Son Thai Nguyen, in Saigon during January 1971. Despite the difficulties which still exist in attempting to find published proof to substantiate Son Thai Nguyen's account, the information which he provided is circumstantially possible, and is not in conflict with other evidence on developments which is available. Some of the information given to the author by Son Thai Nguyen was published in an article by the author in the Melbourne *Age* (12 January 1971).

12. See *Réalités Cambodgiennes*, 30 January 1971.

13. On the basis of information from a private source, there is some reason to believe that Lon Nol was finally prompted to action by the failure of Prince

Sihanouk to give serious consideration to matters which Lon Nol raised with Sihanouk in the course of a meeting between the two men in France in February 1970.

14. Based on my interview with Son Thai Nguyen. If Son Thai Nguyen's account is correct, this appears to be a solid reason for believing that the South Vietnamese military authorities, and through them United States military authorities, must have had some advance notice of the intended confrontation (and subsequent coup), in Cambodia. This is *not* an argument for United States instigation of the confrontation and coup. The fact, however, that there had been some ill-defined but widely accepted association between United States Special Forces and the Khmer Serei in the past (see *New York Times*, 28 January 1970), and the difficulty of believing that Son Ngoc Thanh's promise of material aid would not have been known to United States authorities in Vietnam, does provide significant circumstantial reasons for believing that the events in Cambodia in March 1970 may not have been such a complete surprise as officials in Washington have suggested. See, for instance, Neil Sheehan's account of the Washington position in *New York Times*, 30 June 1970.

15. Thanh's appointment was announced in the semiofficial press, *Réalités Cambodgiennes* of 14 August 1970, and read, in part, "The Government of Salvation has decided to present a united front to its adversary, grouping together all those who are against Sihanouk and his Communist allies. Monsieur Son Ngoc Thanh was one of the first of those to align himself against the Sihanouk regime. He has partisans within the country and a degree of credit abroad. He cannot, therefore, be left indefinitely outside of a government whose first goal is the unity of all nationalist Cambodians."

16. In December 1970 there was reliable information that Lon Nol was holding fifteen senior colonels under house arrest; not for suspected loyalty to Sihanouk, but rather because of suspected disloyalty to him.

17. *Hsinhua*, 16 February 1971.

18. Whatever occurred in March 1970, it was not a social revolution. Personal observation of life in Phnom Penh and Battambang during December 1970 revealed the continued use of deferential greeting styles for members of the royal family, even if the use of royal titles no longer took place. Similarly, the much-used term "Excellency," bestowed upon anyone who at any time has held high government rank, appeared to flourish despite recommendations for its abolition handed down by the new regime.

19. The term is not entirely accurate in relation to both these men, since Yem Sambaur and Douc Rasy are lawyers; but the sense of a technocrat making his contribution in terms of technical rather than political areas does not seem misplaced.

20. Recounted by Douc Rasy, in *Réalités Cambodgiennes*, 11 September 1970.

21. Two qualifications of detail should be made here. Both Douc Rasy and Yem Sambaur do enjoy the respect of sections of the conservative and intellectual circles in Phnom Penh. The size of those involved in this support is, however, difficult to estimate. In addition, attention should be given to the fact that during the parliamentary elections of 1966, Douc Rasy was elected to the Na-

tional Assembly as a deputy despite the very considerable efforts made by Sihanouk, and those acting on Sihanouk's behalf, to discredit him.

22. No extensive biographical treatment exists of this fascinating figure in Cambodian politics. A French account written in 1952 denounced Thanh as a tool of the Communists—an extremely doubtful judgment. See Pierre Christian, "Son Ngoc Thanh," *Indochine: Sud-Est Asiatique* (Saigon), 11 October 1952, pp. 48-49. The account provided of Son Ngoc Thanh by Martin Herz in his *A Short History of Cambodia* (New York: Praeger, 1958), gives too favorable an estimation to a number of Thanh's acts.

23. By no means all felt the impact of discrimination, and some rose to very considerable heights within the government structure. Prince Sihanouk's most important economic adviser for most of his rule, Son Sann, was of Khmer Krom origin.

24. In part, these observations are based on personal research between 1966 and 1970 during various visits to Cambodia. For some commentary on the Khmer Krom group in Phnom Penh, the author is also indebted to discussions with Dr. Gerald Hickey of The RAND Corporation.

25. See *Réalités Cambodgiennes*, 4 September 1970. Thanh was reported as saying that 5,000 former Khmer Serei troops were fighting on behalf of the Lon Nol regime. Additional information on Son Ngoc Thanh's activities in this respect was given to the author in his January 1971 interview with Son Thai Nguyen.

26. For Khim Tit's commentary on Son Ngoc Thanh, see *Réalités Cambodgiennes*, 9 and 16 June 1967.

27. Some discussion of the problem as it existed in 1966 and 1967 will be found in the author's "Regional Disunity in Cambodia," *Australian Outlook* 22 (December 1968), pp. 317-33. The term intellectual as used in Cambodia is not susceptible to any exact definition. A fair judgment would appear to be that all those who obtain the equivalent of a high school diploma, and any higher scholastic qualification, could be classed as intellectuals. Many such persons would not, of course, choose to use such a description of themselves.

28. The most notable of those defecting were Dr. Thioun Thioeun, the surgeon in charge of the Cambodian-Russian Friendship hospital in Phnom Penh; Ros Chetthor, a Cambodian journalist who had been the editor of Prince Sihanouk's Cambodian language newspaper, *Neak Cheat Niyum* (The Nationalist); and Men Nitho, an engineer with the Ministry of Public Works. Telegrams said to have been sent by these men to Prince Sihanouk in Peking have been released by the Agence Khmère d'Information, the news agency associated with Prince Sihanouk's United Front organization.

29. For some instances of government solicitude, see *Réalités Cambodgiennes*, 22 August 1970; and *Agence Khmere de Presse*, 24 January 1971.

30. Information concerning these practices first came to the author's attention in 1966, and was confirmed over a wide range of discussions in subsequent visits to Cambodia. It is a sad reflection of the immense gap in foreign knowledge of Cambodia that no serious scholarly study of Cambodian Buddhism exists. The work by A. Leclère, *Le Buddhisme au Cambodge* (Paris, 1899), which is still occasionally cited as an authority for the history of Buddhism in

Cambodia, is both sadly out of date and far from accurate in its account of historical developments.

31. These observations were made to the author in December 1970.

32. As has been the case with Vietnam, one of the tragic accompaniments of the extension of the Indochinese war to Cambodia has been the sudden influx of refugees into Phnom Penh to escape from areas which are subject to heavy aerial bombardment, and to avoid living in areas dominated by ethnically antipathetic Vietnamese. The best estimate of the number of refugees in Phnom Penh at the end of 1970 was 500,000.

33. For internal and external propaganda purposes, the Phnom Penh Government has denied that any substantial number of Cambodians are fighting with those who oppose the regime. The enemy is always described as Vietnamese or more generally as Viet-Cong. Such an approach does have certain difficulties for Phnom Penh, since it also wishes, when possible, to highlight the fact that numbers of Cambodians have rallied to live under Government administration after a period of fighting with the Vietnamese Communist troops operating in the country.

34. Both in terms of population attitudes and the areas claimed to be, respectively, under Cambodian Government and anti-Government forces, the statements of the Phnom Penh regime and of Prince Sihanouk's government-in-exile must be treated with the greatest reserve. In the author's experience, at the end of December 1970 even the estimates offered in private conversation by both Cambodian and foreign observers were so widely varying in magnitude as to be scarcely worthy of consideration.

35. The author's own research into the March 1970 period, particularly the week between 11 March and 18 March, tends to support the argument that those who finally overthrew Sihanouk had far from made up their minds to take this ultimate step when demonstrations were mounted against the North Vietnamese and PRG embassies on Phnom Penh on 11 March. At the same time, there is a puzzling aspect to Sihanouk's own failure (or apparent failure) to recognize the extent of the danger which confronted his position within Cambodia in the first two or three days of this tumultuous one-week period.

36. The author's own strong inclination is to accept the estimation that these three men are, in fact, no longer alive. Discussion of the subject in Cambodia in late 1967, shortly after the deputies disappeared, gave little reason for believing Prince Sihanouk's own claim that the men had taken to the *maquis*. Political assassination was not unknown in Sihanouk's Cambodia and represented the dark and seldom-mentioned underside of his regime. As early as 1960, the death of the editor of the left-wing newspaper *L'Observateur* was believed to have followed a "Will no one rid me of this turbulent Priest?"-style remark from Sihanouk. In the case of the three deputies, the allegation is that Sihanouk's role was much more direct. Since discussion of three deputies and their fate has developed, the Cambodian Ambassador to the United Nations, Khim Tit, has stated that in 1967, he saw a security document which reported the execution of the three men; Khieu Samphan was said to have been burnt to death with acid, while Hou Youn and Hu Nim were crushed under a bulldozer; *New York Times*, 22 August 1970; for a discussion of the disappearance of the deputies in 1967, see *Réalités Cambodgiennes*, 5 and 12 May 1967.

37. Sihanouk has made this statement on frequent occasions. See, for instance, *New York Times*, 25 September 1970, which gives an account of Sihanouk's interview with a representative of AFP. Some of Sihanouk's more effusive utterances since he has been in China are taken as further evidence for the proposition that he is manipulated by and not manipulating Cambodian leftists. See Sihanouk's speech in Shanghai broadcast over Radio Peking, 22 February 1971.

38. For the "Declaration" presented by Sirik Matak on the occasion of the new cabinet's inauguration, and the "Message" delivered by Lon Nol after the inauguration, see *Cambodge Nouveau* (Phnom Penh) 2, no. 11 (June 1971).

39. *New York Times*, 20 and 25 September 1970.

5

Lao Politics Under Prince Souvanna Phouma

Arthur J. Dommen

Prologue: The Dynamics of Lao Politics

Several years ago, a Hong Kong magazine published a vision of the Laos of the future in which a visitor found that the grateful citizens of Vientiane had erected a huge statue on the bank of the Mekong in memory of their late Prime Minister, Prince Souvanna Phouma. The prince was represented in a characteristic pose holding a finger to the wind.

Whatever may be one's view of the morality of Prince Souvanna Phouma's aptitude for conforming to the prevailing wind, it is evident that this aptitude has served him well in terms of political longevity, for in his present tenure as Prime Minister (his fourth), he has held office continuously for more than nine years, a record that is equalled only by Prime Minister Lee Kuan Yew of Singapore in a region of the world where change often occurs suddenly and unpredictably. This record is due in no small measure to Souvanna Phouma's personal qualities of tolerance and perseverance, as well as to the near-indispensable role he plays in internal Lao politics and in the foreign relations of Laos.

The prince, who was 70 years old on October 7, 1971, has been the fulcrum of politics in Laos since the formation on June 23, 1962, of the tripartite Provisional Government of National Union which included representatives of the three Lao factions, called for the sake of convenience the rightists, centrists, and Neo Lao Hak Sat (NLHS). Under a formula worked out in a meeting on the Plain of Jars preceding the announcement of the government, the rightists, who had previously formed a government led by Prince Boun Oum na Champassak and General Phoumi Nosavan, received four seats; the centrists, being members of Prince Souvanna Phouma's 1960 government who had welcomed him back to the Plain of Jars, where the allied armed forces of Captain Kong Le and the NLHS held control, in the spring of 1961 following a brief exile in Cambodia, held 11 seats; and the NLHS, or Laotian Patriotic Front, held four seats.[1]

Prince Souvanna Phouma has stuck doggedly to his position as the middle man in Laos—the upholder of the policy of national reconciliation among the Laotian factions and of the policy of neutrality in relations with foreign powers written into the Geneva Agreement signed by Laos and 13 foreign governments in 1962. The record of these nine years shows that he has been successful beyond expectation in weathering the storms through which Laos has passed in that period, and that the principal threat to his continuation in office has come not from the adventures in armed force undertaken in Laos by foreign powers, but from the adventures engaged in by one or another of the factions within Laos itself. Indeed, one might say that the more the second Indochina War has escalated and the more obvious have become the evidences of the presence in Laos of foreign armed forces, the more indispensable Souvanna Phouma has become to the contending political factions in the country and to the foreign powers.

This is not to say that there have not been times when Souvanna Phouma has expressed pessimism at being able to continue to shoulder the thankless task he has assumed and which exposes him to accusations from his left of being a puppet of the American imperialists in their war of aggression in Indochina and to accusations from his right of mortgaging the survival of the Lao nation to the encroachments of North Vietnam on Lao territory in the name of an ineffective policy of national reconciliation and international neutrality. Souvanna Phouma has on occasion been deeply pessimistic.

Perhaps his pessimism reached its nadir in April 1964, when, having returned home from visits to Peking and Hanoi with all his hopes of being able to preserve Laos from involvement in escalation of the war crushed, and having failed in his efforts to restore the unity of the government, he announced his intention of resigning. This was at a time when Hanoi, reacting to the overthrow of President Ngo Dinh Diem in Saigon and to the coming to power of General Nguyen Khanh, was already thinking in terms of sending units of its regular army southward in a bid to clinch a victory in the confused, indeed, chaotic, conditions then prevailing all over South Vietnam.[2] Negotiations were very far from the minds of the men in Hanoi at that point, and General Vo Nguyen Giap, North Vietnam's Defense Minister, realized that he would have to build up the trail complex (later to become famous as the Ho Chi Minh Trail) through Laos to carry the heavy armaments required to cope with the stepped-up American commitment. Prince Souphanouvong, the leader of the NLHS and a half-brother of Prince Souvanna Phouma, declined the latter's invitation to return to Vientiane to resume talks aimed at making the coalition a whole once more.

The word that Souvanna Phouma intended to resign precipitated action by two generals, Kouprasith Abhay and Siho Lamphouthakoul, who proceeded to arrest the Prime Minister and form their own revolutionary committee. They may have been misled by the renewed American military aid the Government of National Union was receiving and the hardening attitude of Washington toward North Vietnam into concluding that a change of American policy in Laos was imminent; as it turned out, Washington was not in the least anxious to have a "strongman" running Laos, and Souvanna Phouma was quickly restored to a position he had never in fact relinquished. Invitations to attend Cabinet meetings continued to be addressed to the absent NLHS ministers, and the Soviet Union, China, and North Vietnam continued to maintain their embassies in Vientiane.

Since the April 19, 1964, coup attempt, the generals[3] in Vientiane have understood that an initiative on their part to stage a coup against Souvanna Phouma would not meet with favor by the United States, and since they depend on aid from the United States to pay their troops and retainers, they cannot risk cutting themselves off from their source of supply. In grabbing for a larger share of the pie, they may lose it all. This has been an unwritten, but nonetheless real, rule of politics in Laos ever since.[4]

The Challenges to Neutralism:
the Politics of Stabilization

The sudden overthrow of Prince Norodom Sihanouk in Cambodia on March 18, 1970, and the entry of American and South Vietnamese troops into the border sanctuaries in Cambodia posed the question of whether American support for a neutralist government in Vientiane would change. For a few days in May, Vientiane was abuzz with rumors that the United States would be prepared to see the generals take over and declare the Provisional Government of National Union and the policy of neutrality at an end. These rumors proved to be empty, however, as it became clear that the United States had not changed its policy. However, Souvanna Phouma faced another challenge beginning in May in the National Assembly, where rightist politicians who control the machinery decided to subject the government to a trial of strength. Whereas in previous debates the National Assembly deputies had made the large budget deficit and the government's dependence on American aid the principal targets of their criticism, this time they struck at the policy of neutrality.

Souvanna Phouma was in a vulnerable position because of the fact that the Royal Lao Army had lost two provincial capitals in southern Laos. On April 30, the town of Attopeu, which controls the middle reaches of the Se Kong, fell to the combined Pathet Lao-North Vietnamese forces as the latter strove to consolidate their supply lines in the wake of their loss of the use of the Cambodian seaports. Then on June 9, the town of Saravane fell. The loss of these towns carried great political significance for the Royal Government. Although they had for years been cut off from ground communication with the government's positions in the Mekong Valley, they represented enclaves recognized by the NLHS ever since the June 24, 1962, ceasefire. NLHS statements about the capture of Saravane spoke of the need to foil American plans to use the town as a base for military operations behind NLHS lines. The capture of the two towns at that particular moment was a potentially unstabilizing development that placed the merits of the whole policy of neutrality in question, as the Prime Minister acknowledged in a statement in the National Assembly on June 12.

The action of the enemy puts the situation in Laos into a new stage which has become extremely serious. Such North Vietnamese actions clearly indicate that North Vietnam undoubtedly intends to abrogate the 1962 Geneva Agreement.

The loss of Attopeu and Saravane also had the effect of increasing the rightist pressure on Souvanna Phouma's government at this critical juncture. The towns are located deep in southern Laos, the traditional fief of Prince Boun Oum na Champassak. Prince Boun Oum had retired from national politics in 1962, when he relinquished the titular as well as actual leadership of the rightist faction to General Phoumi to devote himself to commerce and regional politics. The two are inextricably interwoven among the southern Lao, who continue to regard Boun Oum, the heir to the defunct throne of Champassak, with something akin to veneration.[5] It is noteworthy, for instance, that the likelihood of success of any commerical venture in southern Laos is automatically measured by the standard of whether it will have Boun Oum's blessing, or whether on the contrary, it will trespass on his sizeable commercial preserves, in which case it will be doomed to failure.

Attopeu and Saravane had existed for years as captive markets for the Boun Oum interests. With the roads cut, every commodity that was to be sold in the towns had to be flown in, which raised its price and raised proportionately the cut taken by the middle man. By 1970, it had become notorious that not only were officers of the Royal Lao Army receiving profits from this trade, but the NLHS as well. Now these two markets were lost, and Prince Boun Oum was not happy. There was renewed talk in the south of bringing back General Phoumi Nosavan, who has lived in exile in Thailand since 1965; the southerners felt that General Phoumi was a leader who would be able to stop the whittling-away of the territory still held by the non-Communists.

Souvanna Phouma reacted adroitly in the face of this situation. He announced the appointment of Sisouk na Champassak, who is a nephew of Boun Oum and who had been Minister of Finance since the 1965 Cabinet reshuffle, to be his delegate at the Ministry of National Defense. The still-respected formula prescribing distribution of ministerial portfolios among left, right, and center prevented Sisouk, a rightist, from being named actual Minister of National Defense, a portfolio reserved for Souvanna Phouma, but that was in effect what he became. The appointment demonstrated that the Prime Minister was resolved to deal firmly with the military crisis and took some of the wind out of the sails of the rightist politicians in the National Assembly who criticized the government for its lack of decisiveness. At the same time, the appointment allowed Souvanna Phouma to place a trusted civilian over the generals to keep them in check.

Nevertheless, Sisouk's appointment was not accepted immediately by all. The Prime Minister had acted completely on his own and this caused great resentment, even among the southerners. In Vientiane, the appointment drew initial expressions of disfavor from members of the Sananikone family, the most powerful force in Vientiane politics. Ngon Sananikone, the Minister of Public Works and Transport, angrily complained that the Cabinet had not been consulted. He told friends, both Lao and foreign, that if he wished, he could bring about the downfall of the Prime Minister, but the problem was he had no generally acceptable substitute candidate. The threat was not an empty one; the Sananikone family had its members well placed in the National Assembly, where Ngon's elder brother and leader of the clan Phoui held the chair and another brother, Oun, was an influential deputy from Borikhane, and in the army, where the commander of the Fifth Military Region headquartered in Vientiane, General Kouprasith Abhay, was allied to the Sananikones by marriage.

Seeing the opposition to his appointment, Sisouk set about smoothing ruffled feathers. To the National Assembly deputies, he made it clear that his purpose would be loyalty to the Prime Minister rather than self-aggrandizement. Sisouk then did some frank and subtle talking to the generals. At the same time, the Defense Ministry announced a series of promotions; Laos now had a total of 38 generals, compared to five in 1959.

In the debate in the National Assembly on government policy, Souvanna Phouma's assurances that the government intended to take measures to raise the effectiveness of the army and planned to launch new appeals to the Geneva Co-Chairmen and to the United Nations Secretary-General to use their influence to preserve Laos' status of neutrality had a disarming effect on the opposition. A number of compromise resolutions were drafted which, while stating the criticisms that had been made by the deputies, did not go so far as to censure the government. This face-saving draftsmanship was largely the work of the chairman of the Finance Committee, Phan Norindr, a deputy from Luang Prabang.

The situation remained still so unsettled, however, that Souvanna Phouma found it wise to postpone his departure to take his annual *cure* at the springs of Plombières in France, planned for early July. Partly, this was due to the need to appoint a delegation to hold preliminary talks with representatives of the NLHS in order to seek a political solution to the Laos problem, as had been proposed by the NLHS Central Committee in a statement issued on March 6, 1970. Rightist politicians in Vientiane had initially reacted with skepticism to the NLHS proposal and warned Souvanna Phouma against offering concessions to the NLHS until the good faith of the latter had been demonstrably proved. However, Souvanna Phouma was probably in a better position to judge the good or bad faith of the proposals since he had a long experience of negotiating with his half-brother and at the same time had been intimately involved in dealings with the North Vietnamese during his days at Khang Khay on the Plain of Jars.

After the proposal was delivered to him by a messenger from Sam Neua, Souvanna Phouma set about methodically consulting the politicians about it— less, one suspects, to gain their advice than to preempt any opposition to his follow-up and to assure himself as much freedom to act as possible. He thus made sure that he had at least the formal concurrence of Prince Boun Oum, of the National Assembly, of the King's Council, and of the Cabinet. After a series of meetings in Vientiane with Tiao Souk Vongsak, Souphanouvong's special emissary, Souvanna Phouma announced the appointment of a delegation headed by his Minister of Interior, Pheng Phongsavan, who had headed the centrist dele-gation to the Ban Namone truce talks in 1961. In his meetings with Tiao Souk, Souvanna Phouma appeared to accept the abandonment of strict tripartism im-plicit in the NLHS statement's reference to "a political consultative conference of representatives of the interested Lao parties."

Although Souvanna Phouma's Neutralist Party, the Phak Pen Kang, continued in existence, it had lapsed into inactivity, a victim of the blurring of the lines between the centrists and the rightists in the policies and day-to-day conduct of the affairs of the Royal Government. The party itself, according to its secretary-general, General Soukan Vilaysarn, had been rent by a division of opinion over whether to maintain the party's separate identity in spite of the fact that it exer-cised little visible influence, or to merge the party into a broader nationalist front of parties of the type that would be required to prevent defeat in the event of elections contested by the NLHS.[6] There was also a splinter neutralist group that had rallied to the NLHS side following the withdrawal of Prince Soupha-nouvong from Vientiane in 1963. This group, which was referred to in NLHS statements as the "patriotic neutralists," comprised soldiers and officers of Kong Le's army who had deserted under the leadership of Lieutenant Deuan Sun-nalath. Two members of the original coalition Cabinet, Minister of Public Health Khamsouk Keola and Secretary of State for Veterans Affairs Heuan Mongkhon-vilay, who had been expelled from the Phak Pen Kang and dismissed from their Cabinet posts in Vientiane during 1964, were announced as assuming the leader-ship of the "patriotic neutralists" in the NLHS-controlled area. The question of whether tripartism still represented political realities in Laos in 1970 when the NLHS launched their initiative to resume political negotiations was thus an open one. In his exchanges with Souvanna Phouma, Souphanouvong referred to the former as the "leader of the Vientiane party." Souvanna Phouma, however, defended the right of his delegation to speak in his name as Prime Minister of the Royal Government whether or not this government was still the Government of National Union, as the NLHS contended it was not. The final formulation chosen here appeared to hinge mainly on how anxious the two sides were to get the negotiations started.

Intra-Elite Conflict and the War

With these political matters put in order, if not definitively settled, and with the rainy season putting a stop to major military action throughout the kingdom, Souvanna Phouma departed in September on a world tour that took him to the Lusaka conference of nonaligned states and to the United Nations General As-sembly and was not to bring him back to Laos until the end of October. By that time, the political atmosphere in Vientiane had improved noticeably because of a significant development: the Sananikone family had swallowed its pride and had decided to accept Sisouk na Champassak in his new post of authority. Though the two families are age-old enemies, the Sananikones had no alternative. Ngon, speaking for the family, let it be known that he considered it likely that Sisouk would become the next Prime Minister of Laos.

Sisouk's rise to power and the new-found peace between Sisouk and the Sananikones had in the meantime caused unrest among another section of the Laos political scene. Among the followers of General Phoumi Nosavan, who have always been wary of the ambitions of the Sananikones (and particularly since it had been General Kouprasith Abhay who had sent his troops to crush the attempted coup in 1965 that had ended in Phoumi's flight into exile), there was considerable alarm at the new combination in Vientiane. On December 10, there occurred an abortive bid for power in Savannakhet in southcentral Laos, Phoumi's birthplace and the headquarters of his American-backed rebel government in 1960. The whole affair was officially hushed up after the attempt failed, and considerable mystery continues to surround it. What is known is that a band of armed mercenaries recruited in Thailand by Colonel Bounleuth Saycocie, an exiled officer who had triggered the sequence of events that led to Phoumi's flight from Vientiane in February 1965,[7] was arrested on the Thai bank of the Mekong opposite Savannakhet by the Governor of Nakhon Phanom Province. This band was reportedly preparing to go across the river to carry out a plan to seize control of the headquarters of the Third Military Region in the town. The plan reportedly involved the assassination of General Bounpone Makthepharaks, the regional commander, and his replacement by one of his subordinates, General Kot Venevongsos, a man close to Phoumi. Even more alarming, the plan reportedly also involved the kidnapping of the Prime Minister, who had been scheduled to make a stopover at Savannakhet in the course of a flying visit to southern Laos.

General Phoumi, in Bangkok, denied involvement in the "Savannakhet plot." Whatever its origin, the affair was taken extremely seriously by Souvanna Phouma, who viewed himself as the principal target and said "I might have been killed." January 1971, found him in a new mood of depression that bordered on fatalism. He remarked to one foreign ambassador that he sensed he was doomed to die a violent death. He said that if the politicians and the generals wanted him out of the way, he would gladly resign. On January 22, amid indications of a new North Vietnamese offensive in northern Laos, the preliminary talks with the NLHS came to a halt and Tiao Souk departed for Sam Neua blaming the Sananikones for having sabotaged the peace effort. The talks were to resume again after the events of February.

On January 14, Ngon Sananikone had presented the Prime Minister with a written "suggestion" for establishment of a defense community among South Vietnam, Cambodia, Thailand and Laos. This would amount, he wrote, to "a Saigon-Phnom Penh-Bangkok-Vientiane axis aimed at Communist aggression." Such an axis would be something short of a formal military alliance, prohibited under the terms of the Geneva Agreement, but would represent rather "a union of strategic means for legitimate self-defense and for safeguarding the freedom of the peoples of the Indochinese peninsula." Ngon wrote that such a defense community "is not contrary to the Geneva Agreement."

Ngon's suggestion was discussed at a meeting of the Cabinet, where Souvanna Phouma announced that it would not be implemented so long as he remained Prime Minister. It was also discussed in the National Consultative Council, a forum bringing together representatives of political parties, youth groups, student groups, professional and community associations, and so on, and chaired by the Prime Minister.

It had long been accepted by the Lao, and by the Prime Minister himself, that the Ho Chi Minh Trail had become the key to the balance of forces in the second Indochina War. North Vietnam could not expect to win a decisive advantage in the war unless it continued to control the means of access through the mountains to the population centers on the coast. Conversely, the Saigon government could not expect to win the war so long as the Trail remained open. It was with no great surprise, therefore, that President Nguyen Van Thieu's announcement was heard in Vientiane on February 8 that South Vietnamese forces had crossed the border of Laos in the Tchepone region. Souvanna Phouma, without waiting for the South Vietnamese ambassador to deliver the official text of Thieu's announcement, issued a statement in the name of the Royal Government deploring that "once again foreign troops belonging to countries whose governments have committed themselves to guarantee and defend the sovereignty, neutrality, and territorial inviolability of Laos have chosen deliberately to make Laos their battlefield."

This statement was in accordance with the policy of neutrality. The Prime Minister's confidence in his own ability to make this policy prevail had been sufficiently restored by mid-February so that he was speaking of "the difficulty of abandoning my task." Asked on February 13 about rumors he might resign, he replied:

Obviously, if the National Assembly votes a censure motion against the Government, the Government will hand in its resignation. But it is difficult for me in present circumstances to abandon my task because I consider it my duty to remain in office in these difficult times through which Laos is passing. However, if the deputies, the politicians want a change, wish to see the policy of the Government change, they can request an extraordinary session of the Parliament and vote a motion of censure against the Government. In that case, I confess I would be happy to give up my functions. But as for quitting of my own free will, I would consider myself a coward fleeing before the present difficulties.[8]

By this time, Souvanna Phouma knew that the rightists had nothing to hold against him, since they were seeing happen in Tchepone precisely what they had imagined a rightist government in Vientiane would have worked to achieve.

Moreover, the North Vietnamese, Chinese, and Russians had not left Vientiane, meaning that the policy of neutrality would survive. Indeed, the Chinese *chargé d'affaires* told one foreign ambassador in Vientiane while the South Vietnamese operation against the Trail was still going on that Peking would keep its embassy in Vientiane "because we respect the persons of the King and of the Prime Minister."[9] Nor had the permanent representative of the NLHS, Soth Pethrasy, decamped. In conversation, Soth took a hard line in predicting that the South Vietnamese operation in Laos would be a failure, but he shifted the blame for the Vientiane government's acceptance without protest of the state of affairs at Tchepone to the "Sananikone clique." The Prime Minister thus seemed safe on all sides.

The politicians in Vientiane watched the unfolding of the Tchepone operation from afar, as it were. Because of their government's proclaimed policy of neutrality, they could not permit themselves to welcome it openly, although many instinctively did welcome it. They feared, however, that the result would be to drive the North Vietnamese to swallow up more territory west of the present Trail in order to secure their supply routes. Here, there would be problems, for the area was more heavily populated and this made bombing operations on the scale of those against the present Trail impossible. For reasons of security, the Saigon government gave the Lao government no details of operational plans, and Royal Lao Army troops took no part in the operations.

On February 12, the Prime Minister proclaimed a state of emergency over the whole territory of Laos. The effect of this, as the Prime Minister himself described it, was to place the security duties that in normal times resided in the hands of the police into the hands of the military. One assumes that the military had exerted pressure for this move. This meant that in general terms the military had gained influence at the expense of the police, and thus of the Ministry of Interior. The military set about using their newly granted powers to recruit youths off the streets of Vientiane, but the Prime Minister intervened to halt this practice after several incidents had revealed the abuse of these wide powers. This demonstrated again his determination to curb the military.

A North Vietnamese diplomat in Vientiane had told a journalist in October 1970, that there existed a danger that a South Vietnamese and American move to cut the Ho Chi Minh Trail would provoke a reaction by Communist forces against Luang Prabang.[10] It was not altogether surprising, therefore, when Communist pressure around the royal capital began tightening noticeably during February and March. North Vietnamese forces moving down the Hou River valley chased the small Royal Lao Army garrison out of Pak Hou on the Mekong, and Pathet Lao guerrillas appeared on the farm of King Savang Vatthana at Pak Suong about ten miles north of Luang Prabang, telling the villagers they meant no harm to the King but would resist any move against them by the army. On March 21, there occurred the first rocket and mortar attack on the Luang Prabang airfield in several years. The atmosphere of siege that prevailed in the town was heightened by the departure of some Chinese merchants, the cancellation of civilian air services, and the rushing in of troop reinforcements from Vientiane in aircraft that had to approach the airfield through the firing pattern of the artillery pieces positioned there. The town itself, with its many pagodas and the royal palace, was not shelled, however, and the King remained unharmed, a witness to the seige.

Diplomatic sources in Vientiane reported that the Central Committee of the NLHS opposed the launching of the Luang Prabang operation, but was overruled by the North Vietnamese. At all events, when the King made his first visit in many years to south Laos in early July, he seized the occasion to express an unusually explicit condemnation of the North Vietnamese. Speaking at Savannakhet, the King said "The North Vietnamese have used every means to bring our country to ruin in order to turn it into their colony." At Thakhek, he said "We have come here to visit the population and the refugees fleeing from the North Vietnamese, who have invaded our national territory and committed aggression against our country." The North Vietnamese, he said, were using Laos as a screen for their own interests. "We must not accept this role. The North Vietnamese do not have the right to interfere in our internal affairs." The King tempered the force of these remarks by saying at Pakse, "In spite of the open aggression of the North Vietnamese against our beloved country, we will continue to treat them as if they came from a friendly neighboring country."[11] Following these remarks, Prince Souphanouvong is reported to have sent a message to the King in an effort to redress the balance. The text of the message has not been published.

The preparations for the King's southern trip lasted several weeks, and at one point, it was announced that the trip had been postponed altogether. The reason for this delay was the King's uneasy relationship with Prince Boun Oum. The latter continued to tell visitors to the south that he considered King Savang Vatthana to be the King of Luang Prabang, nothing more. Boun Oum told friends that if the King journeyed to south Laos, he would be glad to receive the sovereign at Champassak, the seat of the ancient kingdom of the same name. Boun Oum had been persuaded by the French to give up his claim to the throne of the defunct kingdom and had received the title of Inspector General of the Kingdom of Laos for life, but his resentment against the King of Luang Prabang remained deep. The two men had not met for ten years.

King Savang Vatthana, for his part, was determined to proceed with the planned trip to the south in order to demonstrate that as King, he could not be received by any one of his subjects, but was prepared to receive any of them, including Prince Boun Oum. Finally, the arrangements for the trip were completed. When the King disembarked from his aircraft at the Pakse airport, Boun Oum was the first to greet him. The two shook hands and embraced briefly. Boun Oum did not kneel in the royal presence, as did all others present. Later, the two men held talks at the residence of the *chao khoueng* (provincial governor), which served as the king's official residence during his stay. The moment was propitious in a perverse way for burying the ancient rivalry between them: gunfire could be heard clearly in the town from the hills to the east as government forces sought to contain the most serious military threat the town had ever experienced and many citizens had temporarily fled from the place.

The visit to Pakse showed how the king's immense, but rarely used, influence could be brought to bear. King Savang has stuck firmly to his position as a constitutional monarch who leaves the responsibility of government to his Prime Minister. "The King rules but does not govern," he is used to telling foreign ambassadors. King Savang and Prince Souvanna Phouma have maintained a close relationship within this stricture; the latter consults the king and keeps him informed of all major decisions, and in his turn, the king occasionally gives his Prime Minister advice, which is never made public.

The royal visit to Pakse took place barely a fortnight after a reverse suffered by government troops striving to hold a defense line across Route 23 against North Vietnamese troops, who, coming down the road from the Bolovens Plateau following their capture of the town of Paksong on May 16, were approaching the outskirts of Pakse itself. When North Vietnamese tanks appeared in the fighting, the Lao soldiers flung away their rifles and disappeared in the forest and it appeared for a moment as if all was lost. A counterattack by a special guerrilla unit, organized by Colonel Soutchay Vongsavanh, the deputy regional military commander for the Fourth Military Region, succeeded in blunting the North Vietnamese advance at the cost of 28 killed in one company alone (as compared to four soldiers killed in all the other Lao forces engaged). The next few days saw considerable destruction inflicted on the North Vietnamese force by Royal Lao Air Force T-28's, but the momentary reverse contributed to the dissatisfaction of the government with the performance of General Phasouk S. Rajphak, the commanding general of the Fourth Military Region. General Phasouk had held the same post for almost ten years and was widely known to be deeply involved with Prince Boun Oum's business interests in south Laos. His military performance was lackluster, and moreover, his attitude that the soldiers under his command were faced with insuperable odds and might be forced even to evacuate Pakse and withdraw to the right bank of the Mekong to escape annihilation (as he told a visiting Australian delegation in 1970) was an important factor in weakening morale both among the troops and the civilian population. The Defense Ministry had decided to replace General Phasouk as regional commander. The general resisted the plan to remove him from his fief in southern Laos. More talking was required, and it was the King that did the talking. At a meeting among the King, the Prime Minister, Sisouk, and General Phasouk, the general was informed in no uncertain terms that he was being transferred. The King bestowed a decoration on him at the same time.

General Phasouk's removal was one of a series of interlocking shifts in the military command in Laos effected during the summer of 1971. Never before in the modern history of Laos had such a sweeping shake-up of the military hierarchy been attempted. It demonstrated that where there was a will, the dominance of civilian politicians over the generals could be asserted. The main object and the net result of the reshuffle was to increase the efficiency of the army under civilian control. Sisouk again did much of the actual negotiating with the generals, but Prince Souvanna Phouma's position emerged strengthened.

The occasion for the shifts in military command was the retirement of General Ouan Ratikon, commander in chief of the armed forces, after 30 years' service. General Bounpone, the next senior general according to the system of seniority by years of service, moved from command of the Third Military Region to commander in chief. General Kouprasith moved from command of the Fifth Military Region to become deputy commander in chief, and thus into position to succeed Bounpone when the latter retires in turn in a few years. General Oudon Sananikone moved from his post as chief of staff to become director of planning, and General Phasouk took his place in a post that deprives him of any command of troops. General Kot Venevongsos, the man known to be close to Phoumi, was also brought to Vientiane from Savannakhet and given a staff job as deputy inspector general of the armed forces. Colonel Soutchay took over as commander of the Fourth Military Region and General Nouphet Daoheuang became commander of the Third Military Region in Savannakhet. The commanding generals of the First and Second Military Regions remained unchanged. General Vang Pao, notably, retained his command of the Second Military Region which includes Xieng Khouang Province and the Meo country, one of the hardest fought-over battlefields in Laos in recent years. Despite severe losses suffered by his forces, General Vang Pao has managed to hold the North Vietnamese and Pathet Lao at bay in that strategic region for a decade, during which time he has achieved the distinction of being one of the rare Meo leaders in the history of Laos not to embark on an attempt to create a separatist Meo kingdom. Vang Pao, a Meo, has developed an unusual and potentially significant relationship with King Savang Vatthana, who, he is reported to feel, will back him up in his *démelés* with the Lao generals. No Lao soldier will willingly go into the mountains to fight alongside the Meo, and in recent times, Vang Pao has received the reinforcement of Thai troops to make up for his losses among his own troops.

The extent of Phoumist influence within the armed forces remains unclear, but it is generally accepted by observers in Laos that the exiled general still retains the personal loyalty of numerous middle-ranking officers and a few generals. These loyalties came closer to surfacing at the time of the abortive "Savannakhet plot" and in another affair, equally abortive, involving a Thai politician from Roi Et in the early part of 1971 that resulted in several arrests in Vientiane. The general himself has avoided direct implication in any of these affairs and has disavowed ambitions to stage a *coup d'état*. "I will only return to Laos by legal means," he told a recent visitor. "This implies an amnesty of my conviction to 20 years of hard labor for desertion by a military tribunal, and above all the withdrawal of Prince Souvanna Phouma's complaint against me with a view to bringing me before the High Court of Justice."[12] He has told visitors that he considers himself to have been the victim of a frame-up in 1965, but his repeated pleas to Souvanna Phouma to be allowed to return to Laos to resume his function in the tripartite government have fallen on deaf ears; the general's reentry on the scene of Lao politics at this time is judged to be too inconvenient. And so he remains in Thailand.

The commitment of Thai troops in Laos over recent years, under the guise of volunteers recruited from the ethnic Lao living on the right bank of the Mekong, has had the effect of deepening the stake of the government of Thailand in events in Laos. The two recent adventurist attempts mounted from the territory of his neighbor must have impressed Souvanna Phouma, if he needed so impressing, with the imperative necessity of keeping on good terms with the Thais. This is made more difficult for the Prime Minister by the fact that the Thai ambassador in Vientiane reportedly is completely left out of the chain of command of the Thai troops in Laos, which fall under the command of a general in Bangkok working directly in the office of Deputy Prime Minister Prapass Charusathiara.

While it is true that Prince Souvanna Phouma has not so far been able to claim any signal success in his 18-month-old dialogue with the NLHS (despite a steady flow of letters and telegrams back and forth between Vientiane and Sam Neua), the dialogue tends to keep the opposition from the right neutralized. A more moderate tone has been detected in the statements of National Assembly deputies with regard to the Prime Minister's efforts to engage the NLHS in meaningful discussion of what he calls "an equitable settlement, beginning together with an authentic liberal revolution involving necessary reforms."[13] In the 1971 session, the deputies did not stage a repeat performance of the sharp 1970 debate; they showed less suspicion of the good faith of the NLHS proposals and a greater willingness to discuss their substance. A group of ten northern deputies tabled a resolution calling on the government to take serious steps to open negotiations with the NLHS for a political settlement. The idea that the NLHS stood for meritorious change in at least one field was summed up by Souvanna Phouma when he acknowledged in the Assembly: "We are not afraid to say on this occasion that certain social criticisms of the NLHS are pertinent, and that it would be an excellent idea to have a confrontation of ideas for national construction."[14]

The Prime Minister's personal relations with Tiao Souk Vongsak have continued to be good generally, despite some initial impolite language on the part of the latter and the usual hard-line statements that are viewed as a necessary and inevitable feature of the NLHS' style of negotiating. When the widow of Prince Phetsarath, the last Viceroy of Laos and Souvanna Phouma's eldest brother, died in Vientiane at the age of 95, the NLHS permanent representation dispatched a dozen of its guards to the pagoda where the body lay in state to do serving and cleaning work on a 24-hour basis. Both Tiao Souk and Soth attended the wake.[15]

In terms of the spectrum of non-NLHS politics in Laos, the events of recent times have contributed to a gradual shift of power and influence in the direction of southerners away from northerners, and to a reassertion of civilian control over the military to the extent that such a shift is possible in a time of war.

The rise of Sisouk na Champassak to what amounts to the second most powerful position in the Cabinet today and to the preeminence of being the heir apparent to Souvanna Phouma has most forcefully illustrated the rise of the southerners. But it is also apparent in the position achieved by another southerner, Leuam Insisiengmay, who has been the Deputy Prime Minister representing the rightist faction in the Government of National Union since 1965. Leuam belongs to a family that traces its origin to the ancient chiefs of Muong Champhone, one of the nine *muong* of the region lying between Tchepone and the Mekong, today called Keng Kok, a rich rice-growing and cattle-raising area. Through marriage, Leuam is tied to the Champassaks, since his wife is the sister of Princess Boun Oum.

Two northerner members of the 1962 Cabinet have, on the contrary, distinctly lost power and influence. Pheng Phongsavan, who in the period immediately following the formation of the 1962 Cabinet was the man most closely associated with Souvanna Phouma, has gradually lost out in the competition for influence, although he is still considered a loyal follower and a competent administrator. The proclamation of a state of emergency with the consequent transfer of police powers to the military marked a loss for Pheng. Chao Sisoumang Sisaleumsak, also one of Souvanna Phouma's earliest associates, has been under a cloud recently because of prorepublican remarks he is alleged to have made.

Conclusion

Prince Souvanna Phouma is in the position of a man balancing two heavy weights, representing North Vietnamese and American/South Vietnamese/Thai intervention in Laos. He has very little room for his footing, yet he is in equilibrium. If he were toppled through some internal disorder that caused him to lose his footing, the whole structure would come crashing down, with unpredictable consequences for all.

In order to make this arrangement more stable, it would be necessary for Souvanna Phouma to secure for himself a wider footing in terms of the politics of Laos. But in order to secure a wider base, he needs to be able to enter into substantive negotiations with the NLHS, whom he continues to consider part of the national community. But in attempting to reach for negotiations with the NLHS, Souvanna Phouma risks losing his precarious footing. Any attempt to reach such negotiations will have to be made with due consideration for the regional and family-loyalty factors that are important determinants of the direction of Lao politics.

Biographical Data on Some Figures
in Lao Politics

Prince Souvanna Phouma. Born October 7, 1901, at Luang Prabang. Minister of Public Works in the Lao Issara government in Vientiane, 1945. Deputy Prime Minister in the Lao Issara government-in-exile in Bangkok, 1946-1949. Minister of Public Works, Posts and Telegraph, and Plan, February 1950. Prime Minister, November 21, 1951-October 20, 1954. Deputy Prime Minister and Minister of Defense, 1954-1956. Prime Minister, March 21, 1956-August 18, 1958. Ambassador to France, 1958-1960. Elected National Assembly deputy from Luang Prabang, April, 1960. Prime Minister, August 16, 1960-June 11, 1962. Prime Minister, June 23, 1962-present.

Sisouk na Champassak. Born March 29, 1928, at Pakse. Deputy Permanent Representative of Laos at the United Nations, 1956-1958. Secretary of State for Information, 1958-1959, and for Sports and Youth, 1959. Minister attached to the Prime Minister's Office under Prime Minister Prince Boun Oum, 1961-1962. Ambassador to India, March 1963. Minister of Finance, September 6, 1965-present. Delegate for National Defense, 1970-present.

Phoui Sananikone. Born September 6, 1903, at Vientiane. Joined the civil service, 1923. Governor of Nam Tha Province, 1945. Participated in resistance against Japanese forces and reached China safely with Free French forces. Named Minister of Health, Education, and Social Welfare in government of Prince Souvannarath, March 15, 1947. Elected National Assembly deputy from Pakse and became first President of that body, December 1947. Reelected, 1948, 1949. Prime Minister, February 24, 1950-October 15, 1951. Reelected National Assembly deputy from Vientiane, 1951. Headed the Royal Lao Delegation to the 1954 Geneva Conference. Reelected National Assembly deputy from Vientiane, December 1955, and April 1960. Prime Minister, August 18, 1958-December 30, 1959. Headed the delegation sent to the Geneva Conference by the government of Prince Boun Oum, 1961. President of the National Assembly, 1964-present.

Pheng Phongsavan. Born July 19, 1910, at Luang Prabang. Elected National Assembly deputy from Luang Prabang December, 1947. Reelected to National Assembly, August 1951, and December 1955. Joined Prince Souvanna Phouma's government in Vientiane, 1953. Minister of Interior and Social Welfare, June 23, 1962-present.

Ngon Sananikone. Born December 29, 1914, at Vientiane. Joined the civil service, becoming Governor of Khammouane Province. Elected National Assembly deputy from Thakhek, May 1958. Minister of Justice, Sports and Youth, and Cults, 1960. Minister of Public Works and Transport, June 23, 1962-present.

Khamsouk Keola. Born August 8, 1908, at Luang Prabang. Received diploma from medical school in Hanoi. Chief doctor of infirmaries at Pak Lay, Muong Sing, and Nam Tha, 1933-1945. Medical lieutenant in French Army, 1945-1946. Chief doctor of Luang Prabang Province, 1946. Chief doctor of Vientiane Province, 1947-1948. Chief doctor of Khammouane Province, 1949-1958. Minister of Public Health, Education, Social Welfare, and Rural Affairs, 1959. Vice Prime Minister and Minister of Interior, Health, Education, Information and Finance in Prime Minister Prince Souvanna Phouma's government at Khang Khay, January 1962. Minister of Public Health, June 23, 1962-May 22, 1964. Led the Patriotic Neutralist Delegation to the Indochinese Peoples' Conference in Phnom Penh, February 1965. Attended the Indochinese Peoples' Summit Conference in southern China, April 24-25, 1970.

Notes

1. The complete list of the members of the 1962 Cabinet is published in *Select Documents on International Affairs, No. 16, Laos* (Canberra, Australia: Department of External Affairs, April 1970), Document No. 109, p. 109.

2. For documentary evidence of this decision, which has recently come to light in the form of a hitherto secret resolution of the Central Committee of the Vietnam Workers' Party adopted in December 1963, see *Viet-Nam Documents and Research Notes*, No. 96 (Saigon: U.S. Mission, July 1971), pp. 1-41.

3. General Siho lost his life in 1966, having fled from Laos in the previous year following an abortive coup attempt.

4. As two astute American observers have reported: "And on the political front, we gathered from our conversations with various Lao that it has been made plain to all opponents of the present Prime Minister—primarily the southern politicians and generals—that we wish to see him continue in office and that any change in government might jeopardize continued U.S. support." U.S., Congress, Senate, *Committee on Foreign Relations Laos: April 1971* (Washington: Government Printing Office, August 3, 1971), p. 3.

5. Boun Oum's attitude to national politics after 1962 is reflected in the following remark, made to the writer in 1970: "The war in Laos is between a Frenchman and a Vietnamese. I alone am a Lao." The "Frenchman" is, of course, Souvanna Phouma, and the "Vietnamese" Souphanouvong. Boun Oum has had ample direct experience in his lifetime of becoming the plaything of foreign decision-makers, as evidenced by his biography in Charles Archaimbault, *The New Year Ceremony at Basak (South Laos)* (Ithaca, N.Y.: Cornell University Southeast Asia Program Data Paper, 1971).

6. Interview of the writer with General Soukan in Vientiane, 1970.

7. These events are described in the present writer's *Conflict in Laos; The Politics of Neutralization*, 2d. ed. rev. (New York: Praeger, 1971), pp. 286-288.

8. Interview of the writer with Souvanna Phouma in Vientiane, February 13, 1971.

9. Private information to the writer.

10. "If the South Vietnamese and Americans were to launch an operation against the so-called 'Ho Chi Minh Trail,' the Pathet Lao might do something, against Luang Prabang for instance." Dispatch from Vientiane by Jean-Claude Pomonti in *Le Monde*, 21 October 1970.

11. Agence France-Presse dispatch from Vientiane, 5 July 1971.

12. Ibid., from Bangkok, 10 March 1971.

13. Lao Presse Bulletin (Vientiane), 12 May 1971.

14. Ibid.

15. The year 1971 was a tragic one for the family of Phetsarath. On August 15, Prince Vorada Souligna Phetsarath, the Viceroy's only grandson, was killed in a plane crash near Long Cheng. He was 26 years old and was piloting the plane in poor weather. He left one son. Prince Phetsarath died in 1959.

1971 and Beyond:
The View from Hanoi

Konrad Kellen[1]

Whatever anyone may think about any aspect of the Vietnam war, everybody must agree that "the other side" or "Hanoi" or whatever we call them, are—from their point of view as well as ours—capable of unexpected, indeed almost incredible achievements in the face of tremendous odds. What is Hanoi's secret? It is not, first of all, as some observers have always insisted, *technique*, nor is it inherent in the *situation*. To assume that they could do what they did simply because one can frustrate a big power in a guerrilla war if one is the guerrilla, is not the answer; it would appear that others in similar situations have not or would not have been able to do the same. Nor is the secret to be found, as other observers believe, in *organization*. Naturally, organization, technique, and the situation all had something to do with it. But no amount of these could have yielded the same results without the *people* involved; they are at the heart of the mystery. Yet, very little attention has been paid to the people we face. Of course, observers have looked at Hanoi's history, its economy, or its demographic features. But few have tried to find out, even to the extent that such investigations are possible, how the North Vietnamese (or the VC) function, what animates them, what gives them their strength and confidence in this—for them—truly catastrophic yet also so far successful war.

To understand, at least partially, our adversaries in Vietnam, we can look at the aggregate of their actions and their statements. Their actions are plain for all to see, but are not always self-explanatory. Why don't they yield in Paris? Why don't they melt away and try later? Why do they engage in certain modes of attack but not in others? How are they able to do it? How can they sustain the effort, absorb the punishment? We can find some answers to these questions if we look at what the North Vietnamese and the VC say, whether they are leaders in Hanoi making policy statements, or prisoners of war in our captivity in the South. How reliable are such statements? The answer is that the official line promulgated to their own people and army, and also to the world at large, by Radio Hanoi or the army paper *Quan Doi Nhan Dan*, or the NLF's clandestine radio station in South Vietnam, cannot be dismissed as mere propaganda, even though propaganda is one objective of that line. Though what Hanoi says contains, naturally, some exaggerated claims, the Vietnamese Communists, like other Communists, have a great penchant to air their actual theories, views and methods in public in such a way as to permit the foreign analyst a very good

99

look at what they think. On the other end of the scale, there are the prisoner-of-war statements from which we can learn even more.

As far as the latter are concerned, the most frequently heard objection, of course, is that prisoners only tell you what you want to hear. But anyone who has spent some time with prisoner interrogations, knows that this is not the case. To be sure, there are prisoners who think they can ingratiate themselves with their captors by saying the right thing, and there have been some of those in Vietnam, mainly among the defectors; yet even from those we can learn a great deal if we know how. But when prisoners from the VC or NVA tell us exactly what we do not want to hear, i.e., things that indicate that they are devoted to their cause and confident of ultimate success, or well-fed and able to carry on, why then should we assume they are not telling us the truth? In such cases, the skeptics will say that the men are well-indoctrinated or brainwashed, and that they merely say what their leaders wanted them to say. But, in the first place, "indoctrination" is not a serious term, denying as it does the possibility that people on the other side of the fence can go through opinion formation processes similar to our own even if they do not have access to either the *Readers Digest* or the *New York Review of Books*; and second, what some call an "indoctrinated" person may still be a person functioning in a coherent and individually effective fashion. Our staunchest adversaries in Vietnam are usually men who have suffered severe losses in their families and endless hardships themselves, and been witness to terrible things—all caused by the war. Their views are convictions shaped by personal experience.

In the following, the various sources available to us will be probed for an explanation of the success that our adversaries have so far registered, and the confidence that has allowed them to act as they have in the past and may sustain them at present and in the future.

The Sources of Confidence

Viewed by the leadership in Hanoi, the successes of the past must also be sources of confidence for the future. But successes of the past are not enough to inspire confidence in the future unless one is more of a pragmatist than Hanoi's leaders are. They need—and have—more than past successes to fuel and sustain their confidence. Foremost among what they both need and have are their theories of ultimate success.

Hanoi's leaders and their disciples in the Party and Army are very ardent theoreticians. They love and believe in theory, certainly more so than the Russian Communists do at this stage, or the more pragmatic Communists in a dozen other countries, and perhaps even more than their Chinese brethren to the North. To every major foreign or domestic problem, on peace or war, there is a "correct" solution that can be found by applying the Marxist-Leninist scriptures to the situation at hand. This application of theory not only yields "correct" answers to fighting down to the tactical level; or on how to proceed in the Paris negotiations; or on how to deal with one's big wayward allies; but mainly, of course, on the war itself—and the theory shows incontrovertibly that the war will end, if not in formal victory, at least in a departure of the Americans, followed by a united though not altogether unified Vietnam.

At the core of these overall theories is the theory of contradictions, or antagonistic contradictions. This theory is related to the theory of antagonistic and nonantagonistic differences which Mao established after the Hungarian Revolution in 1956, but it gives Mao no credit and seems quite different. Regardless of what the physical power of the United States and its allies may be, this power cannot, according to the theory, be brought to bear upon Vietnam, at least not indefinitely, as several sets of contradictions must dilute and eventually stay that power.[2]

The leaders in Hanoi consider themselves important originators in the area of theory, claiming credit for creative efforts in theory-building.[3]

Hanoi's theoreticians see mainly five sets of contradictions that will eventually make the United States desist and help them gain the peace and unification they seek.

The first set of contradictions (contradictions are discussed here seriatim, not in order of importance), are in the imperialist camp. The various imperialist countries, though war need not necessarily break out among them, being guided by neocolonialist and neoimperialist motives that clash with each other will disintegrate as imperialist blocs. This will leave the United States isolated and therefore less eager or able to fight in Vietnam.

The second set of contradictions pertains to the United States involvement in Vietnam. There are contradictions between the American imperialist war and the civil war in Vietnam, the neocolonialist vs. the national liberation effort; the struggle of the exploiters against the oppressed people; the superior technology against the people's army's tactical superiority. In such a war, there is an unjust and a just side, with the people eventually winning over weapons. This contradiction is also seen as causing the war to escalate either in intensity or to spread: escalation or United States broadening of the war is a result of preceding failure which was caused by the contradiction, but cannot be overcome by the escalation.

The third set of contradictions pertains to contradictions in the United States society. The American people cannot support a war waged by their ruling classes. To the extent that the people give this war any support, they do so because they are forced to or are misled by propaganda that cannot have a lasting effect. The war will deepen these contradictions in the United States society and make the United States Government desist eventually.

The fourth contradiction is between the United States and Saigon. Even though the Saigon leaders are, in Hanoi's words, lackeys and puppets of the

United States, they cannot consolidate their power without United States support. Nor can they attain that degree of independent power which the Americans desire, precisely because their visible support by the Americans weakens them in Vietnamese eyes.

The fifth contradiction is between the United States and the South Vietnamese people (and presumably the Cambodian and Laotian people) whose puppet governments have fallen into disrepair for reasons inherent in contradiction four. This De-Vietnamization as one might call it, which the Hanoi leaders foresee as a probable sequel to a failing Vietnamization, will be a more direct takeover by the United States in the area and will create more antagonisms between the Americans and the Vietnamese.

Another factor, though not an additional contradiction, is the Hanoi leaders' belief that the Americans, besides being plagued by these contradictions, have no tools for assessing the situation in Vietnam and therefore do not understand it. American science of war, in their view, lacks an entire dimension in that it deals seriously only with weapons and strategies. Hanoi's leaders, however, think they can correctly assess the situation.

In some long and sweeping perorations on military science, General Giap has over the years revealed his own views on the war and how to conduct it. Giap believes—though he does not use the word—that the war must be total, i.e., it must be conducted with all the material and nonmaterial resources of the nation, throughout all of Indochina.

Our military science does not treat lightly the material and technical factors, but it pays great attention to the moral and political factors. Our military science does not treat lightly the problem of quantity, but it attaches great importance to the problem of quality and combat efficiency. Our military science not only pays attention to developing the strength of each force, of each form of struggle, and of each separate combat form, but it also pays great attention to developing the combined strength of all forces and forms of struggle which are closely related to each other.[4]

This is a rather long way from, presumably Mao-inspired, much simpler earlier theories that people and the just cause always prevail automatically over weapons and armies. Giap, and the rest of the Hanoi leaders, are not paper tiger theoreticians by any means. But Giap thinks that people who have not shaped their views of the world and of war on the basis of what Marx and Engels have said on the subject, cannot conduct war against their adversaries in Vietnam successfully.

Marx and Engels established the basis for scientific theories on war and armies as well as on military art . . . . The military theories [of Westerners] —founded on the realities of unjust wars—have a reactionary and unscientific content . . . .[5]

Armed with these (and more) theories on the one hand, and supported by a willing population and a cohesive army on the other, as well as by two big contributing allies, the Hanoi leaders appear to be confident. But are they really? This question must be divided: Are they confident that the United States will desist? If so, are they confident they can carry the burden until that time?

As they are human, one may assume that they go through periods of strain and gloom. On balance, there is no evidence to conclude that they do not feel confident, though perhaps not as confident as they claim.[6] Since they see the war as ultimately global, i.e., as one between the two camps rather than between a tiny country and the mighty United States, and as they see the enemy camp and particularly its leader, the United States, torn and weakened by the contradictions delineated above, they may well feel all the confidence they pretend to have. They are reinforced by confidence that Vietnamization cannot work since everything the Americans or their allies do in Vietnam, including Operation Phoenix, will be rejected by the people. However, they do not appear to see any automaticity in these developments. Unless they assassinate collaborators—which they do—or infiltrate ARVN—which they do—or inflict casualties and setbacks on the United States—which they do—nothing they think can work for them.

The Sources of Success

Army Morale.[7] The greatest source of strength for the Hanoi leadership in its struggle against us had been the morale and motivation of its soldiers. The vast bulk of prisoner statements (over 1000 interviews) over the years in RAND's files show clearly that the VC or NVA soldier has maintained a surprisingly high level of morale throughout, a level of morale not equalled by the Nazi soldiers in World War II or the Chinese soldiers in the Korean War,[8] particularly after those wars had produced some heavy reverses for the attackers. Such findings of high VC and NVA morale, dating back to 1965, have been consistently confirmed by events: there have been few NVA prisoners—and very few cadre—taken in this war; there have been rather few defectors, despite the Chieu Hoi program, and many of those were refugees; there have been no unit surrenders, (a single NVA battalion has been mentioned as surrendering, but this has never been confirmed). The warfighting capacity of the NVA soldiers in almost any engagement has been astonishing, particularly in view of the discrepancy in arms. NVA soldiers still fight when engaged, just as they fought lately again in Laos, often under the most incredibly adverse conditions—without air cover of their own, pounded by B-52s, and showered with napalm. How can they maintain their morale under such conditions?

Their morale is not, it must be emphasized, that of robots or fanatics, which might be fierce but brittle. On the contrary. These soldiers and their cadre emerge from interviews as undramatic, laconic, matter-of-fact people, dedicated but perfectly capable of becoming frightened and discouraged. But when they do, their system of morale restitution goes into action. This system includes almost daily criticism-self-criticism sessions (Khiem Thao), at which the worries of a man or feelings that he has done wrong are laid bare and discussed. A few prisoners have complained of the emotional rigors of the system, but most insist that the system redresses their morale when it sags, which they appreciate. The system also anticipates and alleviates possible future morale troubles. With the three-men-cell that obtains in all VC and NVA forces, providing great emotional and physical support to its members in their virtually symbiotic relationship, the system of criticism and self-criticism is the effective group therapy that lends great resilience to the soldiers' morale. Resilience, rather than mere strength, describes the morale of the NVA and VC forces. The NVA soldiers have indeed learned to "bend like bamboo in the wind," as they like to put it.

There are other important elements that sustain the men in battle. One is their relationship with the people in the countryside. It has been contended, frequently, that the fish must be and in fact already have been deprived of water. Aside from the physical evidence to the contrary—the VC and NVA forces could not operate the way they did and do without considerable public support even in Laos and Cambodia—prisoner interrogations have revealed that, despite some problems between soldiers and the population as a result of the long war, the bond between them has reamined close enough to provide physical and emotional support to the soldiers. The explanation seems to be that despite the rigors of the war, the soldiers continue to treat the local population with respect and otherwise attractive behavior.

Next, there is the relationship between the cadre and the men. The cadre often are men who, in their words, have decided to devote themselves entirely to the revolution; they have made the clean break with all ordinary facets of daily life whose bourgeois features and temptations are as prevalent in communism as in other societies. Having made the break, these men devote their energies or, in Freudian terms, their libido to the army and its cause, and are both mother and father to the fighters, i.e., the privates who often miss their families and shrink from the great hardships under which they live and fight. The relationship between the cadre and the men, in and out of battle, is a great source of strength to both, leading to great faith in the leadership at all levels. It also leads to independence and initiative in battle on the lower levels. Studying the relationship, one is surprised how much give and take there is between the cadre and the privates—much more than one would expect to find in a totalitarian system, and indeed much more give and take than in our own army.

Further, one of the most sustaining elements in the soldiers' morale is their astonishingly uniform and strong belief in their cause, both abstractly and concretely: they do believe, as they are told in education sessions every day, that they are fighting the just war; that they are fighting for Vietnam's freedom and independence; that just wars will be won; that people are more important than weapons. But they also have a deep personal hatred, a true abhorrence of their enemy, the United States. They see the United States in starkly simple terms: invaders who have come from thousands of miles away, who destroy what the local people have built up in their country, kill them and their families, and try to prevent them from pursuing what they consider patriotic and constructive duties and tasks: revolution and unification. Most NVA soldiers have personally suffered grievous losses as a result of the war which they attribute unhesitatingly to the Americans whom they generally regard as worse than the French.

In their view of us, there is no redeeming feature or ambivalence of any kind. (This ambivalence could be found even in some dedicated Nazi soldiers during World War II who often had a certain half-suppressed admiration, envy or curiosity about the Americans whom—much to Goebbel's chagrin—they never brought themselves really to hate or fear.) If one can make a comparison, NVA soldiers feel about Americans as Wehrmacht soldiers felt about the Russians, and even this refers only to the Nazi soldiers' hatred of the Russians; but NVA soldiers feel neither the slightest guilt toward us, such as many Nazis felt toward the Russians, nor the same fear. What little fear of us they seem to feel, their leaders try systematically to exorcise, and they are quite successful at this. Of course, as we have such multifarious capabilities of inflicting death on them, to eradicate fear of us means for them to eradicate fear of death itself, and on this they work assiduously. In quite a few of the captured company records, one finds notations about this or that soldier by a cadre to the effect that "he still fears death"; and in some of their self-criticism (practiced often also in writing), one finds, in captured documents, statements to the effect that "I was still afraid of death."

NVA interrogations reveal no trace of guilt by soldiers for fighting in South Vietnam. There seems to be no doubt in the minds of NVA soldiers that the Americans are entirely at fault in this war and must be made to leave the country whatever it costs and however long it takes. To our objection that they invaded the South, they reply that North and South are one country, inhabited by one people, so how could they invade it? The war, they feel, is defensive, and therefore necessary. That is always the most important element in an army's high morale.

Another source of strength for NVA cadre as well as simple soldiers is the ideological simplicity of their cause. While part of that cause is that the imperialist Americans must be driven out, it is not really ideological in most aspects. Few NVA soldiers seem to regard themselves as Communists. They see themselves as defenders of their country against yet another Western intruder who can be made to desist. He must cease his physical destruction and political pressure. Further, NVA soldiers see themselves as crusaders for unification, independence and a better life for all Vietnamese.

There are other pillars in the soldiers' morale; it would lead us too far to enumerate them all. The point is that all these elements are strong and tend to reinforce each other. The soldier can go on also because, as a result of what his leaders tell him, his expectations are realistic and he does not become disillusioned by setbacks. As one soldier put it in that simple and straight language with which Vietnamese surprise their interrogators: "The instructor taught us that the revolution is not a short-term business." Another said, revealing the equanimity that can only be the result of many things other than indoctrination: "Frankly, I was never disappointed with the result of any battle. Fighting the war we always think there will be times when we win and there will be times when we lose, and we should not be too optimistic when we win and not too pessimistic when we lose. When we lose we must find out what caused us to lose and gain experience for the next time."[9] The NVA soldier is told that this will probably be a long war, and that before it ends it will become fiercer. But he is also told that it may end sooner, even suddenly, if the American people tire of the war as a result of their basic reluctance to continue it and his success in battle which alone can sufficiently increase that reluctance.

Thus, while there are many underlying reasons for the success of the Lao Dong in the struggle against us, the prime element—in turn a composite of many other elements—is the military machine at its disposal, spurred on by an incredibly resilient morale and composed of men of remarkable intelligence, matter-of-factness, and practical ability on all levels. So well-grounded seems their morale, and so self-ressurrecting, that it is not really possible to see how it can be broken. One RAND report concluded in 1967 that short of the NVA (and their VC allies) being physically destroyed, "collapse, surrender or disintegration was—to put it bizarrely—simply not among their capabilities." And unless, concluded that study at the time, we "killed more of them than could be in anybody's interest, they could not be overcome."[10] A subsequent study (1969) concluded that morale had not deteriorated and was not likely to deteriorate.[11]

Finally, NVA soldiers, just as their VC companions, are sustained in their firm belief that they cannot and will not lose this war. This does not mean they expect to win it in the conventional sense, by driving out the Americans. Rather, they feel convinced that sooner or later, in some as yet indistinct form, the war will come to an end and the Americans will depart, leaving the Vietnamese to settle their own differences. Almost uniformly, prisoners, when asked during the days of the largest American troop commitments in Vietnam, what in their view the effects were of so many American troops with perhaps even more coming in, would reply: "This will make the fighting fiercer and prolong the war." None ever said, "Well, that settles it, the Americans will win." Only a few defectors felt differently. In fact, a striking thing about most defectors is that they had given up the fight for personal reasons, such as fear, fatigue, quarrels with their cadre. Most had retained both their conviction that their cause, i.e., the cause of Hanoi and the NLF, was just and that it would eventually prevail. Such unshakable belief in eventual war termination in one's own favor is, of course, both cause and result of very high morale among troops.

Other Sources of Strength. Aside from their trump card—their armed forces— the other principal secrets of the Lao Dong's success in the war would appear to be great intelligence and flexibility in the management of their two big allies and of their own leadership problems, and in the conduct of their total war.

To some extent, the present leaders were lucky: they inherited a Communist party which had not been ruined by Ho Chi Minh, as other parties had been by their leaders. After Ho's death, they were remarkably successful in maintaining an effective collective leadership. No serious Hanoi-ologist has ever been able to detect any serious friction between Le Duan and Truong Chinh, or the war firsters and the North Vietnam firsters, or the Moscow faction and the Hanoi faction.[12] John Donnell, a qualified observer of the Lao Dong, has stressed this point. Yet, if we consider the challenges faced by the leaders over the years, their difficult and fateful decisions, such as how to conduct the war; whether or how to rebuild industry while the war still progressed and heavy bombing resumption remained a possibility; how to deal with eccentric and obstreperous major allies, we are impressed by their ability to reconcile their differences as they apparently have. There have been no shake-ups in the Party or high command, no sudden zigs or zags in the propaganda line, no other signs of instability. Nor have the leaders resorted to pressures against the population in the North that might have alienated them. In the spring of 1969, there was a decree that spies and saboteurs had to be caught and punished, which led some observers in the West to believe that rebellion in North Vietnam was close at hand. Actually, as reflected in many prisoner interviews, the Hanoi regime is perhaps one of the most genuinely popular in the world today. The 20 million North Vietnamese, most of whom live in agricultural cooperatives, like it there, find the system just and their labor rewarding. While it may seem hard to believe, prisoners have spoken convincingly in this vein until at least 1969, i.e., the duration of the RAND interviews; and there has been no subsequent indication that people have changed their minds in the North concerning the Revolution, the war, or living conditions. As in the case of the soldiers, a strong point for Hanoi is that the people in the North, particularly since the bombing, regard the United States as the aggressor who must be fought until he desists, so that no burden of propaganda proof devolves upon Hanoi.

Partly because of the apparently inexhaustible courage and morale of their armed forces and the dedication of the population in North Vietnam to the Revolution, the leadership has been able to mobilize the human and material resources for the kind of total war Hitler spoke of but never attained. The North Vietnamese population, just as the NLF and VC in South Vietnam and the Pathet Lao in Laos, are devoting their entire lives to the war in one form or another. They accept the war and all its facets. The French journalist Jacques Decornoy (admittedly not an impartial observer) reports that a Vietnamese sitting with him in a Hanoi hotel lobby during the regular bombings said: "This lobby in which you are now sitting—we already consider it destroyed. We are ready. We are accepting it all beforehand."[13] It is presumably this particular spirit that explained why Hanoi did not plead for peace in the face of continuous bombing of the North. There is no reason to assume that bombings or the threats thereof would not be equally ineffective again, or at least in the sphere of morale. In fact, the renewed bombings and threats of much more to come already have failed to frighten Hanoi into abandoning what it considers the correct way of fighting this war.

The other important aspect of total war, one might postulate, is that it must be in the minds of its participants altogether open-ended, i.e., everybody must be ready to do his share in it as long as it takes. In producing this open-ended view of the war, Hanoi has been conspicuously successful. Some army cadre even say that they have no expectation of survival. As one of them put it: "I decided to sacrifice myself for the Revolution." Of course, not every one of North Vietnam's citizens will be equally dedicated. But to the extent that we know, the soldiers and people are resigned to fighting on as long as it takes against the Americans, due to their deep-seated view that the war is purely defensive. Nor are they fed extravagant promises by the local media. On the contrary, the North Vietnamese media generally speak of a long war. In specialized journals, there are articles on how to do agricultural tasks, commercial fishing, or cope with medical problems caused by bombs in a detached, timeless way, as though the war were simply part of life, and everybody must simply adjust to it.

Thus, while tactics, strategies, outside support, United States mistakes, NVA organization, terrain and many other factors may have helped our adversaries in Vietnam, these factors cannot have compensated for the vast military, economic and political resources that we employed against them with considerable tenacity over many years. Rather, what maintained them was the extraordinary cohesion, resilience and apparently unwavering dedication on the part of the people, soldiers and civilians, and their firm conviction that they had absolutely no choice but to endure the hardships of what seemed an entirely defensive war against a foreign invader intent on building, only more so, the colonialism of the French.

It has often been asked whether the high morale of soldiers and North Vietnam civilians does not attest to the failure of our psychological warfare. Could the American case not have been made, or still be made, in such a way as to convince substantial numbers of North Vietnamese that this war is not necessary, that they will lose or at least not successfully conclude it? Could the case be made that this in turn would not hurt them, that the United States has other aims in Vietnam than the French had? From the interrogations at hand, that would appear next to impossible; neither the psychological makeup of the NVA forces nor of the people in North Vietnam show any psywar vulnerabilities in the ordinary sense, i.e., while they do of course show the toll taken by the hardships inflicted upon them, they do not reveal any susceptibility to alternate appeals.[14]

The Prospects. In the light of Hanoi's past success and confidence for the future, what are they likely to do? This, of course, is squarely in the area of speculation. As to how they see the American role, we have already pointed out that they see United States strategy as doomed to failure if they apply their own correct strategy. But what, specifically, do they think we have in store for them?

The following answer is a highly condensed summary from recent radio broadcasts, press reports and major speeches.

They say (and apparently think) that the American policy of Vietnamization and withdrawal is designed to deceive the American people into supporting the continuation of the war. They think that Americans are in error as to what their Saigon partners can or will do for them. The Americans grossly overestimate Saigon's military and political capabilities and, when this becomes apparent, the Americans will try to resume their own military efforts, perhaps in modified form, but will be increasingly hampered by the contradictions under which they labor. As for ultimate aims, they seem to think that the United States wants to subdue Indochina permanently, for neocolonialist reasons, i.e., to turn it into a strategic outpost in Southeast Asia, and into a political outpost against the spread of Communism. Above all, they do not think that any conciliatory behavior toward us can save them hardships, such as bombings of the North. They must, they seem to think, inflict at minimum cost continuing losses, delays and other setbacks upon the United States and Saigon, even if that may bring down bombings upon them. They seem to feel that any strategy they can possibly embrace is a high-risk strategy in any event which is undoubtedly the reason they have defied throughout—though with moderation—the threats made against them by the Administration since 1969.

To begin speculation on what they might do, it is useful to speculate first on what they are not likely to do.

1. They are not likely to make concessions in Paris (or elsewhere) which would amount to giving up the game. This means they will not make any substantial concessions at all, as that would be tantamount to giving up the game. Contrary to Americans who believe that a compromise can be reached, they appear to see the situation as an all-or-nothing one in which no concession by either side except surrender of the central war aim can possibly be perceived. They could, of course, give up formally in Paris and resume their efforts five years later. But they could have done that all along the line and never did, so this seems unlikely in the future. Moreover, such action would create too many internal propaganda problems for them.

2. They could locally escalate in the form of terrorist acts or by inflicting great or humiliating damage on some United States forces. This they are unlikely to do, mainly because it would contradict a theory: not to humiliate the enemy, not to hit him harder than is absolutely necessary, particularly if the enemy can do such great immediate damage in retaliation. Ho, in particular, always tries to avoid this.

3. They could call upon the Chinese who might or might not come in. But they are not likely to do this either since, aside from their well-known aversion to being too dependent in general, and to the Chinese, in particular, they would have to fear the results of hostilities between the United States and Chinese armed forces on their soil.

4. They could sit still and wait until the Americans, committed more or less to leave altogether, will have left. This they cannot do, as the war also takes place in the form of Pacification and Operation Phoenix. They must react against these or lose all chance of staging a comeback in the South after the considerable time it would take the United States to get out in any event. Pacification and Phoenix are particularly hard for them to cope with, as they are mainly invisible as forms of war to the world at large, so that their response to these operations looks easily like wanton aggression or terror. While the Americans withdraw men, the war goes on just as before, throughout Indochina. Thus, it is incorrect for them to wait for the American departure, even if it should eventually come (it would be all the less likely to come, and also take longer, if they did nothing).

5. They could stage a major offensive, with or without a new attempt to stage a national uprising, on a similar or larger scale than at Tet 1968. This they are most unlikely to try, because of the "preserve manpower" theory laid down by Ho and so far followed by them.[15] Also, it would probably fail to have the desired result and would bring down heavy bombing on the North.

What then can or will they do? Unsensational though it sounds, they are most likely to do just more of the same, i.e., engage ARVN when they feel they must, occasionally for demonstration and demoralization purposes, and keep their own fighting machine sharp; inflict on United States forces the kind of casualties that will neither be too little to go unnoticed in the United States, nor so heavy as to bring down on them heavy retribution and, worse, a renewed resolve by the American people. Further, since they are aware of the problems of the cost of the war to the United States, not only in casualties but also in dollars, they will try to keep the war expensive for America.

Above all, they will try to keep the war open-ended in every way, with regard to their military preparations, their strategy, their tactics, their economy, their domestic propaganda, and the attitude of their people and soldiers. In a classic answer to the famous German prelate Martin Niemoeller who visited Hanoi in 1966, Ho, when asked whether he would fight on to final victory said: "If by 'final victory' you mean the departure of the Americans, then we will fight to final victory. Everything depends on the Americans. If they want to make war for 20 years, then we shall make war for 20 years. If they want to make peace, we shall make peace, and even invite them for tea afterwards."[16] This open-ended, defensive and counterattacking posture is likely to remain their posture, and they are likely to support it in the field with moderate but more or less constant defensive fighting and continuing sporadic attacks on villages and officials. This may be a high-risk strategy for them, but all strategies for them are high risk. By comparison, this seems the lowest-risk strategy they can pursue with any hope of success.

Will they, as so many observers think, strike in a big way once United States forces are down to, say 100 thousand or less? *Nothing seems more unlikely*.

What purpose could it possibly serve for them? It would almost surely lead to heavy retribution or coercive efforts against the North, and renewed United States efforts in the South. At the same time, it could not possibly bring tangible success, such as an American Dunkirk. It cannot speed the end of the war, as it would surely not accelerate American departure. Unless greatly pared-down United States forces should suddenly engage in a course of action, alone or together with ARVN, that they were entirely unable to tolerate from their point of view (and one cannot imagine what that could be), they would only harm themselves if they launched such an offensive. No matter how the United States proceeds, their plan is most likely to neither lie low nor to stage dramatic attacks, but to continue

1. to fight Pacification, i.e., "security for the people" and the building of a rural base for the Saigon leaders, with the help of terror;
2. to fight Operation Phoenix by evasion of the police, infiltration of the police, and the training of new cadres;
3. to keep infiltrating ARVN so as to weaken it and have insurance against surprises (presumably the operation in Laos was well signalled to them beforehand by their agents in ARVN, aside from the fact that staging activities in the border area were easy to observe);
4. to keep up combat in the field at more or less current levels (depending, of course, on levels initiated by us and/or ARVN) for the same range of politico-military purposes which such combat has always had.

Will they be able to follow this course if they have selected it as their correct strategy? That, of course, will not just depend on their physical and nonphysical capabilities and on their intentions, but also on what we and even others will or will not do.

Notes

1. Any views expressed in this paper are those of the author. They should not be interpreted as reflecting the views of The RAND Corporation or the official opinion or policy of any of its governmental or private research sponsors.

2. In general, the North Vietnamese leaders are apparently fiercely independent and practice that self-reliance that Lin Piao demanded in an article on September 3, 1965. They also have imbued their soldiers with the feeling that they can fight this war alone. The latter, when interrogated on this point, usually say: "When we need the Chinese, we will ask them to come in. So far we don't need them." Therefore, early United States psywar to the effect that "you are being let down by your Chinese allies" was a psywar blunder.

3. For an excellent discussion of Hanoi's theories, see Melvin Gurtov, "Hanoi on War and Peace," in *Vietnam and American Diplomacy*, edited by John Boettiger (Lexington, Mass.: D.C. Heath and Company, 1968).

4. Vo Nguyen Giap, "The Party's Military Line is the Ever-Victorious Banner of People's War in Our Country," *Nhan Dan* and *Quan Doi Nhan Dan*, 14-17 December 1969 (FBIS No. 31, 13 February 1970, Supp. 5).

5. Ibid.

6. The war itself is for them a sort of shield against a host of contradictions they may have to face eventually, such as questions of succession in Hanoi, of relations with Moscow and Peking, and of reconstruction. The war may keep the lid on these contradictions at least for a time—no one can tell.

7. Most of the passages on Army morale are based on three RAND studies in that area: J.C. Donnell, G.J. Pauker, J.J. Zasloff, *Viet Cong Motivation and Morale in 1964: A Preliminary Report*, The RAND Corporation RM-4507/3-ISA, April 1971; Konrad Kellen, *A View of the VC: Elements of Cohesion in the Enemy Camp*, The RAND Corporation RM-5462-1-ISA, November 1969, and Konrad Kellen, *Conversations with Enemy Soldiers in Late 1968/Early 1969: A Study of Motivation and Morale*, The RAND Corporation RM-6131-1-ISA, September 1970.

8. See A.L. George, *The Chinese Communist Army in Action: The Korean War and Its Aftermath*, New York: Columbia University Press, 1967, ch. 9.

9. A deputy squad leader, in Kellen, *Conversations with Enemy Soldiers*, p. xiii.

10. Kellen, *A View of the VC*.

11. Kellen, *Conversations with Enemy Soldiers*.

12. For the dexterity with which Hanoi leaders have dealt with conflicting pressures by their allies, see John C. Donnell and Melvin Gurtov, *North Vietnam: Left of Moscow, Right of Peking*, in *The Communist Revolution in Asia: Tactics, Goals, and Achievements*, edited by Robert A. Scalapino (Englewood Cliffs, New Jersey: Prentice-Hall).

13. *Le Monde*, 25 November 1966.

14. From a review of the actual psychological warfare efforts that we have made, better psywar would also appear next to impossible. From what I have seen (as a psychological warfare officer in World War II), our psywar efforts in Vietnam were quite versatile, eloquent and to the point, both to the NVA and in leaflets dropped over the North. They could not be much better. They just failed to score.

15. They only expended considerable manpower in Laos and probably considered that inevitable because the battle, from their viewpoint, was defensive and offered an opportunity to meet ARVN under reasonably favorable circumstances.

16. *Der Spiegel*, 17 January 1967.

7 Leadership and Organization of the Pathet Lao

Joseph J. Zasloff

Any discussion of Pathet Lao leadership and organization must be set within the sociocultural context of Laos.[1] The least developed country in Southeast Asia, Laos is more a geographic expression than a nation. With a population estimated at 3 million, its peoples differ widely in social organization and political identity. The lowland Lao (Lao Loum) who live along the Mekong River valley, share a lifestyle, a common language, Therravada Buddhism, and wet rice agriculture. They have developed political loyalties to the powerful families of the various regions, and only in recent years have these regions been joined, still loosely, into a single nation. There are even greater differences among the peoples of the mountains which cover more than half the country. At the middle altitudes are a great variety of Mon Khmer peoples, known in Laos as Lao Theung, and at the higher altitudes are Sino-Tibetan peoples, the Meo and Yao, each group with its own language and social organization.

There has been little modernization in Laos. The brief, indirect French colonial rule did not break down the traditional institutions of the society in the same manner as in Vietnam. In its sparsely populated area, there has been no serious land alienation, and there is a relative abundance of food. Visitors to Laos have noted consistently the gay and carefree quality of its peoples and their relative lack of acquisitiveness and tension. However, the tragedy of war, raging intermittently since 1946, with savage intensity in some areas since 1964, has changed this harmonious image.

Within this social and cultural context, the Lao Communist movement, commonly referred to as the Pathet Lao (PL), has been nurtured. New Communist institutions have been established whose leaders, with guidance from North Vietnamese advisers, wield the power. However, traditional political patterns still persist, and combine with the new Communist forms. For example, some of the PL leaders have accumulated their authority primarily as members of the important families of lowland Laos or as chieftains of tribal minorities in the highlands, deriving their power as much from ascriptive sources as from the Communist institutions they have established. The account which follows will examine the Pathet Lao leadership and their principal instruments of rule, the Party, the Army and the governmental and administrative organs.

113

Leadership

Top PL leaders generally come from one of three social categories, suggesting the major influences in their rise to power. One group springs from influential Lao Loum families, some with aristocratic origins like those of Prince Souphanouvong or Prince Souk Vongsak, others with mandarinal backgrounds or otherwise prominent roots, like Phoumi Vongvichit and Singkapo Chounramany. Tribal chieftains comprise a second category and include such figures as Sithone Kommadam, a prominent Lao Theung leader from South Laos, and Faydang, a Meo dignitary from North Laos. Members of a third category, which includes two of the most powerful leaders, Kaysone Phomvihan and Nouhak Phomsavan, have more modest backgrounds, but have established close ties with the Vietnamese Communists, either through birth, education, or early career association. Despite their social diversity, the striking feature of the Pathet Lao leadership is their cohesion and stability.

Like the North Vietnamese, the current PL leaders have served together, with apparent harmony, since the founding of their revolutionary organization in the late 1940s. Several factors help to explain this remarkable cohesion over the past two and a half decades. PL leaders have been fighting together in a revolutionary struggle, often under great hardship and personal danger, circumstances which weld strong personal ties among men and link their thoughts and sentiments in a common cause. The cause has been essentially a nationalist one—fighting against the two foreign "imperialist" enemies, France and the United States, and their domestic "lackeys"—subsumed into a larger Marxist-Leninist ideology transmitted principally by the North Vietnamese. The Communist organizational doctrine which they adopted from the North Vietnamese has been another factor in promoting their cohesion. The doctrine, which is taught assiduously to all cadres, stresses the obligation of the leaders to serve the revolution selflessly and provides a set of techniques, such as criticism and self-criticism, that effectively regulate behavior. Another crucial ingredient has been North Vietnamese guidance and support given since the initiation of the Pathet Lao movement. As a strong, respected outsider, commanding resources important to the movement's growth, the North Vietnamese have provided a firm guiding hand which has attenuated or resolved some of the social, ethnic, and regional conflicts inherent in the PL movement.

The cohesion of the PL leaders has been tested by the numerous opportunities offered them to defect to the RLG side. At several periods in Lao political history, particularly after the Geneva Agreements of 1954, during the temporary RLG-PL political accommodation prior to the 1958 elections, and within the coalition period from 1962 to 1963, PL leaders could easily have joined their RLG competitors. Yet, none of the top echelon, and but a handful of lower echelon cadres, did so. Abandoning their cause would have meant abandoning not only their ideological commitments, but also their power and prestige, since it is unlikely that they would have been named to positions of importance by their opponents. In addition, they had created a web of family commitments and personal interests which committed them to their posts. Many have children studying in North Vietnam, the Soviet Union, China, and other Communist countries who would not necessarily have followed them to the RLG side. Moreover, the RLG itself was hardly attractive to them. Many saw the RLG elite as "comprador bourgeoisie" or as "feudalists," riven by cliques and factions, using public office for family advancement, engaging in corruption, and living a soft life—not an inspiring cause for a revolutionary to join. Further, the strong dependence of the RLG elite upon the United States, whom the PL saw as consistently engaged in nefarious operations (particularly during the period of active United States intervention on the side of the right-wing elements during the latter part of the 1950s), would hardly endear them to their opponents.

There are important gaps in our knowledge about the PL leadership. While the most influential group of PL leaders can be identified, individuals cannot be ranked in order of importance with certainty. There are indications that, as Secretary-General of the Party and Minister of Defense, Kaysone is the principal figure and that his deputy in the Party, Nouhak, may be second in command. Prince Souphanouvong, Chairman of the Lao Patriotic Front, is presented to the public, both within Laos and internationally, as the leading NLHS spokesman, but his decision-making power seems to be less than Kaysone's and Nouhak's. While Souphanouvong is given greater public prominence than Kaysone and Nouhak, there has not been an attempt to build a cult of personality, as in the days of Stalin, or to create the adulation enjoyed by Mao Tse-tung or Ho Chi Minh. Although Souphanouvong may not have power equivalent to Kaysone and Nouhak, it does not seem likely that, as some analysts contend, he is simply a figurehead manipulated by the Communist movement because of his aristocratic origins and personal appeal in Laos and abroad. Rather, his popularity within Laos, his strong personal qualities of leadership and his long-standing prominence in the movement, make it probable that he does still wield significant influence

Any question regarding power of individual Lao Communist leaders must be put in the context of another question—the role of the North Vietnamese in the Lao Communist decision-making process. It is clear that the North Vietnamese have played a decisive role in the founding, growth, and persistence of the Pathet Lao's organization.[2] They continue to play a critical military and political role, with some 50,000 to 67,000 troops serving in the country and a network of advisers placed throughout the most important PL institutions, including the Party, the Army and the Front. While there is little question that the North Vietnamese exercise critical influence on PL decisions, an insider's view of the decision-making process is not available. Obviously, the crucial decisions affecting NVA troop deployment, strategy and tactics are made by the North Vietnamese. When matters are more clearly identified as within Lao Communist jurisdiction, it appears that the North Vietnamese work through the Lao leadership, with relative sensitivity to Lao nationalist sensibilities. However, no information is available about which leaders the North Vietnamese may consistently favor or which they may distrust. It seems likely, nevertheless, that as the North Vietnamese military investment has increased in recent years, and the war has escalated, North Vietnamese influence in the PL decision-making process has correspondingly increased.

Cohesion and stability notwithstanding, a number of important issues might provide a source of factionalism within the PL leadership, as has been the case in North Vietnam, China, and other Communist systems. Is there a difference of opinion regarding the pace and scope of the war, as there seems to be in North Vietnam? Would some leaders favor reducing the military conflict in favor of a political offensive, possibly offering temporary accommodation with the RLG? Are there differences on the question of alignment in the Sino-Soviet dispute? Most importantly, are there differences concerning the PL relationship with the North Vietnamese?

It is reasonable to assume that the world-wide trend within national Communist parties toward diversity and autonomy has influenced the thinking of certain Lao Communist leaders. Moreover, dependence upon the Vietnamese runs counter to Lao historical sentiment, based on fear of Vietnamese expansion into Laos. The split in 1949 of the PL wing from initial Lao independence movement, the Lao Issara, concerned the issue of cooperation with the Viet Minh (an issue which still divides the PL and the RLG today). Some PL leaders, as Lao nationalists, must entertain misgivings about such heavy reliance upon their traditional enemy, even when—or perhaps especially when—they receive scarce resources but abundant advice. Some PL leaders must be pondering the painful question as to whether Lao interests always coincide with those of the Vietnamese, whose decisions must be based first upon their own national interests and purposes. Indeed, some PL leaders might well believe that the intensity of the war on Lao soil is a product of their intimate involvement with the Vietnamese. On the other hand, the Lao Communist leaders have developed a habit of dependency upon the Vietnamese and must feel that they share common interests and a beneficial partnership. Further, since their RLG opponents receive massive support from the Americans and, to a lesser degree, the Thai, PL leaders must recognize that their small and relatively weak movement badly needs external assistance. These latter elements make it likely that they will continue to lean heavily upon their North Vietnamese neighbors. Indeed, it is possible that, in view of the deep North Vietnamese involvement in their system, they have no other feasible choice.

Another question about which little information is available concerns the state of morale of the PL leaders. In their public pronouncements, they understandably strike heroic poses and express confidence in victory. We have no reason to surmise that they are now any less committed or constant in revolutionary zeal than in the past, even though the war in Laos, especially the bombing in their zone, has intensified. Still, we do not know what they really believe regarding the outcome of the war and the prospects for a solution favorable to them.

Another question about which we can only speculate concerns how the next generation of PL leaders will differ from the current one. It seems likely that, if the current PL-RLG separation continues, more future PL leaders will come from the ethnic minorities. Highland tribes populate roughly 80 percent of the PL-controlled zone, where a campaign of recruitment for education and Party membership, selecting the brightest and most ambitious youth, has been under way for nearly a decade. As these younger cadres return from their studies in North Vietnam, China, the Soviet Union, and other Communist countries, what changes will they bring to the leadership? With more technical education and a stronger, more formalized dose of Marxism-Leninism than present incumbents, how will their policy inclinations differ from the present leaders? What will be the nature of their nationalism? How committed are they likely to be to reunification with the lowland areas of Laos? From an RLG perspective, it is likely that an anti-Communist Lao Loum elite will be even less enthusiastic about sharing power with Marxist-Leninist ethnic minority leaders than with the current, predominantly Lao Loum, PL leadership, which includes relatives, former classmates, and associates in government.

The People's Party of Laos

Since its official founding in 1955, the Party has been steadily consolidating its role as the commanding institution of the PL movement. Enduring over a decade and a half, with an estimated 12,000 to 14,000 members in a PL-controlled zone of approximately 850,000 to 1 million inhabitants, it is a unique political accomplishment within Laos. By contrast, on the non-Communist side, political parties have been short-lived alliances of the leading members of traditional family and regional groupings which have had little cohesiveness and less organization.

While the Party has not succeeded in extending its influence equally to all areas of the PL zone, it has reached out in all directions in an attempt to impose its authority and extend PL rule. In the manner of incumbent Communist parties elsewhere, cadres guide the execution of policy from cells within the other institutions of rule, most importantly the Army, the Front, and the government administrative apparatus. In its recruitment of new members, the Party has been stressing youth, ability, lower class social origins, and susceptibility to learning the Party doctrine and developing revolutionary zeal. Thus, as these young cadres move into positions of greater authority, new criteria of leadership will have replaced the ascriptive criteria of traditional Laos, in which important family or tribal leadership offered the route to power.

The Marxist-Leninist doctrine of the PPL, which closely resembles the North Vietnamese version, provides the guidelines for the PL struggle. The enemies are defined as the United States imperialists and their lackeys, who comprise bureaucratic and military elements, comprador bourgeoisie, and reactionary feudalists. A "worker-peasant alliance," drawing some petty and "national" bourgeoisie into the struggle is paid to lead the "national and democratic" revolution against imperialism and feudalism. The "genuine revolutionary party" which leads the revolution is said to have followed a correct military and political line. It has established and consolidated a broad united front, and drawn upon "huge support and assistance of the socialist countries." Elaborating on the Party's strategy and tactics, Kaysone Phomvihan, the PPL Secretary-General, declared the following.

The Party has mobilized the masses to wage a struggle in many forms closely combining armed struggle with political struggle, making use of various forms of struggle—legal, diplomatic, parliamentary, several negotiations, two national coalition governments . . . but the party always regards armed struggle and political struggle as the two fundamental ones, the former being the most important form to win victory.[3]

Party organizational principles follow the pattern of Communist parties elsewhere, again particularly the North Vietnamese version. The official doctrine is inculcated into Party members with the aim of creating a corps of dedicated, selfless cadres who are committed to achieving success of the revolution. As mentioned before, criticism and self-criticism and other techniques of Communist organization are employed in training, instilling discipline, and building a cohesive Party.

The Party has maintained a semisecrecy about its commanding role in the PL movement. Members do not disclose their Party affiliation, even though, as interviews show, fellow workers and soldiers are generally aware of their membership. This semisecrecy follows the united front strategy of the Vietnamese Lao Dong Party of camouflaging the leadership role of the Communist Party to give the impression, both within the country and externally, that the Front guides the revolution. In Laos, the Lao Patriotic Front (NLHS), under the chairmanship of Prince Souphanouvong, is said to speak for the Lao revolution. In recent years, there has been intermittent public reference to the role of the commanding Party in NLHS radio broadcasts and publications. The reasons for the Party's emergence from the penumbra of secrecy are not altogether clear. Some references may have been inadvertent. However, it seems that as the Party grows in size, strength, effectiveness of control and confidence, it will increasingly expose its true leadership role, and in doing so, follow the DRV's pattern of revealing party's vanguard role to ensure that non-Communist groups, particularly bourgeois elements, would not gain ascendancy. At the present time, this policy of semisecrecy in the PPL in Laos is similar to that practiced by the People's Revolutionary Party in South Vietnam, which still operates in the background, leaving the public role to the National Liberation Front and the Provisional Revolutionary Government.

Politics and Administration

The PL authorities, operating within extremely difficult physical and cultural conditions, have developed a political and administrative capacity generally superior to the RLG's. They have mobilized their population into a variety of associations which function as agencies of training, indoctrination and social cohesion, and as groups for the performance of work tasks. Although the PL claim publicly that voluntarism is their organizing principle, they stimulate social pressures to guide people into suitable organizations. Much time and effort in these associations is devoted to political indoctrination. Youth especially, whose organizations receive much more attention than those on the RLG side, are encouraged to spread the Lao Communist gospel throughout their communities. The Lao Patriotic Front, working under the direction of the Party, has an apparatus at each echelon of government down to the village level and coordinates the efforts of these associations. In addition, the Front, proving a flexible instrument of policy, has served as the open political party during the brief periods of accommodation with the RLG, and in the one relatively free election in 1958, it scored impressive gains over its non-Communist opponents.

The PL administrative system, varying widely from region to region, seems most developed nearest its central headquarters in Sam Neua and least in the more distant tribal areas in the mountains. In these latter regions, tribes are tied to the PL Center by bargaining between PL emissaries and local chiefs, although these traditional patterns seem to be giving way to more centralized forms of Communist rule as tribal youth are recruited and indoctrinated into the PL system. To a much greater degree than the RLG, PL leaders can exert authority in the villages, demanding and expecting compliance with orders. This is due, in good part, to their success in creating dedicated cadres. The PL system offers considerably more opportunity than the RLG for able youths, especially poor farmers and minority tribesmen, to acquire training and rise in the ranks.

Again in contrast to the RLG, a rather elaborate system of propaganda has been constructed by the PL authorities. NLHS propaganda is directed from a ministry at the Center and all echelons of the administration and Front, as well as the Army, must ensure that each cadre takes seriously his propaganda duties. In addition, special mobile propaganda teams, often armed, are assigned to operate throughout PL-controlled and contested areas.

There are other forms of PL social control which are more pervasive than the RLG's. At the lowest level of society, the interfamily group, modeled on the Vietnamese Communist technique, links about five families under the leadership of an elder to whom village officials can refer for information or tasks. A judiciary system has been organized in which "people's courts" are convened, sometimes by a visiting cadre when infractions are too serious for village authorities to judge. In meting out punishment and regulating behavior, PL authorities stress "reeducation" rather than open coercion. Secret agents are placed throughout the PL zone, as well as in contested and enemy-controlled areas, to report on suspicious political behavior, and a system of passes and checkpoints to control population movement has been established. The relative success of PL authorities in recruiting soldiers, collecting taxes and assigning work tasks in their zone is some measure of the effectiveness of their administrative controls.

As for technical competence, because of American, and to a lesser degree, French and Thai assistance, RLG ministries are probably more able to deliver services in such fields as agriculture, irrigation, and public works, and RLG technicians have had more training and experience in dealing with advanced machinery and equipment, such as automotive, radio, and telecommunications devices. In addition, members of the RLG bureaucracy are likely to have more formal education than PL administrative cadres. On the other hand, as we have pointed out, the PL system shows a greater political capacity.

Life in the PL zone is one of hazard and severe hardship. American bombing of selected areas of the PL zone has been the heaviest in world history, and tens of thousands have fled to the RLG areas to escape it. According to William H. Sullivan, Deputy Assistant Secretary of State for East Asian and Pacific Affairs and former Ambassador to Laos, testifying before Senator Kennedy's subcommittee on refugees on April 22, 1971, over 700,000 residents of Laos had been displaced at least once since 1962.[4] The overwhelming majority have come from the PL-controlled zone. While these figures, which include others besides refugees from the bombing, can be taken only as gross indicators of flight, they do emphasize the widespread hardship in the PL zone and the enormity of the refugee problem. In some areas, inhabitants spend their daylight hours in damp caves or underground dugouts, emerging only at night to conduct their necessary activities. Devastation has been enormous, and the burdens placed upon those who remain have been heavy. Most able-bodied men, and some women, have been conscripted into military service; tax levies are high; the requirements of porterage and other corvee labor are onerous.

While this tragic picture of life in the PL zone is clear, the political attitudes of the population are not. Refugees, who may wish to appear friendly to the RLG authorities, often stress the oppressive aspects of PL rule, especially the heavy work assignments, monotonous political propaganda, limitations on personal movement, heavy taxes, and interference by Vietnamese advisers. However, there is reason to believe that those who have stayed, and perhaps some who have fled, respect and are committed to the PL authorities—an attitude similar to that of the North Vietnamese population toward their leaders. The bombing and other hostilities may have created a feeling that people must rally around their leaders and fight against the Power which seems bent on bombing them to capitulation. If this is true, the bombing becomes an important factor in forming political attitudes in the PL zone since, in less besieged times, no centralized authority—neither PL nor RLG—would be likely to arouse strong political support from the ordinary peasant.

Another factor in assessing public attitudes in the PL zone is the popular feeling toward the presence of North Vietnamese troops and advisers. The North Vietnamese make significant efforts to maintain a low profile within Laos. They endeavor to post their troops out of the population centers and have generally refrained from making onerous direct demands upon the local population. The advisers, who are normally adept at learning the local language and customs and live at the level of their hosts, make a strong effort, in the words of several refugees, not to let themselves be seen. Even though these measures seem to have succeeded in reducing popular resentment, a certain amount of popular antipathy toward the active North Vietnamese role in Laos remains.

The impact of the war and the flight of the refugees raise a series of questions which we can only pose but not answer. How severely has the drain of population affected the PL authorities and the remaining population? What is likely to be the effect of continued bombing and warfare on those who have stayed—what are the limits of their endurance and how will they react to the strain? Looking ahead to happier prospects of peace or simply to reduced hostilities, which refugees are likely to return to their home territories?

The PL Fighting Forces

Unlike their competitors in the RLG Army, whose inclination for coups d'etat increased during the latter 1950s as their forces expanded, military leaders of the Peoples Liberation Army (LPLA), as the PL military forces are designated, have adhered to the Communist principle of Party dominance. However, there can be no question that the military exercises an important influence in policymaking. The LPLA is the largest PL organization, absorbing the major portion of the PL's scarce resources, and it probably makes the largest impact upon the life of the inhabitants in the PL zone. The Minister of Defense, Kaysone, is also the Secretary-General of the Party, and most of the founding members of the Pathet Lao organization, who are also the current leaders, have been intimately involved in military affairs.

Despite the serious drain upon the population of the PL zone since the commencement of American bombing in 1964, the LPLA, starting at 20,000 during that year, has increased to the present estimated 45,000 to 50,000 (at which point it seems to have leveled during the past few years). A growing, or even stable troop strength at the present level, in the face of a declining population, suggests the prodigious effort invested in recruiting and maintaining the military forces. (It should be noted that North Vietnamese troop commitment in Laos during this same period of LPLA growth has increased from 10,000 troops in January 1966 to between 50,000 and 67,000, according to various United States estimates.)

During the conflict against the French and in the postindependence military engagements, the North Vietnamese have consistently played the major role, generally providing the more competent first-strike forces with the LPLA serving as support and auxiliary forces. In the past few years, as the fighting in Laos has intensified and as the North Vietnamese troop investment has increased, the NVA has further overshadowed the LPLA. This is not to say that the combat role of the LPLA has declined, since there has been increased fighting for everyone.

The PL military forces are divided into three principal categories: regular forces, which serve under center, region, or province commanders; regional (or popular) forces, which are drawn from and serve at the district or canton; and the militia (or guerrilla) forces, from the canton or village. As this organizational pattern suggests, the military performs a great variety of functions at all echelons of government in addition to fighting. They are responsible for maintaining internal order and control as well as for local administration. For example, the posts regulating the movements of inhabitants are manned by soldiers who also collect and transport rice, mobilize groups for labor duty and conduct propaganda. Troop units are assigned to planting and harvesting rice, as well as to other agricultural duties. Engineering units build roads and bridges and repair war damage. The army also provides a major part of the transportation and communication services for the zone.

The LPLA performs an important educating and socializing function within the PL zone, shaping the habits, values and political orientation of its members. For a majority of the troops, the literacy training they receive in the army, joined with lessons on geography and arithmetic, constitutes their only exposure to formal schooling. Indoctrination concerning rules of personal behavior inculcates important modern sanitation practices, good behavior toward the people and respect for the various ethnic groups, and encourages notions of self-improvement. Most of the rank-and-file recruits enter military service with little knowledge of Laos and few political ideas. They are taught a new conception of their country and often work with diverse ethnic groups under the doctrine that all are fighting for the same cause. The enemy—the United States imperialist—is defined for them, and they are pressured into assuming an identity as a Lao citizen. Taken from a kinship group or tribe whose habits and values are determined by tradition, they are instructed to conform to the rules of a relatively modern military organization. This is clearly an effort to alter parochial attitudes and create a larger identity for the new soldier. The results are not yet clear, although it seems probable that he is significantly influenced by his military experience.

We have already pointed out that present PL capacity—political, administrative, and military—is attributable, in good part, to North Vietnamese guidance and assistance. An interesting question is what would happen if this support were seriously diminished or removed. As for the administrative and political institutions, their competence would surely decline. But, since it is not clear how firmly these institutions have taken root in Lao soil, it is not evident whether the loss would be disastrous or merely serious. Speculating about the effect on the PL military capacity following the removal of North Vietnamese assistance is even more elusive. It seems likely that if the RLG maintained its external support from the Thais and the United States, including the massive bombing, while the LPLA was stripped of North Vietnamese assistance, the LPLA could be routed. But the reverse is equally, indeed, even more likely—that is, if external assistance were stripped from the RLG, while the NVA support to the LPLA remained constant, the RLG Army could be easily overrun. There is no empirical way of measuring a third possibility—how the LPLA would fare against the RLG Army if neither had outside support. Certainly, the level of violence in Laos would decline if the outsiders departed. However, it seems much more likely that, in the near future, weak and fragile Laos, situated in the center of the Southeast Asian conflict, will continue tragically to be subject to intervention by the more powerful external nations.

Notes

1. This essay draws upon interviews made in 1967 with Lao and foreigners who had knowledge of the Pathet Lao, as well as with Pathet Lao and North Vietnamese prisoners and defectors. For a selected list of persons interviewed or consulted, see Paul F. Langer and Joseph J. Zasloff, *North Vietnam and the Pathet Lao: Partners in the Struggle for Laos* (Cambridge: Harvard University Press, 1970), Appendix A. More recent information was drawn from an examination of PL radio braodcasts and published materials, as well as statements emanating from Hanoi, Moscow and Peking, reports of Pathet Lao and North Vietnamese prisoners and defectors, refugee interviews, and translations of captured PL and North Vietnamese internal documents.

2. See Langer and Zasloff, ibid., for an account of this relationship.

3. All quotations on doctrine in this paragraph are taken from an article by Kaysone Phomvihan, Secretary General of the PPL, written on the occasion of the twenty-fifth anniversary of Laos' proclamation of independence (October 12, 1945). See PL News Agency in English, 5 October 1970. For a further authoritative discussion of PPL doctrine, see Phoumi Vongvichit, *Laos and the Victorious Struggle of the Lao People against U.S. Neo-Colonialism*, (Neo Lao Haksat Editions, 1969).

4. U.S., Congress, Senate, Subcommittee to Investigate Problems Connected with Refugees and Escapees, Committee on the Judiciary, *Hearing on Laos and Cambodia*, 92nd Cong., 1st sess., 21, 22 April 1971, pt. 2, p. 47.

Exporting Insurgency: The Communists in Cambodia

David E. Brown

Prologue: Mounting Pressures

In the last years of Prince Norodom Sihanouk's reign as Cambodian Chief of State, the delicate *modus vivendi* which he had negotiated with the Vietnamese Communists came under increasing stress. Growing Communist difficulties within South Vietnam and the Cambodian government's hardening position made some sort of a confrontation virtually certain, whether or not Sihanouk had remained in office.

The Vietnamese Communists saw Cambodia as a source of supplies, a conduit for arms and ammunition and, as they lost ground in South Vietnam, increasingly as a safehaven. Without the use of Cambodia's convenient seaport, Sihanoukville (now Kompong Som) and Cambodian Army cooperation, it would have been vastly more difficult to refit Viet Cong and North Vietnamese Army (VC/NVA) units with modern Russian and Chinese weaponry in 1967 and to launch the large-scale offensives of early 1968. And, as Communist regular forces were slowly driven from the heavily populated South Vietnamese lowlands and then from the mountains and jungles as well, sanctuaries in Cambodian border areas became vital havens. By 1968, COSVN–the Communist general staff for southern Vietnam–and its appended fronts and bureaus were largely situated in the thick jungles and rubber plantations near the Cambodian towns of Krek, Mimot and Snoul. In the triborder area of northeast Cambodia, a major logistics complex grew at this southern terminus of the Ho Chi Minh Trail. To the south, the Communist commands for the Saigon area and the upper Mekong Delta worked in the salient now immortalized as the Parrot's Beak. In these bases, VC/NVA units rested, refitted and trained before returning to action in South Vietnam.

These urgent military interests far outweighed Hanoi's long-term ideological and political interests in Cambodia itself. The indigenous Cambodian Communist movement was to Hanoi primarily an embarrassment. The Khmer Communists and their sympathizers, known collectively as the Khmer Rouge, seem never to have numbered more than a few thousand. Their ill-timed initiatives agitated Sihanouk and thereby jeopardized the VC/NVA's sanctuaries and supplies. Thus, while the Vietnamese Communists could not wholly reject comradely pleas for aid–and apparently went so far as to spirit away to Hanoi leftist Khmer forced into hiding in early 1967—they seem to have provided little or no help to the Khmer Rouge bands which tried to ignite an insurrection in scattered parts of the country, notably the mountains of western Cambodia, from 1967 on. Until sometime in 1969, the Vietnamese Communists' limited political activities in Cambodia were directed almost entirely at organizing the ethnic Vietnamese minority, scattered groups comprising less than 10% of Cambodia's population, to provide funds, foodstuffs and recruits for the struggle in South Vietnam.

Sihanouk, meanwhile, had sought to keep Cambodia out of the war while profiting from it. Central to his strategy was an attempt to balance between the contending forces while favoring the likely victor. By 1968, the Cambodian government was well aware of the increasing use Hanoi was making of its border areas—and that this reflected a significant shift in the political and military climate within South Vietnam. Although the Cambodian Army (FANK or *Forces Armées Nationales Khmères*) was too feeble to do much more than monitor Vietnamese Communist activity, Sihanouk sought to apply pressure in other ways. Shipment of war goods was embargoed; the last Chinese arms delivery reached Sihanoukville in April 1969 and was doled out to the NC/NVA over a six-month period beginning about September. Relations with the United States improved fitfully. Phnom Penh became increasingly less concerned by US or South Vietnamese Army (ARVN) clashes with the VC/NVA in remote areas. FANK operations against dissident Khmer Leou montagnards and Khmer Rouge were intensified and Sihanouk grew prone to denunciation of Vietnamese Communist use of Cambodian territory and to accusations that Hanoi was sponsoring the home-grown rebels. In this context, the less cautious demarches of Lon Nol and Sirik Matak to the Communists once Sihanouk had fallen carried Sihanouk's maneuvers to their logical conclusion.

Hanoi's Response

With the storm signals prior to March 1970, the Vietnamese Communists may have anticipated an eventual collapse in the *modus vivendi*. In any event, they rapidly shifted to tough tactics once Sihanouk fell on March 18. They refused to bargain with Lon Nol, unveiled the National United Front of Cambodia (FUNK or *Front Unifie Nationale de Kampuchea*) on March 23, and moved to expand and strengthen Communist positions in the border areas, steps which permitted the evacuation of COSVN agencies and key facilities further into Cambodia before the (US/ARVN) incursion began on April 30th. The proclamation of FUNK's formation was necessary to put a nationalist veneer on the VC/NVA assault on FANK. It signalled Hanoi's intent, once faced with a thoroughly hostile Phnom Penh government, to patch together a responsive liberation movement from whatever building blocks could be found, and thus legitimize their continued use of Cambodian territory and resources.

Indeed, by late 1969 the first Khmer militias and village administrations seem to have been organized by the VC/NVA in border base areas from which higher Cambodian officials had been effectively excluded. The significance of this modest, and probably experimental, prototype of FUNK is that it may have satisfied COSVN that a Khmer infrastructure could be rapidly created in Cambodia. As early as April 1970, the Vietnamese Communists began to launch "armed action teams" deep into the Cambodian countryside, with the mission of creating FUNK from scratch. Although the armed action teams appear to be the lineal descendants of the agit-prop teams pioneered by the Viet Minh in 1944, they were nonetheless in scale and function an audacious initiative. COSVN agencies and subordinate echelons in South Vietnam were levied for experienced political cadre beginning in March 1970. Two of these cadre, joined by a medic, one or two interpreters and an armed squad, formed an armed action team; within a few months a great many—perhaps several hundred—of these teams had been hastily trained and deployed to Cambodian villages, usually in proximity to VC/NVA units but sometimes unsupported.

Within this context, Prince Sihanouk's adherence to the Communist camp seems to be a fortuitous event. When FUNK was proclaimed, Sihanouk, who had come to rest in Peking, embraced it, and not *vice versa*. Not until the "Indochinese People's Summit Conference" on 23-24 April did Hanoi endorse Sihanouk's titular leadership of the Cambodian liberation movement. Nor, since that time, has Hanoi rendered more than half-hearted lip-service to Sihanouk's princely pretensions. It now seems well established that the Vietnamese Communists regarded Sihanouk's wounded pride as a useful device to rally Cambodian support, and nothing more. On top of many private comments by Vietnamese and Khmer Communist spokesmen have come Sihanouk's own admissions, beginning in September 1970, that he does not control FUNK. For example, he told a French reporter "I am giving everything to the Red Khmers. They are pure. They will do what is necessary for the people. They are patriots." Moreover, he continued, newly-appointed "vice-ministers" inside Cambodia "are not under the authority of the titular ministers [members of Sihanouk's entourage] in Peking. . . . They are not Sihanoukistes; they are Khmer Rouge."[1]

Building FUNK

Communist directives captured during the Allied cross-border operations in May and June 1970 contain detailed, rather cynical instructions to the cadre of the VC/NVA armed action teams. Except when dealing with the special problem of overcoming Khmer antipathy to the Vietnamese, the instructions are tested Vietnamese Communist formulae for "liberation" of a village. Although the Vietnamese cadre were instructed to work in concert with preexisting Khmer Rouge elements where possible, it was recognized that ordinarily a team would find no such allies on its arrival in a village. The armed action teams were to call on villagers to rally to FUNK, stressing the themes of loyalty to Prince Sihanouk, protection of life, property and Khmer culture against foreign (i.e., United States and South Vietnamese) invaders, and opposition to local tyrants (i.e., Cambodian government officials and soldiers). Monks, village chiefs, and teachers were to be singled out for special proselyting. Once the COSVN teams succeeded in identifying "individuals with prestige . . . (including monks) . . . who have decided to oppose the Lon Nol reactionary clique" and who "agree with all actions of the [national] Front Committee," their election to village and hamlet FUNK committees was to be arranged by a show of hands at a mass meeting. Then the village committee, guided by its Vietnamese advisors, was to recruit a FUNK village militia (to be trained by VC/NVA cadre) to organize the village farmers, women and youth, into "liberation associations," to levy modest taxes and to eliminate "enemy tyrants and intelligence personnel,"—e.g., those village leaders who had resisted the blandishments of the COSVN cadre—through selective terrorism. On this base, the Vietnamese Communists were supposed to erect district FUNK administrations and try to build up local force companies.

The COSVN directives seemed confident that Khmer-Vietnamese antipathy and the inherent difficulty of directing activity while ostensibly remaining advisors could be overcome. The Vietnamese cadre were instructed to keep a low profile; no more than two were to be present at any FUNK meeting and they were cautioned repeatedly to "strive to avoid bad attitudes before the committees under all circumstances." The democratic facade was to be maintained. Not coercion, but persuasion, was required: "all actions, and especially the neutralization or elimination of bad elements, are to be decided by the local FUNK committees." If the people insisted on electing independent-minded leaders to the FUNK administrations, the COSVN advisors were to "accept them temporarily and later use the authority of higher echelon to dismiss them."

It appears that the VC/NVA were rather successful between April and September 1970 in erecting a village-level FUNK structure in large areas of the countryside, largely because the armed action teams were able to operate in a near vacuum.[2] The government, staggered by the VC/NVA onslaught, was evicted from much of northern and eastern Cambodia and in some other areas was forced back into province and district towns. The COSVN teams moved in; rural elites by and large fled into Phnom Penh and other towns. Within a few months, a FUNK framework heavily dependent on its Vietnamese advisors—the cadre of the armed action teams and complementary VC/NVA structures at province and district level—emerged.

Very little is known about the higher echelons of FUNK. It is apparently modeled after the National Liberation Front of South Vietnam, with a hierarchical system of village, district, and provincial committees presumably culminating in a national committee located in close proximity to COSVN, i.e., somewhere in southern Kratie province. Initially, the higher FUNK committees, like those at village level, seem to have contained mostly Sihanouk loyalists and such other "individuals with prestige" as could be found for the Vietnamese Communists.

Khieu Samphan, Hou Yuon and Hu Nim, three Cambodian leftists who dropped out of sight in 1967 (and in Phnom Penh are widely believed to have been liquidated at Sihanouk's command) have been featured by Asian Communist media as the leaders of the Cambodian resistance. According to Sihanouk, They represent the Pracheachon (the Cambodian Communist Front of the late 1950s and early 1960s) in FUNK and also hold key positions in the cabinet of his Royal Government of National Union (RGNU). It seems likely that within Cambodia, the RGNU and FUNK are only theoretically distinguishable, and that the half-dozen less well-known Cambodian leftists whom Sihanouk identified in September as RGNU vice-ministers present in the liberated zone are also in the FUNK inner circle. These appointments coincide with and probably signalled an apparent purge of Sihanoukistes in the upper reaches of the FUNK organization. Refugee reports from scattered Communist-controlled areas suggest that this was no isolated occurrence; that in the autumn of 1970, Khmer Rouge (i.e., Khmer Communist) influence within FUNK increased and was reflected by deemphasis of the "rally-round-Prince Sihanouk" propaganda theme.

It also appears that Communist emphasis in the autumn of 1970 shifted away from the creation of the FUNK structure to fleshing it out. Various rallier reports had suggested that the Viet Cong advisors considered their FUNK counterparts generally incompetent, and it is not surprising that numerous training courses for specialized cadre seem to have been organized in the liberated zone.

Finally, although not all of the information on this point is consistent, it appears that late in 1970, Vietnamese advisors to FUNK committees were instructed to assume a lower profile. In some cases, it is said that the FUNK administrators let it be known that the Vietnamese cadre would henceforth be "tolerated only as advisors," while other sources ascribe hesitant transfers of decision-making responsibility to a Vietnamese initiative.

Building the Khmer Liberation Army (KLA)

The VC/NVA have also labored to create a Cambodian military force. In this regard, they seem to be following a two-track strategy. On the one hand, Khmer have been recruited—or, more often, impressed—into understrength VC/NVA units, and now seem to comprise a substantial fraction of certain regiments. On the other hand, an attempt to organize a multilevel, essentially Khmer force, the Khmer Liberation Armed Forces, (KLA) seems also to be underway. Insofar as can be determined, the KLA is to adhere to the standard Vietnamese Communist pattern of village guerrillas, district and province local force units and, finally, mainforce units available for service on any front. Order of battle information on the KLA, however, is very sketchy, and it seems doubtful that it is yet a force of much consequence. The KLA seems to have been employed primarily as a second-class auxiliary to the VC/NVA, fit mainly to move supplies and to garrison towns liberated by their allies. Although reports cannot always be authenticated, the Cambodian government has reported frequent defections to its forces. In the few instances where predominantly Khmer units have been identified in battle, they seem to have been badly battered, and privately Hanoi may well regard its experience with the KLA quite disappointing so far, the elaborate praise heaped on it by Asian Communist media notwithstanding. Recently, a scattering of Khmer officers have been identified; however, defectors report that these officers are invariably dominated by their more experienced VC/NVA advisors. Still the more common practice, it appears, is for the Khmer rank and file to be led directly by VC/NVA officers and political cadre detailed to the KLA units.

VC-FUNK Relations

Traditional Vietnamese-Khmer animosity and mistrust has been endemic in Communist ranks from the beginning of the VC/NVA assault on Cambodia. Though less well reported, such ethnic friction between allies probably is as great a headache for higher Communist echelons—and the VC/NVA advisory structure—as it is for the GVN and the Cambodian government. From at least March 1970, internal propaganda and indoctrination directed at VC/NVA troops operating in Cambodia has laid remorseless stress on winning behavior toward the Khmer population and comrades-in-arms. All this rhetoric about pan-Indochinese brotherhood notwithstanding, reports of clashes between VC/NVA and KLA elements are legion. As told by refugees and defectors, these incidents stem mainly from Vietnamese Communist arrogance and insensitivity, and from levies on the Khmer population for free food, labor and shelter.

A circular issued to VC/NVA units in the three key provinces of Kompong Cham, Prey Veng and Svay Rieng illustrates COSVN concern. After reiterating the importance of "modest, patient, tactful, persuasive, positive and considerate" behavior toward KLA troops, it notes that "in certain areas, there are still some cadre and troops who sometimes [do] not follow prescribed guidance. . . ." Getting to the point, it then explains that the circular has been issued "in accordance with the spirit of a joint meeting held on 7 October [1970] . . . [between] the friendly forces [KLA] and ourselves," and details in admonitory language the several points of friction. The VC/NVA units are adjured to (1) establish contact with local FUNK authorities when entering an area; (2) issue travel orders to all personnel assigned to procure food or perform other duties before "borrowing" trucks, etc.; and (3) to return or pay for borrowed trucks and materiel. Then in particular: "In no circumstances are we to permit our troops to encircle and open fire on [KLA] troops, as was done by a unit in the Xang Tuc area." Rather, the VC/NVA are admonished to arbitrate their differences with their Khmer comrades. Finally, in a sort of postscript, the circular reveals another problem: Khmer serving in VC/NVA ranks should not be misled by enemy propaganda that they won't be eligible for benefits extended to KLA personnel when the liberation government comes to power. Rather, "when the liberation of the country is achieved, they will participate in the unified Khmer government."

Refugees from the Communist-controlled areas are perhaps prone to exaggeration, but nonetheless it appears—despite orders from higher VC/NVA echelons—that FUNK officials suffer considerable humiliation at the hands of their allies and mentors. The attitude of the low-level VC/NVA soldier, a common one in any expeditionary force, seems to be that the Khmer population should gratefully sacrifice for the common struggle, and not be too sticky on points of protocol. FUNK officials, for their part, evidently resent seeing their prestige undercut by Vietnamese exactions upon the populace or disregard for local mores. Not infrequently, it appears, they seek to resolve this dilemma by siding with the population. In a recent and typical instance, FUNK officials in one district reportedly intervened on behalf of Buddhist monks when the monks protested that the VC—despite an earlier agreement—insisted on camping in their pagoda. Moreover, the VC had fired on aircraft, causing the temple to be bombed. For their pains, the FUNK officials were beaten up by the Vietnamese; this seems to be a common outcome of such low-level clashes. If they are as frequent as they seem to be, it is difficult to see how FUNK can succeed in building a popular base.

Friction between FUNK and the Vietnamese Communists springs from considerably more than mere xenophobia. Insofar as FUNK enjoys an independent existence, its objectives naturally diverge from those of the VC/NVA. While the Khmer insurgent organization's *raison d'etre* is the defeat and destruction of the Lon Nol government, FUNK adherents seem to be infected with the quite natural belief that their Vietnamese Communist allies are considerably more intent upon exploiting Cambodian resources in their own struggle against the Saigon government.

Although Hanoi certainly attaches greater long-run importance to the struggle in South Vietnam, the relative emphasis which it presently accords the wars against Phnom Penh and Saigon is not easily determined. Nonetheless, it seems that the Vietnamese Communists may now regard the Cambodian theater as the less critical. While the Sihanoukville supply line remains cut and the border bases are no longer sanctuaries, COSVN and its subordinate staffs are considerably less vulnerable than they were in the winter of 1970, land communication with North Vietnam is more secure, the resources of much of the Cambodian countryside are easily available and FANK does not present a major threat. Moreover, since Tet, 1968, Hanoi's ability to recruit troops in South Vietnam has deteriorated precipitately; gaps in VC/NVA ranks perforce must be filled primarily by levies on an increasingly shallow North Vietnamese manpower pool. Thus, even should Hanoi believe an early seizure of Phnom Penh possible, it may well consider it not worth the cost. They would risk heavy casualties. Even if the Cambodian government were to succumb, the VC/NVA could not hope to be immune from aerial interdiction or ARVN attacks. Moreover, Phnom Penh would be a dubious prize unless FUNK should suddenly become a much more reliable prop, for Hanoi would find itself additionally required to defend and govern by proxy a large and hostile urban population.

It is not unreasonable, therefore, that the Vietnamese Communists would accord priority to reviving the flagging effort in southern South Vietnam, while dashing FUNK hopes for an early liberation of Phnom Penh. Low-level reports suggest that the Vietnamese Communists have told FUNK that this is their job, and that it cannot proceed until the FUNK infrastructure and the KLA are equal to the task.

Nor is it unreasonable that FUNK adherents should become bitter as contradictions between their own aims and Hanoi's become more evident. Captured documents, refugee and rallier reports provide evidence of substantial friction over the disposition of Cambodian resources. As the captured circular quoted previously suggests, the respective manpower claims of the VC/NVA and the KLA are one bone of contention; Hanoi has sought to fill gaps in its ranks by levies of ethnic Khmer. Also in dispute are the disposition of captured weapons, the responsibility for opposing ARVN sweeps and, particularly, the VC/NVA's requirements for corvée labor and taxes (or contributions) in kind and cash.

Nowhere, apparently, have these contradictions been more acute than in the heavily populated, contested border districts of the Cambodian provinces of Svay Rieng, Prey Veng, Kandal, Takeo and Kampot. These areas to the Vietnamese Communists are vital terrain; they must be controlled if supply links into the Mekong Delta and the Saigon area are to be reestablished. Moreover, they have been for some time the refuge of a number of intermediate VC/NVA commands forced out of their jurisdictions in South Vietnam proper. One Viet Cong province committee, for example, has sought to annex most of southern Kandal province and to monopolize taxation of the lucrative river trade on the River Bassac there. Similar land grabs have been reported at a number of other points along the border. The local FUNK administrations, despite their dependence on VC/NVA support, have lost none of the historical Khmer sensitivity to Vietnamese imperialism; friction has been constant and armed clashes frequent. Efforts by COSVN advisors to arbitrate these disputes seem to have been largely unproductive. Much of the substantial ethnic Vietnamese minority on the Cambodian side of the border, which in many cases served as a pretext for local VC/NVA claims to joint sovereignty, has fled into GVN-controlled territory.

Conclusion: Force or Figleaf?

The extent and vigor of FUNK's support among the Cambodian rural population remains a matter of considerable doubt. Thus, whatever is known about its genesis, its organization and its relationship to the Vietnamese Communist apparatus in Cambodia, FUNK's potential as an insurgent movement is uncertain. The internal contradictions described above appear to impose severe limits. However, the Cambodian government's present military and political weaknesses, its reliance on conventional tactics, and its uneasy dependence on South Vietnamese support provide the Communists with exploitable opportunities.

It is possible, of course, to identify the zones administered by FUNK. Virtually everywhere FUNK's sway over the population seems to be roughly proportional to the density of VC/NVA forces in an area. The phenomenon so often noted in South Vietnam of government and underground insurgent administrations coexisting in the same village, vying for the support of the population, so far seems to be unknown in Cambodia. In northeast and much of northern Cambodia, where VC/NVA battalions overwhelmed FANK in the spring and summer of 1970, increasingly tight controls have been instituted upon the population. Conversely, in the western provinces of Pursat and Battambang, where VC/NVA units have not penetrated, FANK has been able by and large to limit the Khmer Rouge bands long active there to occasional forays from their mountain camps. In the densely populated delta of southern Cambodia, where the contending forces are most evenly matched, the classic revolutionary warfare pattern of government-held towns and insurgent-dominated villages is being repeated. It is the population here, in the heartland of the Khmer nation, which FUNK must rally to its banner if it is to present a viable political and military challenge to the government in Phnom Penh.

In the south, as elsewhere, most of FUNK's gains seem so far primarily attributable to the umbrella provided by the Vietnamese Communists. Several VC/NVA regiments moved deep into the area in April and May 1970, and since then have constituted the principal threat to FANK's grip on the major towns and roads. The government forces, hastily recruited and usually poorly equipped and trained, seldom venture into the countryside in less than battalion strength. The refugee exodus of the summer of 1970, when most village officials, teachers and merchants decamped on the arrival of the VC/NVA armed action teams, has subsided; travelers from the Communist-controlled zones are now often greeted with suspicion. FUNK administration of the insurgent-held villages is now more largely a Cambodian affair, but the VC/NVA advisors at village level and above seem still to exert substantial and probably controlling influence. Trade with government-held towns is embargoed with varying degrees of effectiveness. Taxes on the Communist-controlled population appear initially to have been light, but to have grown in severity. Men of military age are pressed to join main- and local-force units or, if reluctant, to serve as village guerrillas.

While the typical reaction of the provincial elites to the institution of FUNK control seems to have been avoidance (in the first half-year of the war the population of Phnom Penh alone doubled, an influx of one-tenth of the nation's population), the delta peasant's typical reaction seems to have been reluctant acquiescence. Cambodian farmers, according to Jean Delvert, have not been a greatly oppressed class.[3] They eat very well. Landholding is quite evenly distributed, tenancy uncommon and indebtness of manageable proportions. Nor has the Khmer peasant been, unlike his South Vietnamese counterpart, politicized by thirty years of war or moved to covet a higher living standard by the expansion of mass communications or the market economy.

The VC/NVA armed action teams, then, have had an uphill struggle. Despite the predictions of some western observers, Prince Sihanouk's misfortune apparently did not stir great indignation in rural Cambodian hearts. This provides probably the best explanation for Communist propagandists' pronounced shift of emphasis away from the rally-round-the-Prince theme late in 1970. According to scattered reports, FUNK and VC cadre have gained somewhat better results from depicting the government of Lon Nol and Sirik Matak as a slave of the Americans and the GVN. The Phnom Penh regime, they proclaim, is in collusion with the South Vietnamese to deprive Cambodian farmers of their land and crops. Reports of atrocities perpetrated by ARVN or FANK troops are lovingly embroidered, and there is sufficient direct or grapevine corroboration of these stories to impress the villagers. The rural Khmer are promised that the VC/NVA will leave just as soon as they are no longer needed to help the fledgling KLA defend against ARVN incursions.

There is evidence that in scattered areas of southern Cambodia VC/FUNK propaganda and organizational activity, supplemented by selective terrorism, has begun to generate some popular support. In time, and particularly if the Cambodian government cannot dispense with ARVN help or adapt its military tactics, FUNK's base may broaden and evolve into a respectable insurgent force. Nonetheless, the heavy hand of the Vietnamese Communists in FUNK remains obvious to the rural Khmer. Fear and hatred of Vietnamese imperialism is embedded in the national's historical consciousness, and appears to be as operative against the VC/NVA as against ARVN. As related above, the ethnically, linguistically and culturally alien Vietnamese Communists seem prone to bias and insensitivity, and accounts of friction between FUNK and VC cadre, or incidents between VC/NVA and Khmer villagers, with FUNK caught in the middle, are legion. The Vietnamese Communists' urgent requirement for Cambodian resources—labor, food and cash—to shore up their deteriorating position across the border in South Vietnam injects an extra element of tension. The handful of educated Cambodians who initially joined FUNK from loyalty to their deposed prince has apparently grown increasingly disenchanted.

By the late summer of 1970, COSVN reportedly "considered the speed with which [FUNK] had developed to be phenomenal," and was calling it "the most rapidly developed revolutionary movement in history." However, if this assertion was meant to be anything more than internal propaganda, it appears that COSVN was to a great extent confusing form with substance. As long as FUNK remains vexed by fundamental contradictions—its own dependence on the VC/NVA, intra-FUNK hostility between Communists and Sihanouk loyalists, and, probably of greatest significance, the divergent objectives of the Vietnamese Communists and their Khmer allies—it seems likely that FUNK will remain little more than an elaborate figleaf for Vietnamese Communist military occupation of Cambodian territory.

Notes

1. *Agence France Presse*, 25 September 1970.

2. For a journalistic account of the takeover of a village in Kandal province by an armed action team, see *New York Times*, "Cambodian Describes Life Under Red Rule," 20 July 1970.

3. Delvert's monograph, *Le Paysan Cambodgien* (Paris and The Hague, 1961) establishes him as the leading Western authority; see also his article, "Cambodian Peasants in the Tempest," *Le Figaro*, 2 July 1970.

Indochina in North Vietnamese Strategy

Melvin Gurtov[1]

Introduction

"The American interventionists are not only plotting to turn these three countries [Laos, Cambodia, and Vietnam] into their colonies but to use them as bases for aggression in China, to suppress the liberation movement of the peoples in Southeast Asia, and to plunge the world into a new World War . . . . The basic task of the Vietnam, Cambodian and Laotian revolutions is to drive out the French aggressors and the American interventionists, so as to achieve the genuine independence of Vietnam, Laos and Cambodia." So said the United Front manifesto announced by the Viet Minh radio in March 1951 following a conference of leaders of the three insurgent movements.[2] Nineteen years later, the *dramatis personae* had changed somewhat,[3] but the script was quite similar. Delegations representing the Democratic Republic of Vietnam (DRV) and the National United Fronts of Laos, Cambodia, and South Vietnam held a Summit Conference of the Indochinese Peoples that issued a declaration of mutual purpose on April 27, 1970. The declaration stated in part:

In the face of the treacherous manoeuvres of the United States . . . , the conference calls on the three peoples [of Indochina] to redouble their vigilance, strengthen their solidarity and intensify the struggle against the common enemy—American imperialism and its flunkeys in the three countries—until complete victory. Inspired by the principle that the liberation and defense of each country is the affair of its own people, the different parties undertake to do everything possible to render mutual support in accordance with the desire of the interested party and on the basis of mutual respect.[4]

The similarities in these two declarations underscore the historically close relationship between the Vietnamese Communist revolution and the balance of forces in Laos and Cambodia. To achieve their primary national objective of reunifying Vietnam under the Lao Dong Party's authority, first the Viet Minh and now the North Vietnamese and the National Liberation Front of South Vietnam (the NLFSV) have consistently had to coordinate their Vietnam strategy with their military and political actions throughout Indochina. When Premier Pham Van Dong spoke at the April 1970 conference of Indochinese unity in struggle as being "the decisive factor for our victory,"[5] he was only reiterating a long-standing maxim of Vietnamese Communist strategy.

To be able to state with some precision the nature of North Vietnam's interests in Laos and Cambodia, and their implications for the DRV's strategy in the next few years, I shall recount briefly the highlights of approximately 40 years of Vietnamese Communist involvement in Indochinese affairs.

Developments from 1929 to 1962

Politically and ideologically, the origins of Vietnamese Communist interest can be traced to the Indochinese Communist Party (ICP), founded in Hanoi in June 1929. It was one of three leftist Vietnamese revolutionary groups which, at Comintern's order, merged in 1930 to become a new ICP under Ho Chi Minh's leadership.[6] That the party's interest extended beyond Vietnam in more than name alone did not become apparent until the period of resistance against Japanese rule during World War II. A party central committee conference in November 1940 decided that "the party must prepare to take over the sacred tasks of leading the oppressed peoples of Indochina in armed violence to seize their freedom and independence."[7] At its eighth conference in May 1941, the central committee, in announcing the birth of the *Viet Nam Doc Lap Dong Minh Hoi* (the Viet Minh), also promised that the anti-Japanese, anti-French struggle in Indochina would become a single effort.

... the Eighth Conference ... totally expressed the issue of nationalism within the framework of each of the countries—Vietnam, Cambodia, and Laos—in the spirit of a mutually dependent and closely interrelated national liberation revolution of the peoples of these three countries goading and helping one another to achieve victory. Thus, the conference simultaneously combated the enemy scheme to divide the three nations and enabled two friendly peoples, the Khmer people and the Lao people, to develop their independence and autonomy and to actively contribute to the fight against French and Japanese fascism. . . .[8]

It remained until the immediate postwar period, when the Democratic Republic of Vietnam (DRV) was proclaimed in Hanoi (September 1945) and the Viet Minh-French conflict began (December 1946), for Vietnamese Communist contacts with resistance forces in Laos and Cambodia to be politically and militarily consequential. But such contacts were not entirely successful in promoting the Viet Minh struggle. In Laos, Prince Souphanouvong, returning from central Vietnam in 1946, brought along some Viet Minh advisers to support his attempt to organize resistance against the French authorities. But the prince was apparently more interested than were other leaders of the Lao Issara (Free Lao) movement in cooperating with the Viet Minh. In 1949, the Issara leadership, based in Thailand, ousted the prince.[9] Later that year, it returned to Vientiane to head up the newly independent Laotian Government (which, however, was still tied to the French Union), leaving Souphanouvong to continue in rebellion with Viet Minh support.

In Cambodia during this period, there likewise was disagreement among the nationalist forces that the Viet Minh sought to use to their own advantage.[10] King Sihanouk headed a moderate group that was willing to negotiate with the French for independence, while Son Ngoc Thanh and others in the Khmer Issarak (Free Khmer) movement demanded armed resistance and formed an exile government in Thailand. Some Khmer Issaraks received help from the Viet Minh, whose cadres helped set up a Khmer People's Liberation Army (KPLA) in 1946 and a "resistance government" in southern Cambodia in 1950-51. Sihanouk, in the face of rebellion from two sources and French intransigence on independence, was able to rally some Issaraks to his cause by warning of Viet Minh aggression and by eventually obtaining French agreement (in November 1949) to Cambodia's independence—as in Laos, howeever, on terms that compromised Sihanouk's control of the Cambodian armed forces.

To support their own and outflank French Union forces, Viet Minh activities in Laos and Cambodia increased sharply during 1953 and 1954. This was preceded by more open integration with their allied "liberation" forces in Laos and Cambodia, namely, Souphanouvong's Free Laos Front and Resistance Coalition Government (formed in August 1950 and known collectively since then as the Pathet Lao), and the KPLA. These two essentially puppet movements, which contributed marginally to the Viet Minh's military operations,[11] met in November 1950 and again in March 1951 with their Viet Minh mentors to establish a single united resistance front and military alliance. Since the governments of Laos and Cambodia opposed Viet Minh involvement in their countries, these meetings were probably meant to legitimize the Viet Minh's presence in Indochina, then and subsequently, as supporters of the only nationalist movements willing to fight the French colonial army.

By the time of the Geneva Conference, the Viet Minh had fulfilled its evident intention to make greater use of the Indochina battlefront. Due largely to General Giap's offensives in the spring and fall of 1953, the Viet Minh held sizable portions of northeastern and southern Laos. Viet Minh forces were also strong in northeastern Cambodia. The importance to the Viet Minh of being able to exploit Indochina for mobile warfare was no better illustrated than in Giap's dramatic siege of Dien Bien Phu, which was preceded in December 1953 by a feinting operation toward Thakhek (on the Laos-Thailand border) that succeeded in dispersing French forces from the northwest corner of Vietnam.

At the Geneva Conference, the Viet Minh delegation tried unsuccessfully to use these territorial advantages in Laos and Cambodia to gain political recognition of the Pathet Lao and "Khmer Issarak" (i.e., KPLA) movements. Pham Van Dong argued at the second plenary session (May 10, 1954) that these movements were de facto governments carrying out democratic reforms in the areas their armies had liberated. He demanded that their status as equals of the Laotian and Cambodian governments be recognized, and that they be allowed to participate in national elections.[12] These demands (with the exception of the one concerning elections) were turned aside, apparently with some assistance from China's Premier Chou En-lai.[13] But the agreements eventually reached concerning the regroupment of Pathet Lao and KPLA troops, and the withdrawal of Viet Minh forces from Laos and Cambodia were sufficiently loose as to have satisfied DRV interests in at least two respects: first, in making possible the retention in both countries (though far greater in Laos than in Cambodia) of a capability for renewed fighting; second, by assuring Vietnamese Communist access to and political influence in Indochina, especially desirable at a time of rapidly receding French involvement.

The Geneva accords worked well in Cambodia but broke down in Laos, largely because political leadership was stable in Cambodia (under Sihanouk) but fragmented in Laos, because Communist military forces (indigenous and Vietnamese) were more numerous and better organized in Laos than in Cambodia, because the DRV's security (and Chinese and Soviet interest in it) was related much more closely to developments in Laos than in Cambodia, and because soon after the Geneva Conference, Laos became a setting for international power politics while Sihanouk was moving toward an accommodative neutralism. The result was that whereas, in Cambodia, Sihanouk's authority was publicly affirmed and the Khmer Communists remained weak and politically isolated,[14] in Laos political alignments were fluid, open to competition and bargaining in which the United States shortly became involved.

The North Vietnamese were evidently determined not to reduce their leverage in these circumstances by carrying out their commitment to withdraw completely from Laos. Instead, their military and political advisers helped the Pathet Lao to consolidate the Communist position in the regroupment provinces of Sam Neua (where Souphanouvong had established his resistance government in April 1953) and Phong Saly.[15] North Vietnamese leaders were probably confirmed in their suspicions and their policy by events after the supplementary National Assembly elections of May 4, 1958, in which the Neo Lao Hak Sat (the Laotian Communists' political party, which was legally entitled to compete) was denied the fruits of its sizable gains at the ballot box by the United States-supported government of Phoui Sananikone.[16] The experiment of Phoui's predecessor, Prince Souvanna Phouma, with the kind of coalition government envisaged in the Geneva accords had failed to prevent civil war.

The fighting that ensued and lasted until mid-1962 had a dual significance for North Vietnam. With respect to Communist influence in Laos, it provided both a challenge and an opportunity to consolidate and expand the Pathet Lao's assets at the expense of the United States-supported right-wing generals. At first put on the defensive by RLG attacks and the imprisonment of their leaders, the Pathet Lao responded with a major offensive in the summer of 1959 that was spearheaded by units of the North Vietnamese Army (NVA).[17] The Communists also took advantage of political upheavals in Vientiane that included a coup by Captain Kong Le and a countercoup by General Phoumi Nosavan in 1960, events that pushed the neutralists and Souvanna Phouma to the side of the Pathet Lao. Before the next set of agreements was signed at Zurich and Geneva, Communist forces had government units on the run, and probably would have taken over most of Laos had not the threat of overt United States intervention been so immediate.

Also of importance to the DRV, by 1959, was the insurgency in South Vietnam. What has come to be known as the "second war" in Laos had its origins then: the infiltration of men and supplies into the South over the Ho Chi Minh Trail network in the Laotian panhandle.[18] It was probably no coincidence that in the spring of 1961, as the Geneva Conference got under way, the NVA/Pathet Lao offensive reached south into the panhandle area.

The DRV's position with respect to Laos and South Vietnam was measurably strengthened as a result of the Geneva Conference on Laos (May 1961 to July 1962). Although the Pathet Lao may not have obtained the political representation in the tripartite coalition to which their military gains entitled them,[19] their political status and territorial control were greatly improved. From the DRV standpoint, of particular importance in the accords were the recognition of the Pathet Lao as a legitimate and powerful force in the new Government of National Union, the erosion of the political and military strength of the right wing tied to the United States, the expansion of PL-controlled territory in northeastern and northern Laos, and the assumption by Communist forces of control of the entire border area of eastern Laos approximately from the 19th parallel to the Cambodia border (and thus adjacent to South Vietnam).[20] The fact that the United States had been compelled by virtue of the Geneva accords and the Zurich Agreements (June 22, 1961) to recognize the Souvanna government and withdraw support from Phoumi Nosavan's forces also assisted the Communists' expanding effort in South Vietnam. While United States special forces teams were removed from Laos, a good many North Vietnamese units were not.[21] With the situation thus tentatively stabilized in Laos, the way was cleared for intensified Communist pressure on the Diem regime in Saigon.

Involvement in Laos and Cambodia Since Geneva

The de facto partitioning of Laos after the Geneva Conference provided the geographical setting for the "two wars" that has not changed significantly to the present time. In the north, fighting centered on the Plain of Jars. In push-pull fashion, North Vietnamese-supported Pathet Lao units took the offensive in the dry season, only to yield in the rainy weather to RLG forces backed by United States air power. For the DRV, the pattern was acceptable, since it required a fairly small investment of cadres, soldiers, and logistical support to assure that the Pathet Lao would keep up the pressure on Souvanna Phouma's government.[22] There was no urgency to attempt a takeover of the entire country, which has generally been regarded as feasible with strong NVA involvement but at the great risk of inviting direct American and possibly Thai ground intervention. Meanwhile, North Vietnamese control of access routes from the DRV into eastern Laos and thence into South Vietnam went unchallenged. Although the Saigon government had gained the RLG's agreement to send Vietnamese forces into the Ho Trail area as early as 1964, not until February 1971 did it do so.[23]

Effects of Sihanouk's Removal

In terms of the war in South Vietnam, the Ho Trail network increased in value by 1965, when direct and extensive North Vietnamese and American ground involvement began. The northeast corner of Cambodia, and portions of the Cambodia-South Vietnam border areas, also took on importance for Vietnamese Communist strategy at that time. The Sihanouk government had become increasingly friendly toward Hanoi and Peking, and increasingly hostile toward South Vietnam (with which it broke relations in August 1963) and the United States (with which it severed aid relations in December 1963 and diplomatic ties in May 1965). But Sihanouk's friendship, by which he hoped to keep the Vietnam conflict from involving Cambodia, could not be entirely reciprocated by North Vietnam, especially when the war started to intensify. Hanoi's leaders refused, for instance, to state in writing their respect and recognition of the existing Vietnam-Cambodia border.[24] And, pending the end of hostilities in the South, Hanoi also turned down Sihanouk's bid in 1965 to have the Geneva conferees reaffirm and guarantee Cambodian neutralism and territorial integrity.[25] By then, Vietnamese Communist forces needed the border regions of Cambodia for rest and sanctuary from United States pursuit, for infiltrating men and supplies from the Laotian trails area, and for supplying Viet Cong units in the Mekong Delta of South Vietnam by way of Sihanoukville (now, Kompong Som).

Intensified Vietnamese Communist military operations in Laos and Cambodia beginning in 1968 may have been related to the Tet offensive in South Vietnam and to the DRV's acceptance of President Johnson's proposal (on March 31) of a partial bombing cessation in return for beginning negotiations. Departing from their previous pattern in Laos, Communist forces continued their attacks into the wet season. In the north, they moved within striking distance of the royal capital at Luang Prabang, and in the south, they ranged beyond the Ho Chi Minh Trail area.[26] Viet Cong use of sanctuaries in Cambodia increased at this time, to the point where Prince Sihanouk, faced with the possibility of United States-ARVN forays in pursuit of the insurgents, publicly admitted that Communist infiltrations (which he distinguished from "implantations") were occurring.[27] Early in

1968, with the resurgence of Cambodian Communist dissidence that the Royal Government previously declared had been suppressed, the prince went further. He charged that Viet Cong and Pathet Lao agents were assisting dissident Khmer Loeu and other tribesmen in the northeast; and he allowed that some Viet Cong base camps and hideouts might exist in inaccessible, uninhabited areas of Cambodia.[28] These developments in Laos and Cambodia seem to have been prompted less by Hanoi's desire to improve the positions of its Communist insurgent allies than by a North Vietnamese decision to strengthen their own hand once negotiations began with the United States.

The drive for increased territorial holdings in Laos and for consolidation of the base areas in Cambodia continued during 1969. Again, Hanoi's purpose seemed to be to exploit Communist advantages and capabilities in Laos and Cambodia at the Paris talks. Between March and June in Laos, Communist forces captured the key government base of Na Khang in Sam Neua, successfully maintained their drive to oust government troops from the Bolovens Plateau in the south, and took over Muong Soui (on the western edge of the Plain of Jars) from RLG Neutralist forces.[29] Hanoi coupled the offensive to a diplomatic initiative: its ambassador to Laos, Le Van Hien, reportedly returned there after a lengthy absence to present Souvanna Phouma with a proposal for stopping the offensive and eventually withdrawing some NVA troops if Souvanna would request the cessation of heavy United States air attacks on the Ho Trail area.[30] Had the offer been accepted, it would not only have sanctioned the farthest Communist military advances in Laos to date, but would also have assured their use of the trails area with impunity.

The expansion and consolidation of Viet Cong base areas in Cambodia proceeded simultaneously with the drive in Laos. Investigation by senior Cambodian military leaders disclosed that the Viet Cong had been launching operations from the border provinces into South Vietnam.[31] Protests to the NLF and DRV missions in Phnom Penh only produced repetition of previous pledges to respect Cambodia's territorial integrity. In the fall of 1969, Sihanouk reported the presence of about 40,000 Vietnamese Communist soldiers in the border provinces.[32] These events were not without effect on the prince's policy. In late April, he issued the first order for Cambodian army units to attack Viet Cong encampments; and in June, he agreed to have the American Embassy reopened.

Nineteen hundred and seventy began in much the same way as the two previous years. North Vietnamese and Pathet Lao forces retook the Plain of Jars and Muong Soui, and advanced on other strategic outposts in central and southern Laos. Once again they coupled these moves to a peace proposal. On March 6, the NLHS issued a five-point plan whose main feature was the suggestion that an all-Laotian political conference be convened to establish a provisional coalition government and to decide the conditions for general elections. A subsequent telegram from Souphanouvong to Souvanna Phouma indicated that the complete halt of United States bombing was a precondition to negotiations.[33] Before further action on the proposal could develop, however, the overthrow of Prince Sihanouk (March 18) occurred.

Sihanouk's removal had a profound impact on North Vietnamese strategy in Indochina. It meant the end of Cambodian cooperation to ensure that the port of Sihanoukville would be open to Communist ships delivering war materiel for use in South Vietnam. It meant the start of collaboration between Cambodian and South Vietnamese army commanders along the border in actions (some jointly, most by the ARVN alone) against Viet Cong units in the Cambodia sanctuaries. By the end of April, with the entry of United States and ARVN units into the sanctuaries without Phnom Penh's formal approval, Vietnamese Communist forces in Cambodia were in retreat, forced either to move deeper into the interior, thus threatening to isolate Phnom Penh, or to solidify their hold over the northeast at the junction of Laos, Cambodia, and South Vietnam. Cambodian neutralism had changed from friendly to hostile toward the Communist world, and with that change, Cambodia became—as Sihanouk had warned just prior to his ouster—a "second Laos."

The initial North Vietnamese and NLF reaction to the overthrow of Sihanouk was to attempt to negotiate with General Lon Nol, the new leader. But Lon Nol, in no mood to compromise and probably encouraged by the prospect of receiving military support from the United States and the GVN, demanded the complete and rapid withdrawal of Communist troops from Cambodia. Negotiations never really got started, the DRV and NLF withdrew their diplomatic missions, and, on March 21, Radio Hanoi vowed solidarity with the Cambodian people's struggle. In response to Sihanouk's five-point declaration from Peking on March 23 that announced plans to form the NUFK and an exile Royal Government of National Union (both of which were later revealed to have pro-Hanoi Khmer Communists in key positions), Hanoi quickly issued a statement of strong support. The statement made clear that North Vietnam's future strategy in Indochina would be geared to the new situation of three fronts:

The more the United States imperialists intensify and expand the war and the more they resort to perfidious manoeuvres to divide the Indo-Chinese peoples, the tighter the Vietnamese, Khmer and Laotian peoples will close their ranks and the higher will be their determination to fight and defeat them. . . . The coup d'etat of March 18, 1970, in Cambodia can in no way save the United States imperialists, but will on the contrary cause them to sink deeper in the quagmire of a still more disastrous defeat.[34]

The strong possibility implicit in this statement that North Vietnamese forces would respond elsewhere in Indochina to loss of the sanctuaries in Cambodia soon became a reality. They gained control of large areas of north-central and western Cambodia, and speedily cut off access routes to the capital. The made northeast Cambodia and southern Laos a single massive new sanctuary following the seizures (for the first time since 1962) of Attopeu and Saravane in southern

Laos. By gaining control of these towns and the surrounding areas, the North Vietnamese were able to direct supplies to units in Cambodia and South Vietnam over the Se Kong and Mekong Rivers. Southern Laos soon became a major NVA logistical and troop development center—a natural consequence of the United States-ARVN Cambodia operation that led to the ARVN invasion, with United States air support, of the Ho Trail area in February 1971.

Until the invasion, the North Vietnamese and the Pathet Lao, without public Chinese support, had continued their efforts to begin peace talks with Souvanna Phouma. But in view of events in Cambodia, the previous NLHS terms for negotiations stood no chance of gaining acceptance unless modified to suit Souvanna and his military supporters.[35] Toward the end of 1970, the NLHS proposal did change significantly: instead of demanding a complete halt to the United States bombings throughout Laos, the Pathet Lao were willing to begin talks if the bombing was stopped only in Sam Neua and Xieng Khouang Provinces.[36] In terms of North Vietnamese strategy—and it is very unlikely that the new proposal, any more than previous ones by the NLHS, originated without Hanoi's approval—the concession on the bombing may have reflected Hanoi's reassessment of feasible alternatives in Laos in light of the changed Cambodia situation. Now, a cease-fire limited to the Plain of Jars (but without requiring a prior NVNA withdrawal) would be preferable to no cease-fire at all.[37]

North Vietnam's Future Strategy

In the aftermath of the United States-ARVN incursions into Cambodia and Laos, repetition of which might be repeated in future dry seasons, how are North Vietnamese interests in Indochina, and their Indochina strategy in the next few years, affected? According to figures presented in February 1971 by President Nixon, the NVA has committed about 90,000 men to Laos, over 50,000 (including Viet Cong) to Cambodia, and approximately 100,000 to South Vietnam.[38] He stated then that "Hanoi has made the war an Indochina conflict." But the war has been an Indochina *conflict* since 1946; and the close relationship of Laos and Cambodia to Vietnamese Communist strategy has been recognized since the founding of the ICP in 1930. It is precisely because of the interdependence of the three countries in that strategy that North Vietnam cannot be expected, any more now than in 1954 or 1962, to withdraw completely from Laos or Cambodia so long as the objective of reuniting South Vietnam under Communist control is still unsatisfied.[39] In the absence of an ability to react in any of several locales in Indochina to United States-ARVN military moves, North Vietnamese leaders seem to believe they would risk losing the initiative in the war. The balance of forces, a key concept in their military thinking, would then tip in the opponent's favor.[40]

The cruciality to the North Vietnamese of maintaining an Indochinese dimension in their strategy relates not only to their paramount objective of bringing about a rapid and total United States withdrawal and completing the Communist revolution in Vietnam. It also relates to their objective of eroding, and preventing the restoration of, the United States presence and influence in Laos and Cambodia. The governing of those two countries by compliant regimes that are friendly to North Vietnam and hostile to United States policies is thus a major interest of the DRV. In the event of Communist control of South Vietnam, the DRV probably would want to assure that, in return for pledges of noninterference (such as Pham Van Dong gave at the April 1970 summit conference), Cambodian and Laotian governments are not hostile to Communist Vietnam. Military aid or advisory relationships with the United States would have to be terminated. North Vietnam's ties to Communist insurgent movements in Cambodia and Laos would be a powerful source of leverage to assure that they act in conformity with DRV interests. It is also conceivable that some kind of loose Indochinese federation might be proposed by Hanoi as a means of monitoring its neighbors' behavior.[41] Not to be omitted either is the possibility of a tacit DRV-Thailand arrangement to divide Laos into two spheres of influence that would satisfy each country's security interests at Laos' expense.

Speculating more specifically, however, about North Vietnamese policies and objectives in Laos and Cambodia over the next few years is a hazardous undertaking for a number of reasons. American tactical and financial support of South Vietnamese, Cambodian, and Thai military operations in Indochina seems certain to continue, but at what level and with what objectives—hence, with what impact on those governments' strategy and on North Vietnamese planning— remain unclear. The state of Sino-Soviet relations would affect Hanoi's policies if relations should so deteriorate as to jeopardize their respective military and economic assistance programs for the DRV.[42] Division in the North Vietnamese leadership could also occur, for instance, over the priority to be accorded the armed forces and domestic reconstruction—although the post-Ho leaders seem determined to meet the requirements of both, as William Turley's piece argues. Finally, it is always conceivable that North Vietnamese and allied insurgent forces, whether faced with an abundance or a scarcity of external aid, might suffer a serious loss of will to continue their struggle. It must be stressed, however, that all the evidence, present and past (see the essay by Konrad Kellen), indicates that Communist forces in Indochina can maintain high morale and the determination to fight on, even under conditions of material deprivation and the necessity to lower tactical objectives.

These contingencies need to be kept in mind, but they do not pose insuperable obstacles to looking slightly ahead of the present. In Laos, North Vietnamese policy will probably continue to be guided by considerations of strategic advantage (relative to South Vietnam), the security of the DRV's borders, and the political compatibility of the Vientiane government. VNA and Pathet Lao forces can be expected to maintain military pressure in northern Laos until they can gain the RLG's agreement to at least a partial bombing cessation.[43] A major offensive westward against the RLG-held Mekong Valley towns (including Luang Prabang) must always remain a possibility, despite prospects of direct United States, ARVN, and/or Thai intervention. Should North Vietnamese leaders decide that significant new territorial gains are necessary in Laos in order to outflank the United States Vietnamization program, compel a cease-fire that would enable the NVA to concentrate resources elsewhere in Laos or Cambodia, and demonstrate that Hanoi retains the initiative in Indochina, they might make the attempt. Such a move, of course, would have implications for China and the Soviet Union in the event the United States response in northern Laos should raise the risk of a direct confrontation of major-power forces. But so long as a Laos offensive is in reply to allied military pressure (in Laos or, perhaps, in North Vietnam itself), the DRV could probably count on China's and (less enthusiastically) the Soviet Union's political and material support.

Politically in Laos, it is difficult to imagine the NLHS and Hanoi accepting a settlement that would merely restore to the Pathet Lao the four cabinet seats they gained in 1962. The growth and increased territorial holdings of the Pathet Lao, their establishment of effective administration in the northeast, and their superior military assets (when linked to North Vietnamese support) make it probable that they would insist upon being accorded a dominant position in any new coalition. Hanoi could then expect to deal with a "neutral" government that would recognize North Vietnam's security interests in the eastern border provinces, would be receptive to North Vietnamese operation of the Ho Trail area, and would reflect the DRV's international policy views. The time might also be propitious for Hanoi to bargain with the Thai Government over their respective "spheres" on terms that might assure the DRV of Thailand's nonintervention in Laos in exchange for de facto Thai control of Laotian territory west of the Mekong.

In southern Laos, the NVA command must now take into account future United States-supported South Vietnamese incursions to attempt to frustrate Communist buildups. North Vietnamese planning with respect to a major offensive in I Corps and the central highlands of South Vietnam may consequently have to be reconsidered. Although it is apparent that Hanoi can count on Moscow and Peking to refurbish materiel losses sustained in Cambodia and Laos,[44] Hanoi's leaders may have to reevaluate how they will allocate their resources in view of the continued extensive involvement of United States air power in Indochina while ground forces are being gradually reduced.

One possibility is that priority in North Vietnamese strategy will, temporarily, be given to rebuilding the Cambodia sanctuaries after solidifying control over southern Laos and northeastern Cambodia. Without writing off support of the Viet Cong, North Vietnam might deemphasize prospects for generating high-level military action in South Vietnam and instead concentrate on expanding Communist holdings in the border areas of Cambodia.[45] Pressure on South Vietnam would, in this strategy, be applied mainly from outside rather than from within the country. Compared with the post-Tet (1968) calls from Hanoi for a "general offensive," the strategy would mark a further scaling down of Communist ambitions and activities within South Vietnam; but it would also be in keeping with China's oft-stated preference (which the Soviet Union would also have grounds for supporting) for protracted, low-level fighting in which United States and ARVN strength can be eroded primarily by guerrilla warfare.

As for the Communist movement in Cambodia, the North Vietnamese will probably continue to use it as a means of exerting pressure on the pro-United States government in Phnom Penh, as a front for Vietnamese Communist military activities in Cambodia, and, over the long run, as the basis of a pro-Hanoi alternative to either the present regime or the unpredictable and popular Prince Sihanouk. For the moment, Hanoi and the NUFK have rejected in advance any compromise solution that would bring the fighting to a halt, partition Cambodia, or imply recognition of the Lon Nol Government.[46] Instead, it is claimed (as in 1954) that a people's administration already exists in Cambodia, the head of which is Khieu Samphan, a Khmer Communist who has been Sihanouk's bitter enemy in recent years.[47] From Communist sources, the impression is strong that Hanoi prefers gradually to build up the Khmer Communist movement, exploiting Sihanouk's sympathetic statements from Peking while developing the tight organization, leadership, and base areas that (it is hoped) will undermine Phnom Penh's authority and reduce the movement's need of Sihanouk's support.

A deal with Phnom Penh is much more likely to be offered when the indigenous Communist movement is strong (as in Laos) and when circumstances in South Vietnam are favorable to Communist forces than, as at present, when the NUFK is patently Vietnamese-controlled and when success in South Vietnam is still uncertain. Hanoi, through the NUFK, might then insist upon the formation (as in Laos) of a coalition government that would reflect Communist territorial predominance and military superiority. As with a Pathet Lao-dominated government, North Vietnam would seem to prefer a coalition responsive to Vietnamese Communist political and security needs to a purely Communist regime whose claims to neutrality and independence would lack international or domestic credibility.

Implications for United States Policy

The depth and longevity of North Vietnamese involvement in Indochinese affairs, and the high probability of their continued involvement for as long as the fighting in South Vietnam necessitates it, raise questions about the wisdom of American policy in recent years. Since the end of the 1954 Geneva Conference, four American administrations have contributed massive amounts of material assistance to rightist governments in Indochina, have matched if not outdone Communist violations of the Geneva accords, have supported clandestine as well as conventional military operations in each of the countries, and have committed United States ground forces (now declining) and air power (now expanding) to achieve favorable balances of forces for anti-Communist regimes.

It might be argued on the basis of my primarily historical presentation that these United States policies, though costly and unable to produce security for America's Indochinese clients, are still preferable to accepting what might amount to a North Vietnamese sphere of influence in Laos and Cambodia. Without a large American investment, the dominoes would assertedly long since have fallen.

I will offer here only two short answers to this argument.[48] The domino hypothesis assumes that American policy has consistently been defensive and reactive. But Communist strategy in Indochina has frequently turned on United States-initiated pressures, such as in Laos in 1957-1958 and 1964, and Cambodia in 1970. The United States bears considerable responsibility for the character and breadth of North Vietnamese involvement in those countries.

Furthermore, the desirability and feasibility of American support—overt and covert, political and military—to governments mainly on the strength of their proclaimed anti-Communism may be doubted. Debate will always be inconclusive concerning the popular credentials of the contending factions in each of the Indochinese countries at war; but there should by now be little doubt that the American attempt to influence these internal struggles through primarily military means cannot resolve them, weakens and even destroys the possibilities for national reconciliation through local political accommodations and negotiations, and brings new suffering to the present populations trapped in the middle of the battle. Unless and until the United States acknowledges these circumstances—by rejecting further intervention in Indochinese politics and discontinuing its own and proxy military activities there—the future is likely to see a gradual erosion of the positions of the governments it supports, with decreasing prospects for the survival of sovereign Laotian and Cambodian nations.

Notes

1. Any views expressed in this paper are those of the author. They should not be interpreted as reflecting the views of The RAND Corporation or the official opinion or policy of any of its governmental or private research sponsors. Papers are reproduced by The RAND Corporation as a courtesy to members of its staff.

2. Quoted in Ellen J. Hammer, *The Struggle for Indochina* (Stanford, California: Stanford University Press, 1954), p. 262.

3. Ton Duc Thang, now President of the DRV, represented the Viet Minh in 1951; Premier Pham Van Dong led the delegation in 1970. Prince Souphanou-

vong represented the Lao Communist movement on both occasions. The Cambodian representation marked the only historical discontinuity: a pro-Viet Minh Khmer Issarak (Free Khmer) named Sieu Heng was the principal figure in 1951, but in 1970, the just-ousted Prince Norodom Sihanouk, who had fought to maintain independence from both the French colonialists and the Communists (Vietnamese as well as Cambodian), headed the delegation of the NUFK (National United Front of Kampuchea).

4. Text of the declaration in *Peking Review* (May 8, 1970): 3-6.

5. Ibid. (April 25, 1970), p. 29.

6. See Truong Chinh, "Ho and the Introduction of Leninism into Vietnam," *Nghien-cuu lich-su* (*Historical Studies*, Hanoi), May-June 1970, trans. Joint Publications Research Service (JPRS) No. 52240 (*Translations on North Vietnam*, No. 857), January 25, 1971, p. 17. The Comintern directive was republished in *Nhan Dan*, January 6, 1970. The new ICP was founded in October 1930 in Hong Kong and, in 1931, was officially recognized by Comintern. Ho Chi Minh declared in November 1945 that it was being dissolved, but in fact, the ICP remained active underground.

7. Lao Dong Party Central Committee, Historical Research Department, *The August Revolution (1945)*, trans. JPRS No. 52097 (*Translations on North Vietnam*, No. 844), January 4, 1971, p. 8.

8. Ibid., p. 13.

9. See Hugh Toye, *Laos: Buffer State or Battleground* (London: 1968) Oxford University Press, pp. 77-80, and George Modelski, "The Viet Minh Complex," in *Communism and Revolution: The Strategic Uses of Political Violence*, edited by Cyril E. Black and Thomas P. Thornton (Princeton, New Jersey: Princeton University Press, 1964), p. 195.

10. This paragraph relies on Roger M. Smith, *Cambodia's Foreign Policy*, (Ithaca, New York: Cornell University Press, 1965), pp. 26-51.

11. In Laos, for instance, the most careful study of the Pathet Lao states that "the Lao troops were never a significant factor in the Viet Minh's ultimate success. (Estimates of their troop strength ranged from 1500 to 3000 troops at the time of the 1954 Geneva Conference.) Most of the Lao units . . . were used merely for support activities." Paul F. Langer and Joseph J. Zasloff, *North Vietnam and the Pathet Lao: Partners in the Struggle for Laos*, (Cambridge, Massachusetts: Harvard University Press, 1970), p. 51.

12. Geneva Conference, Second Plenary Session (Indochina Phase), *U.S. Verbatim Minutes*, pp. 61.

13. Sir Anthony Eden, in *Full Circle* (Boston, Mass: Houghton-Mifflin, 1960), p. 145, revealed that Viet Minh withdrawals from Laos and Cambodia were not agreed to by the Communist side until mid-June, when Chou told Eden the Viet Minh could be persuaded to withdraw, and the royal governments recognized, provided the United States did not establish military bases in the two countries.

14. Sihanouk's personal rule was overwhelmingly approved by popular referendum in February 1955, and his political movement—the Sangkum Reastr Niyum—won handily in National Assembly elections held in September 1955 under the supervision of the International Control Commission. The Communist

Party in Cambodia—the Pracheachon—neither then nor later was a significant source of opposition. But at the time, Sihanouk did charge that a number of Viet Minh soldiers had not withdrawn from Cambodia and had in fact stayed in the countryside or merged with the Vietnamese minority in the cities.

15. See Langer and Zasloff, p. 62. These provinces were formally restored to the king's authority in November 1957, with Pathet Lao officials, however, retaining a considerable voice in province affairs. Souvanna Phouma and Souphanouvong also agreed at that time, in return for legalization of the NLHS and two cabinet seats, to demobilize about 4300 Pathet Lao troops and to integrate about 1500 into the Royal Laotian Army. See Arthur Dommen, *Conflict in Laos: The Politics of Neutralization*, (London: Pall Mall Press, 1964), p. 86.

16. Nine of the 13 NLHS and allied candidates who ran in the elections won, and Prince Souphanouvong was the top vote-getter. But Phoui, after replacing Souvanna Phouma as prime minister in August 1958, excluded Souphanouvong and another NLHS minister, Phoumi Vongvichit, from his cabinet, and thus allayed American concern about growing Communist influence in the Laotian government. For further detail and comments on the United States role, see ibid., ch. 6.

17. Ibid., pp. 68-69.

18. Ibid., pp. 70-71.

19. It was agreed in June 1962 that Souvanna Phouma would be prime minister, the rightist Phoumi Nosavan deputy prime minister, and Souphanouvong also a deputy prime minister. Of nineteen cabinet posts, eleven went to neutralists and four each to representatives of the NLHS and the rightists.

20. See the map in ibid., p. 75.

21. Dommen, pp. 239-240. At the checkpoints set up by the ICC in Laos, 666 American military personnel passed through and only 40 North Vietnamese. Several thousand NVA troops did leave secretly, but several thousand probably remained behind.

22. The reversal of Communist support of Souvanna's prime ministership occurred after the right-wing coup of April 19, 1964, when Souvanna authorized United States reconnaissance flights and jet air attacks on Pathet Lao positions. Since then, Hanoi and the Pathet Lao have maintained that Souvanna is only qualified to represent the Vientiane faction, not the national union government, which has ceased to exist.

23. The agreement was reached in March 1964 between General Phoumi and South Vietnamese Premier Nguyen Khanh (Dommen, p. 255). South Vietnam's invasion of the Ho Trail area in 1971 was not, however, based upon exercise of the 1964 agreement.

24. Several discussions involving Cambodian, North Vietnamese, and NLFSV spokesmen took place during the 1960s. Sihanouk did not obtain their written agreement until mid-1967—and then, apparently only because the Soviet Union committed itself on the issue, forcing the DRV, the NLF, and China to follow suit.

25. This occurred at the Indochinese People's Conference (March 1965) of Cambodian, North Vietnamese, and leftist Indochinese delegations. Sihanouk had also then hoped to elicit support for his proposal to neutralize Cambodia,

South Vietnam, and Laos in exchange for United States withdrawal from the region. Because of opposition from Hanoi and Peking, the prince did not deliver the speech containing his plan; but it was published. See Royaume du Cambodge, *Discours de S.P. Norodom Sihanouk Upayuvareach, chef de l'état du Cambodge, à l'occasion de l'ouverture de la conférence plenière des peuples indochinoises*, Ministry of Information, Phnom Penh, February 25, 1965.

26. Robert Shaplen, "Our Involvement in Laos," *Foreign Affairs* 48, no. 3 (April 1970): 485.

27. In a letter to the *Christian Science Monitor*, 27 October 1967.

28. These charges were made in broadcasts by Sihanouk over Phnom Penh domestic service on 23 April, 24 May, and 17 August 1968.

29. A strong RLG counterattack in September recaptured the Plain, however.

30. Shaplen, "Our Involvement . . .", pp. 485-486.

31. See, for example, the report of Lieutenant General Nhiek Tioulong, commander-in-chief of the army, in *Neak Cheat Niyum (Le Nationaliste*, Phnom Penh), 24-30 March 1969.

32. Phnom Penh radio broadcast by Sihanouk, 18 October 1969.

33. Arthur Dommen, "Laos in the Second Indochina War," *Current History* 59, no. 352 (December 1970): 331.

34. Statement of the Government of the DRV, March 25, 1970, in *Peking Review*, no. 14 (April 3, 1970): 19.

35. Arthur Dommen has described the Laotian generals' exhilaration at the United States-ARVN incursions in Cambodia, and their anticipation—which may have worried Hanoi—that the United States might be prepared to acquiesce in the overthrow of Souvanna and thus put an end to the neutralization experiment. Even though their expectations have not been met, the generals probably continue to exert influence against Souvanna's acceptance of peace talks while North Vietnamese troops are still in Laos. The ARVN operation in Laos in 1971 could only have strengthened the rightists' hand. But Souvanna's own reluctance to debate the NLHS and the North Vietnamese, because of his past experiences in negotiating with them, should not be discounted. Dommen, *Laos*, p. 332.

36. Vientiane domestic service, 29 November 1970. The proposal was to hold the talks in Khang Khay, on the Plain of Jars, and to suspend the bombing in the two provinces for a number of days before, during, and after the talks. The RLG's counterproposal was for North Vietnamese troops to withdraw from these provinces and for the bombing to be suspended in and around the towns of Khang Khay and Sam Neua. Radio Pathet Lao, 16 December 1970.

37. See R.P.W. Norton, "The Rocky Road to Peace," *Far Eastern Economic Review* (January 23, 1971): 43-45.

38. In the President's 1971 State of the World Message; *New York Times*, 26 February 1971, p. 12. See the map on p. ix for North Vietnamese troop strength.

39. Thus, for instance, proposals to the DRV for cease-fires and mutual withdrawals in Indochina prior to a political settlement in South Vietnam will invariably be rebuffed by Hanoi. See the DRV Foreign Ministry's statement on President Nixon's five-point proposal of 7 October 1970, broadcast by VNA (Hanoi) international service, 14 October 1970.

40. North Vietnamese commentaries on the significance of Communist military actions in Laos and Cambodia to the balance of forces may be found, for instance, in Radio Hanoi domestic service, 24 May 1970; and in the NVA publication, *Quan Doi Nhan Dan* (*People's Army*, Hanoi), June 1, 1970 and October 26, 1970. These commentaries make the point that as United States troop withdrawals proceed under the "Vietnamization" program, American forces will lose the manpower and the mobility to cope with Communist armies on three fronts. Incursions by ARVN and United States forces, such as into Cambodia, are explained as desperate efforts to resurrect the balance of forces before Vietnamization thoroughly depletes United States combat strength.

41. The federation concept was raised at the aforementioned Indochinese People's Conference in 1965. When the conference agenda was set up in February, one of the items included for discussion was creation of a permanent secretariat of the Indochinese states to symbolize and promote the area's solidarity. (Phnom Penh broadcast to Southeast Asia, February 18, 1965.) Sihanouk subsequently elaborated that periodic conferences would take place at which common economic and political problems would be discussed. (In an interview with a correspondent of *Mainichi Shimbun;* see *Kambuja* (Phnom Penh), No. 38, 15 May 1968, p. 14.) But the prince apparently feared that a federation might exacerbate rather than alleviate Cambodia's border problems with a Communist Vietnam. As an unsigned editorial in the Sihanoukist weekly, *Réalités cambodgiennes*, said on 31 May 1968, there existed the danger that a federation might be "dominated by a Communist neighbor country," and that Cambodia's territorial integrity might be harmed as a result. During these years, no concrete steps seem to have been taken to implement the federation idea.

42. Short of that circumstance, however, North Vietnamese leaders have demonstrated time and again in recent years their ability to capitalize on Sino-Soviet differences to meet the DRV's aid requirements without sacrificing independence in policymaking. The political and ideological competition between the two Communist powers, the Hanoi leadership's cohesion and determination to act independently, and the DRV's ability to maintain neutrality toward (while urging unity of action in) Sino-Soviet relations help account for North Vietnam's successful "blackmailing" of its larger partners. North Vietnamese policy in wartime is a classic illustration of how a small power can exert leverage over larger powers despite being highly dependent on them for material assistance.

43. The DRV Foreign Ministry at first reacted to the ARVN invasion of the Laos panhandle by saying it was "wrecking the meeting between the representatives of the two princes in Laos and all the NLHS efforts to peacefully settle the Laotian problem." (Hanoi domestic service, February 5, 1971.) But interviews by Japanese correspondents with Pathet Lao representatives later on elicited confirmation that the NLHS would continue to seek negotiations and would not set up a provisional government of its own. On April 27, 1971, Souphanouvong made a new proposal to Souvanna Phouma (Vientiane domestic service, May 13, 1971), in the wake of new Communist advances in the Bolovens Plateau. In return for a United States bombing halt throughout Laos, the NLHS would agree to a total cease-fire in place, to be followed by political consultations on a provisional coalition government. Souvanna rejected the offer.

44. After the allied incursions in Cambodia, the Soviet Union signed a supplementary military and economic aid agreement with the DRV on June 11, 1970. Additional Soviet assistance to meet new North Vietnamese needs was probably also involved in a technical aid agreement signed a few days after the South Vietnamese invasion of Laos. Both agreements were in addition to annual Soviet aid commitments. Supplemental Chinese economic and military assistance was announced by Hanoi in February 1971.

45. Although a North Vietnamese-backed effort to overthrow the Cambodian government is also a possibility, there seem to be many more disadvantages than advantages to such an operation, even though Hanoi could probably expect Chinese and Soviet military assistance. The advantages would be that it would lead to the emplacement of a pro-Communist regime in Phnom Penh, erode the confidence and effectiveness of the Cambodian armed forces, and put Communist forces in position to attack the former sanctuary areas from the rear. Against this operation are these considerations: it would probably require one or more additional NVA divisions to be committed to Cambodia (at present, it is generally believed that only about 5000 NVA troops are actually engaged in fighting against the Cambodian army); it would take substantial resources to seize and hold Phnom Penh (especially if the ARVN chooses to defend it); it would amount to a blatant act of takeover that would belie Hanoi's (and Peking's) talk of a popular Sihanoukist liberation movement in Cambodia; and it would not necessarily improve North Vietnam's ability to assist Viet Cong forces in South Vietnam.

46. VNA (Hanoi) international service, 24 October 1970; statement of the NUFK and Sihanouk's Royal Government, as broadcast by New China News Agency (Peking), 27 October 1970.

47. Khieu Samphan is a deputy premier of the exile government and minister of defense. The claim of a people's administration having been established in five liberated provinces was made by Khieu Samphan over Liberation Radio (to South Vietnam), 20 November 1970, and in a Radio Hanoi domestic service commentary on 18 January 1971.

48. For further comment, see Gurtov, *Southeast Asia Tomorrow: Problems and Prospects for U.S. Policy* (Baltimore: Johns Hopkins Press, 1970), pp. 16-18 and 83-87.

10 Cambodia's Foreign Relations: Sihanouk and After

Bernard K. Gordon[1]

In the year since Prince Sihanouk was deposed in Cambodia, there have been revolutionary changes in that nation's foreign policy and its international relations. These changes have transformed relations with both types of states with which Cambodia (now the Khmer Republic) is primarily concerned: the major powers, including China, the United States, and the Soviet Union, as well as with the smaller nations of Southeast Asia and Indochina.[2] What remains unchanged, however, is an important objective characteristic of Cambodia in modern world politics: it is one of that handful of nations (Israel, and perhaps Jordan and Pakistan) whose leaders believe their state's continued national independence and existence is not to be taken for granted. In these few nations, there is an unmatched urgency and immediacy to problems of foreign policy.

For Cambodia, during the years of independence since 1953, this belief in the proximate possibility of national extinction led to a foreign policy style that was both highly flexible and highly successful—given particularly the meager material resources available to sustain Cambodian independence, and the many elements in the Asian environment that threatened its survival. Most prominent among the resources was the diplomatic skill, based on a principle of exploitation, that was developed and deployed by Prince Sihanouk. By "exploitation" I mean the technique by which the Prince manipulated the interests and policies of other nations in ways that would work to the benefit of Cambodia. Because this required much flexibility, Cambodian policy under Sihanouk seemed often to be merely erratic, whereas it was in fact an internally consistent approach. The approach contained at least three elements.

The fundamental *goal* and purpose of Cambodian foreign policy is survival. The *operating principle* designed to achieve this goal is to establish that survival as a value for those other states which have potential control over Cambodia's destiny. The *method* by which to implement this principle is constantly to focus on Cambodia the attention of world leaders directly concerned with Southeast Asia.

Cambodia, because it lacked the "usual ingredients of power and influence, must exploit the one asset it does possess: the mutual interest of other states in Cambodia's continued independence."[3]

Much—but not all—of that approach has continued to characterize Cambodia's foreign policy since March 1970, when the Prince was ousted. The government led by General Lon Nol and Sirik Matak has also sought, in other words, to impress upon other nations that the survival of an independent Cambodia serves several national interests. But in material terms, post-Sihanouk Cambodia has also been able to call upon far greater resources than were ever available to the Prince. It has, in particular, been able to draw upon direct budgetary assistance from the United States for both economic and military purposes, and it has also been given direct combat help—for military operations within Cambodia itself—by the United States and by other nations. In dollar terms alone, the assistance granted Cambodia by the United States in the months since Prince Sihanouk's removal has amounted to more than $250 million, and will very probably approach $300 million in the fiscal year that begins in July 1971.[4] To place that amount in perspective, it should be recalled that during the entire *decade* of United States assistance to Cambodia that ended in 1965, *all* forms of aid totaled no more than $341.3 million.[5]

Relations with Russia and China

This high level of United States assistance to Cambodia by the end of 1970, it needs to be remembered, was developed from a zero figure only a few months before. For American aid had been terminated—at Prince Sihanouk's request—by 1965. In the intervening five years, Cambodia's relations with China had intensified, and from 1967 onward, the Soviet Union in particular undertook a careful and pragmatic cultivation of its relations with Phnom Penh that appears to have been quite effective. As I have pointed out elsewhere, the USSR sent as its Ambassador to Cambodia one of its most senior and experienced diplomats, Sergei Kudryavtsev.[6] As might be expected, however, Cambodia's present heavy dependence on the United States is not seen in Moscow to be altogether consistent with close relations with the USSR. As a result, Ambassador Kudryavtsev (but not the Embassy) has gone home, the Russian aid program he instituted is in limbo, and Cambodian-USSR relations today are neither broken nor active.

Not so for China, which of course has provided a place of exile—some might say house arrest—for Prince Sihanouk. Under Sihanouk, Cambodian relations with China had developed steadily during the 1960s. Peking developed a modest aid program in Cambodia,[7] and probably found it useful to point to Cambodia— like Burma—as an illustration of the point that peaceful relations with nearby Southeast Asian states were entirely consistent with Chinese policies.

From Prince Sihanouk's viewpoint, and although there was at least one important instance when he was quite critical of Chinese activities in his country,[8] the relationship with Peking was considerably more important. Among other things, it provided him with a place to which, like a vassal of an earlier era, he could bring complaints about a neighbor, and appeal for China's help.[9] This he did often, in the hope that China's influence in Hanoi would help inhibit the North Vietnamese from taking too many liberties in Cambodian territory. And the Prince also hoped, of course, that China would act as a counterweight to American influence in the region—for he long believed that Thai and South Vietnamese expansionist ambitions were encouraged by the relative security provided to them by their American defense umbrella.

For restraints against the Thai and South Vietnamese, the present government in Phnom Penh can no longer look to China. From Peking's viewpoint, Lon Nol and Sirik Matak are a retrograde step, and it probably has to be accepted that China will seek ultimately to bring about a change in the foreign policy stance of Cambodia. This does not mean that Prince Sihanouk necessarily will remain China's chosen instrument, for there are probably few illusions there about the extent of domestic support in Cambodia for the Prince. It is a pleasant myth, of course, that the Prince was overthrown because there was a sudden elite disaffection with his foreign policies, particularly his inability to deal effectively with the presence of North Vietnamese forces in Cambodian territory. In fact, the events that led to his removal from power derived as much from internal dissatisfaction with his development and economic policies, and the corruption that surrounded his entourage, as from any upset with his foreign policy.

China's initial reaction to the arrival of the Prince in Peking—only hours after his removal—reflects this knowledge. The meeting at the airport was reserved,[10] and there was no initial mention of his ouster by the official China press agency, *Hsinhua*. Indeed, Peking's official support for Sihanouk's government in exile was withheld for more than two weeks, and diplomatic relations with the government in Phnom Penh were not broken until early May—i.e., until *after* the joint United States-South Vietnamese armed intervention into Cambodia on April 30, 1970. Moreover, some reports indicate that for almost two months after the overthrow of the Prince, China carried on secret negotiations with the Lon Nol government, perhaps in the hope that the North Vietnamese sanctuaries would be respected.[11]

When it became apparent that Lon Nol was instead prepared (as Prince Sihanouk used to predict) to "turn to the Americans," and that the United States would in fact respond with a massive program in Cambodia, China in turn proceeded to make much use of Prince Sihanouk during 1970. His statements throughout the year were given wide dissemination in *Peking Review*,[12] and it is, of course, likely that they were drafted for him—for all followed completely China's line that there is *one* Indochinese struggle in which Cambodia is simply a part. Thus, the Khmer people were called upon by their former leader to undertake a "protracted peoples' war," and "wage revolution and struggle against the imperialist powers of Asia."

The point has frequently been made that the Prince has done little to promote his chances for a return to Cambodia (he denies that he aspires to) by his long stay in Peking, and by his willingness to act as a spokesman for China's policies. These acts are seen in Phnom Penh as profoundly antinational, for they play primarily into the hands of the North Vietnamese. At the same time, and as we have already suggested, the present Cambodian government has forfeited any right to expect future help from China in attempting to deal with the North Vietnamese. On balance, it has to be concluded that one element on which the Prince used to count for support—China's interest in maintaining an independent Cambodia—has been removed during the year since his removal.

The Soviet relationship with Cambodia today is more complex. As part of its efforts to promote what Dr. Gurtov has referred to as the "national-socialist model,"[13] the USSR embarked on a state-to-state relationship with Cambodia under Prince Sihanouk. An impressively pragmatic program of economic assistance, education, and technical aid was begun, and it seems apparent that the Soviet Union is hesitant today to break the connection altogether. As we noted earlier, diplomatic relations continue (a *chargé* is present in Phnom Penh), but like the absent Ambassador himself, more than one hundred Soviet teachers simply have not yet returned to Phnom Penh from their summer vacation.[14] Yet despite this evident freeze in relations, the simple fact of continuing Soviet representation in Phnom Penh, and the concomitant fact that the USSR has not recognized Sihanouk's exile government, is a point of support for the Lon Nol government. The Prince accurately assessed the result of these policies when he complained recently that "Lon Nol pretends that his regime is a popular one, and he tells the Cambodians that the proof that he is not proimperialist is that the Russians . . . choose to stay in Phnom Penh."[15]

Soviet ambivalence to the Khmer Republic is evident in a number of ways, and probably must be explained in terms that have little to do with Cambodia itself. Most important is the Soviet desire not to be ejected altogether from a state in Southeast Asia at a time when the entire pattern of Russian policy in the region has been characterized by a widening involvement—as in Singapore, Malaysia, and the Philippines. Similarly, the extent to which the Prince has associated himself with China's aims and preferred methods makes it simply unacceptable—in the context of Sino-Soviet relationships—for the Soviet leaders also to endorse Sihanouk. To do so would complicate unnecessarily Moscow's preference to build useful relationships with a number of Asian governments—most of which regard Lon Nol and Sirik Matak as the legitimate Cambodian leadership, and which are themselves apprehensive regarding China.

Yet, it is also quite apparent that nothing keeps the Lon Nol government viable as much as its American dollar support, and for the Soviet Union, there are evident difficulties in appearing also to support that government. Thus, when a Japanese correspondent reported recently that the Soviet aid program in Cambodia was continuing, and that Russian trucks were still being supplied for military use,[16] there was a quick denial from the Soviet Embassy in Tokyo.

On a more important scale, the same unease and difficulty was illustrated during the spring and summer of 1970 by the events surrounding the so-called

Djakarta Conference on Cambodia. That meeting, which was inspired by Foreign Minister Adam Malik of Indonesia, was convened ostensibly to find some sort of resolution to the worsening situation in Cambodia. It should be mentioned here because it illustrates the extent to which Cambodia—long ignored—has become increasingly a focus of Asian interest. Planning for the meeting began in April, and in one sense, it was of course upstaged when the United States (with South Vietnamese forces) began its two-mo⟨...⟩ Cambodia. But the conference is an important landmark in post⟨...⟩ way, because it represented the first time since the defeat of 194⟨...⟩ rticipated in an overtly political meeting among Asian nations c⟨...⟩ pecifically with a political problem. The meeting was also a maj⟨...⟩ up for Malik, not only because it was held in so short a time, ⟨...⟩ of the very senior level of representation (there were Prime Mi⟨...⟩ was represented by its Foreign Minister).

Nevertheless, the initial Soviet reac⟨...⟩ he conference was one of denunciation—as voiced by *Tass* press releases and by articles in *Pravda* and *Izvestia*.[17] The argument presented by the Soviets was that there was no need nor justification for an international conference, and even after the conference had concluded, this continued to be Moscow's expressed view. However, a primary symbolic result of the Djakarta meeting was the appointment of a senior three-man committee of Asian diplomats, charged with the responsibility to contact leaders in several world capitals in a follow-on effort to implement the resolutions of the conference. The membership[18] of the committee was important: Japan, Indonesia, and Malaysia. One of its first announced intentions was a plan to visit Moscow, which put the Soviets in a difficult position. On June 11, for example, Moscow had announced an increase in the level of its military and economic aid program to North Vietnam. Yet, less than a week later, Foreign Minister Gromyko agreed to meet with a committee of three appointed by a conference that Hanoi had refused to attend. Not surprisingly, the Soviet press made no mention of the visitors.

Cambodia's Asian Neighbors

Although Cambodia's ultimate fate may be affected most by its great-power relations, the most striking feature of the 1970-71 period is the shift in Cambodia's relations with its Asian neighbors—especially those that are closest. Historically, Cambodia has suffered from the pressures of population and territorial expansion of the Thai and Vietnamese peoples, and as a result, both have been regarded as the main threats to Cambodia's independence, identity, and territorial integrity. As compared between the Thai and Vietnamese, the Cambodians have reserved their special dislike and fear for the Vietnamese, both because of the greater difference in cultural background and traditions, and also because Vietnamese were the agents and minor officials of the French colonial administration in Cambodia.

In the period since independence, relations with both have been troubled and formal diplomatic ties were broken throughout much of the past decade (with Thailand in 1961; with South Vietnam in 1963).[19] The problems involved territorial disputes; money issues deriving from the French colonial period when the the Indochina states were in a single economic unit; personality conflicts (heightened by Prince Sihanouk's ability to attract headlines); and (least important) differences in East-West foreign policy alignment.

With regard to the other states of Southeast Asia, there were no such conflicts, but neither was there much contact. Aside from ceremonial visits—as with Indonesian and Philippines leaders—Cambodia under Prince Sihanouk was much removed from Southeast Asia, and in some respects seemed in process of becoming as withdrawn and isolated as Burma. There was a short period—from 1954-56—when Prince Sihanouk may have considered an altogether different foreign policy posture, and it has long been rumored that at one point he contemplated even joining SEATO. But whatever the truth of that report, it is apparent that by the late 1950s, he had decided upon a policy of so-called nonalignment, which in practice meant that Cambodia increasingly was withdrawn from many aspects—economic and political—of Asian affairs.[20]

Sihanouk's purpose was to insulate Cambodia, as much as possible, from the conflicts and controversies that generally characterized not only Indochina but much of Southeast Asia during the 1960s. Thus, the Prince tended to restrict Cambodia's involvement in the region largely to ECAFE matters, and even participation in meetings of the Mekong Development Committee was often on an uncertain basis. There was outright rejection, of course, of the invitation tendered to him by Malaysia and the Philippines in 1959 to participate in developments that led to the Association of Southeast Asia (ASA), a group that included Thailand as well. Similarly, the Prince refused to participate in the broadened regional group that was formed in 1967, when Indonesia and Singapore joined with the ASA members to form the Association of Southeast Asian Nations (ASEAN).

Against that background, the changes since mid-1970 are little short of revolutionary. Not only has Phnom Penh become the focal point of political interest by many of its neighbors, but Cambodia itself has undertaken a vigorous and active effort to achieve among the nations of Southeast Asia, what the Prince sought only among the major powers: acceptance of the belief that Cambodia's independence is an objective important to others as well. This was the main theme argued by Cambodia's representatives at the Djakarta Conference of May 16-17, 1970, where they lobbied for direct material help, and it has continued to be the argument pressed by Koun Wick, Phnom Penh's Foreign Minister. He has traveled widely throughout Asia in recent months, stressing the most un-Sihanouk-like view that "the [Cambodian] government . . . hopes for closer relations with the countries in this region, and that goes for all spheres."[21]

To some extent, as will be shown later, this effort has been successful, for in addition to the roles of Thailand and South Vietnam, economic and indirect military assistance has also come from Australia, New Zealand, Malaysia, and others. Indeed, it is likely that some leading Indonesians—perhaps even including General Suharto—were initially prepared to extend direct military assistance to Cambodia in the weeks immediately following the ouster of Prince Sihanouk. The Indonesian role deserves special mention, for it is very likely that in mid-April 1970, in direct response to General Lon Nol's appeals, a small group of Indonesian military personnel visited Phnom Penh to evaluate Cambodian needs and potential Indonesian help. Among the roles considered were shipments of arms, training facilities for Cambodian troops, and even the direct deployment of a small number of Indonesian troops in Cambodia. Their visit, which was never publicized, appears to have taken place between April 10-19, while Foreign Minister Malik was in Manila and Bangkok in connection with his plans for the Djakarta Conference.[22] Very probably, the mission (variously reported to include from a dozen to sixteen officers) was organized by General Ali Murtopo, President Suharto's adviser on intelligence matters and head of OPSUS (the Indonesian Army's office for special operations).

Details of this mission are not likely to be known for some time, but General Murtopo did not deny its existence in a conversation with this writer in Djakarta during June 1970. It was apparently composed largely of logistics personnel, and reflected in part the view among Indonesian Army officers that the efforts of Foreign Minister Malik would not be relevant to the real needs of the Cambodians in the period immediately after Sihanouk's ouster. Thus, the OPSUS representative in Cambodia appears to have assured the Lon Nol government that arms aid would be forthcoming from Indonesia—or so Cambodian spokesmen stated to foreign newsmen. The Indonesians, for their part, are likely to have believed that any arms and ammunition shipped to Cambodia would somehow be replaced or compensated by the United States.[23]

In fact, however, Adam Malik put a stop to all this. He learned (reportedly *via* the Soviet Embassy in Djakarta) of the visit to Phnom Penh by Indonesian officers, and no doubt quickly petitioned President Suharto to ensure that no Indonesian military assistance would be provided Cambodia. Among other considerations, Malik's reasoning included the view that the hoped-for Djakarta Conference could hardly be convened if Indonesia itself became a party to the fighting. Thus, Malik issued a formal denial that a special military group ever did go to Phnom Penh in April 1970, and the explanation was instead put out that newsmen must simply have seen members of the staff of the Indonesian military *attaché*.

By early 1971, however, it became apparent that Cambodia's requests for practical military assistance from the wider Southeast Asia region have in fact been heeded—certainly in Kuala Lumpur, and probably in Djakarta as well. In February 1971, Foreign Minister Koun Wick visited a number of Malaysian military and police installations, including the special training center for counter-guerrilla training near Penang. He reported on his return to Cambodia that the Malaysians had expressed a firm interest in training Cambodian police in coun-terguerrilla operations, and only a week later, the Cambodian press announced that a Malaysian delegation (led by the Deputy of Police in charge of training) had arrived in Phnom Penh "in order to [prepare] for the training of Cambodian police in Malaysia."[24]

This direct step by the Malaysian government may become the largest single factor—when the Malaysian role becomes widely acknowledged—in removing the restraints on an Indonesian military assistance role in Cambodia. After the Army-civilian *imbroglio* of mid-1970, whic   onesia on July 2 formally to reject Cambodia's appeal for military help   not surprising that little has been done in this field. Yet, reports con   culate that some Cambodian military personnel are being trained in In   Perhaps these are instructors who will be expected to pass on the rest   leir experience once back in Phnom Penh.[26]

Exchanges and visits among the mili   nations have continued (an Indonesian group visited Phnom Penh   Wick was in Djakarta),[27] and a certain amount of sympathy for Lon   government exists among the senior military in Indonesia. The Indonesians are proud of the special training facilities they have developed at Bandung and elsewhere, and in recent years have had to turn away Asian requests for billets at their Command and General Staff College (SESKOAD) because of insufficient space. It is likely that the Indonesian Army leadership will want to assist the Cambodians, and one of the main reasons for not doing so—that it would compromise Indonesia's nonalign-ment—will be diluted to the extent that the increasingly neutralist government of Malaysia finds no obstacle in providing defense help to Phnom Penh.

Relations with Thailand and South Vietnam

Up to this point, we have dealt largely with only those instances of Cambodia's widening Asian contacts that have been relatively free of major difficulties and tensions. It will be apparent to any newspaper reader, however, that South Viet-nam and Thailand, with which Cambodia shares borders, have either caused diffi-culties for Phnom Penh or have themselves experienced difficulties because of Cambodia's involvement in the Indochina war.

The problems with South Vietnam were readily predictable, and began to re-ceive widespread attention not long after General Lon Nol demanded—on March 13, 1970—that North Vietnamese and associated forces leave Cambodia. Shortly after, when President Nixon announced on April 30 that both United States and South Vietnamese forces would undertake military operations within Cam-bodian territory, the way was open for a host of problems between Saigon and

Phnom Pe⁓ ⁓as been widely reported, the deportment of South Vietnamese
forces wi⁓ ⁓mbodia was often reprehensible, and led the very senior Cambodian ⁓ General Sosthen Fernandez, to complain.

> Sou⁓ ⁓iese troops rape, they destroy houses, they steal, they loot
> pa⁓ ⁓y beat the Buddhist monks. . . . My personal opinion is that if
> we ⁓ ⁓apons, it is better to avoid South Vietnamese help. . . .[28]

There is every indication that this attitude is still held in Cambodia, for there continue to be reports of serious disputes—even armed firefights—between Cambodian and South Vietnamese forces. One incident involved the shelling of a Cambodian border village and a tank attack on Cambodian Army troops by South Vietnamese forces, which in turn led the Cambodian Army to order its aircraft to attack the tanks. It was only the intercession of two American generals that resulted in mutual withdrawals. Apparently, this outbreak in no way resulted from activity of communist forces—it was instead "precipitated by the [Cambodian] arrest of two South Vietnamese soldiers caught stealing bicycles, pigs and chickens. . . ."[29]

Other incidents have occurred, both in Cambodian villages and in Phnom Penh itself. In early February 1971, South Vietnamese marines used their ship docked in the Mekong as a base for rifle and machine gun fire (and grenade launchers), and damaged several Cambodian government buildings. In this case, the violence reportedly arose when the Vietnamese Marines "began stopping all taxi-buses in the street, taking all money and jewelry from the passengers."[30]

Against the background of such events, it seems unfortunate that Secretary of State William Rogers called the military involvement of South Vietnamese forces in Cambodia a perfect illustration of the Nixon Doctrine in action—of Asians helping Asians. Rather, it appears that no binational relationship in Southeast Asia is more prone to ⁓ ⁓nosities and cruel behavior than that between Vietnamese and Cambo⁓ ⁓th the probability of excesses greater on the more powerful Vietnar⁓ ⁓han on the Cambodian. It needs to be remembered that the South⁓ ⁓e forces, which numbered as many as 47,000 during the intervent⁓ ⁓June 1970, have never fully withdrawn from Cambodia. Since ther⁓ ⁓nbers have ranged from 8,000 to 23,000, and reports in February 1⁓ ⁓licated that approximately 21,000 South Vietnamese troops remaine⁓ ⁓bodia—engaged both in the defense of border areas and Phnom Penh i⁓ ⁓well as with planning, training, and supply work in connection with the provision of American military assistance.

Both Indochina governments have instituted special procedures to avoid future incidents likely to result from the continued presence of so large a force of foreigners, who are regarded with deep-seated fears and resentments among the Khmers. On March 6, 1971, for example, a joint commission reported a series of incidents and recommended strong measures to bring an end to South

Vietnamese theft and violence against Cambodian civilians.[32] Moreover, a series of high-level meetings were designed to promote broader cooperation between the two governments. Three Cambodian parliamentary delegations visited Saigon (June and December of 1970, and March 1971), an economic mission was sent in November 1970, and the Cambodian Foreign Minister twice visited South Vietnam. Finally, General Lon Nol personally led a 20-man delegation to Saigon in January 1971.[33]

South Vietnam in return dispatched a number of groups, including three military-assistance delegations (April, July, and September 1970); a parliamentary mission in December; an economic body in October; and in June 1970, Vice-President Ky visited General Lon Nol. This series of meetings resulted in a number of political and economic agreements pertaining to the resumption of diplomatic ties, the treatment of Vietnamese in Cambodia, and the expansion of economic relations. In January 1971, General Lon Nol signed in Saigon a treaty of friendship, and five agreements dealing with border delineation, telecommunications and transportation, and joint use of Mekong River facilities.[34] Apparently, however, there remain unresolved a number of difficult financial issues. South Vietnam, for example, has insisted that Cambodia pay $15 million in troop-support costs incurred during the intervention of May-June 1970. Cambodia has in turn insisted—as Prince Sihanouk did also—that Saigon still owes millions to Cambodia as a result of customs revenues and bank deposits placed, as it were, *in escrow* in Paris at the time of the Geneva settlements of 1954.[35]

Thailand poses an altogether different kind of problem. Cambodia's involvement in the Indochina war has placed significant strains on Thai politics—particularly in the field of foreign policy. Although it has expanded diplomatic, economic, trade and other relations with Cambodia since March 1970,[36] Thailand has shown far greater hesitancy than South Vietnam to undertake military action in Cambodia. The Lon Nol government requested military support from Thailand in the immediate aftermath of the overthrow of the Prince, hoping, apparently, not only for arms, supplies, and advisers, but even for as many as a division of Thai troops.

From the beginning, the Thai response was cautious, although Deputy Premier Praphas agreed to the dispatch of 50,000 sets of "defense support equipment," 20 patrol boats, and aerial reconnaissance assistance.[37] The question of arms and direct troop involvement was then discussed within the Thai Cabinet, and apparently led to intense disagreement—as in Indonesia, partly along military-civilian lines. It appears to be widely believed, especially in the United States, that Thai hesitancy to deploy troops to Cambodia was simply a question of dollars from the United States: that Thai troops would have been sent had the United States been prepared to pay the bill. The realities, however, are far more complex than that narrow and somewhat venal explanation.

To be sure, Thailand must have sought American assurances that a Thai involvement in Cambodia would not work clearly to Thailand's disadvantage, both in security and fiscal terms, but it is also apparent from the public and private debates that took place in Bangkok that the disagreements were substantive as well. For example, there was a most unusual (in the context of Thai politics) panel discussion between Foreign Minister Thanat Khoman and Deputy Prime Minister (and Army Commander-in-Chief) Praphas, before 4000 students at Chulalongkorn University on July 13, 1970. Praphas argued that because of Chinese and Vietnamese aspirations regarding Thailand, "We have to send Thai troops into Cambodia. The Thai government, especially the military officers, feel very strongly that sending Thai troops . . . will serve as a protective and self-helping measure. . . . If Cambodia were taken over, Thailand would face a war."[38]

Foreign Minister Thanat publicly disagreed with that view. In private, he probably argued even more forcefully against becoming involved in a conflict that could interfere with Thai plans to open a dialogue with China, and reinforce the belief in Peking that Thailand is irrevocably tied to the American camp. Moreover, Thanat was sensitive to Adam Malik's argument that the deployment of Thai troops in Cambodia would endanger the then-forthcoming Djakarta Conference and any hopes of a resolution of the conflict in Cambodia that might come from that conference. At minimum, Thai participation would have been endangered.

Thailand's behavior reflects some of these considerations, for Thai policy toward Cambodia from May-September 1970 was quite confused. Initially, Prime Minister Thanom announced that Thailand would send "volunteers" (of ethnic Khmer descent) to Cambodia, and that Thailand would train Cambodian officers within Thailand.[39] Yet, only two days later (in early June), the Thai Cabinet reversed this decision,[40] and Bangkok reports indicated in July—after the Praphas-Thanat panel meeting at the university—that General Lon Nol had reached an agreement with Thanom for the dispatch of some Thai forces.[41] Finally, however, the Thai government announced in September that it had decided against sending *any* forces to Cambodia, including the approximately 2000 ethnic Khmers who had been in training in Thailand since July. Thanat Khoman, who made the announcement, acknowledged the rift that this issue had caused in the Cabinet (some reports suggest that it was resolved only by the King himself) and stressed that Thailand might still have to send troops to Cambodia: but "only in the last extremity, when the question is absolutely life and death."[42]

Since this discussion is not intended to focus on Thailand, little more should be said here about the impact of developments in Cambodia on decisions in Bangkok. It must be stressed, however, that one of the consequences of the formal inclusion of Cambodia into the Vietnam War has been to force the leadership in Bangkok to reexamine some basic foreign policy and national security premises, and the policies that have grown from those premises. In particular, what was a growing tendency to shape Thai policies relatively independent of Indochina considerations may have been arrested.

Historically, of course, Thai leaders have been very conscious of the sensitivity of Thailand's national security to developments in Laos and Cambodia, as well as Vietnam, and I am not suggesting that Thai leaders somehow forgot that sensitivity. In recent years, and particularly in the period since Thanat Khoman has been Foreign Minister, Thai policy has sought to separate Thailand from the Indochina conflic̗ ᵃⁿᵈ ᵗᵒ promote especially close connections with the non-Indochina states   east Asia. Malaysia and Indonesia have been the particular focus of   Southeast Asia interests during the 1960s. In April 1971, Thanat sa   had for some years been trying to develop a "supplementary policy   ᵗlism" to complement Thailand's Western connections.[43] The ref   s policy, of course, is found in Thailand's primary role in the dev̗   of the Association of Southeast Asia (ASA), in 1961, and mor   , of the Association of Southeast Asian Nations (ASEAN), in 19

From the peᵣᵤₚₑ₋₋   United States, and particularly in the context of President Nixon's Guam Doctrine, this long-standing effort of Thailand to promote regional collaboration among the *non-Indochina nations* of Southeast Asia—especially the regional effort among the five nations in ASEAN that includes Indonesia—has been a most welcome development. While it should not be thought of as a goal of immediate practical significance to the United States, the longer-term value of the ASEAN effort in Southeast Asian regional cooperation (for the late 1970s and for the next decade) holds a reasonable promise for helping to reduce the balkanization and conflict potential of much of the area. The nations in ASEAN represent the more developed states of Southeast Asia, and with a population of 204 million, they comprise by far the bulk of the region's population.

From the perspective of Thailand, however, events surrounding Cambodia in 1970 were a forceful reminder to the Thai military leadership—and probably to Thanat as well—of the limits to which Thailand could safely seek to insulate itself from Indochina. In this context, actions of the United States in 1970 were important to Thailand, particularly to the extent that those actions helped intensify the conflict in Cambodia, and brought it to the Cambodian territory proximate to Thailand's borders.

This is not to suggest that the United States brought about the fall of Sihanouk, nor intended to intensify the activities of the North Vietnamese forces in Cambodia—for they had been making free use of portions of Cambodia since at least 1967.[44] But the United States, by virtue of its intervention in Cambodia in 1970, has certainly contributed to broadening geographically the Indochina conflict, and its continued major support for the post-Sihanouk Khmer Republic is also likely, from the North Vietnamese viewpoint, to have heightened the importance of weakening or toppling the regime in Phnom Penh.

These actions brought the Vietnam war closer to Thailand, in a period when Thai leaders were already very worried about the United States commitment to

Thailand's security. Thus, in the Thai view, the threat to its national security has heightened, while the level of support to be expected from its main guarantor—the United States—has appeared to lessen. When the United States also made it clear, in midsummer of 1970, that there would not be direct United States support for the costs of any Thai intervention in Cambodia, nor would any new United States guarantees be forthcoming in the event that a Thai intervention in Cambodia met with heightened North Vietnamese (or even Chinese) responses, Thailand's worries about the United States, and concomitant Thai caution, appear to have increased significantly.

The result is likely to be a Thai policy increasingly emphasizing the need for *rapprochement* with both China and North Vietnam (indeed, that policy course became increasingly evident in Thanat's statements during the early months of 1971). While this goal may be worthwhile, it is also likely to raise inconsistencies—especially with Indonesia and with the goal of regional cooperation. ASEAN in particular may be treated with more caution and less enthusiasm in Bangkok, particularly in the Foreign Ministry. To the extent that progress in ASEAN is slowed and Thailand's heightened concerns with Indochina strain its remarkably easy relationship with Indonesia and Malaysia,[45] the widened war in Cambodia will have caused unanticipated damage, particularly unfortunate from a longer-term American foreign policy perspective.

The Balance Sheet

Is Cambodia today more secure than it was prior to the overthrow of Prince Sihanouk? Do the patterns of international relations in which Cambodia is involved contribute usefully not only to its security, but to the stability of the region and the prospects for peace in Southeast Asia and Indochina?

In any effort to assess the consequences of the shift in Cambodia's foreign relations since Sihanouk, it has to be recognized that the Prince had achieved, to a remarkable degree, the widespread acceptance of Cambodia's right to national existence. To be sure, he had found it necessary to ignore penetration of his nation's borders (largely by the North Vietnamese), and he had also found it necessary to remove Cambodia from most of the developmental thrust in which Southeast Asian nations have been involved. American aid, for example, was foregone, participation in other assistance and development efforts was slight, and the Cambodian economy was increasingly stagnant. Although it is likely that the Prince viewed these sacrifices and the humiliation of Vietnamese encroachment as prices to be paid for independence, ultimately the consequences of meeting these costs led to his overthrow in March 1970.

In the weeks immediately following that event, the prospects for Cambodia's continued political stability, independence, and national existence fell drastically. But by mid-1971, Cambodia's international position had a decidedly up-beat appearance. It may develop, of course, that the internal political instabilities following the illness of General (now Marshal) Lon Nol will prove too much for the new Khmer Republic, but in its foreign affairs, there are a number of credits that must be entered into the balance sheet.

There has been a widening, for example, of the number of nations with which Cambodia has useful dealings. Korea and Taiwan now have regular relationships with Cambodia, and both states have agreed to provide Cambodia with assistance—initially, medicines and related material. Of course, as relations with these two nations were resumed, the Asian communist states broke their ties: North Korea, North Vietnam, and China. Nevertheless, Cambodia's worldwide diplomatic relations remained essentially unchanged for the present government is recognized at the United Nations (only eight of its more than 120 members have refused to accept the credentials of the Khmer Republic), while only 16 governments recognize Sihanouk's exile government based in Peking.[46]

In material terms, however, the roles of Australia and Japan need to be singled out, for the assistance provided by other governments is largely symbolic and some—like the Philippines—have not been prepared to go even that far. Australia, however, had long been providing aid to Prince Sihanouk's Cambodia and is a participant in the Vietnam conflict. Thus, Canberra responded almost immediately to Lon Nol's appeals for military assistance relevant to that conflict, and in June 1970 extended a special grant of A$500,000 to supplement the previously announced 1970-1971 figure of A$600,000. These amounts have been further supplemented, in order to provide for a wide variety of military equipment, including machine guns, radios, trucks, river craft, and so on. An announcement of September 3, 1970, brought the total amount of Australian aid to Cambodia since 1970 to more than $2 million (Australian).[47]

Japan's assistance has been larger, and includes for example the extension of a $2 million grant in June 1970 for medical and other humanitarian aid. An equal amount was then announced in November to provide for trucks and ambulances, and through the provision of such items as leased ferries and the extension of interest-free loans, Japan has maintained a modest but relatively large aid program in Cambodia. The Japanese do not intend to undertake a significantly larger program on a unilateral basis however, and announced in December 1970 that measures were being studied "for reconstruction of the Cambodian economy in the future under a multilateral-international cooperative formula."[48]

All of these figures, of course, become insignificant by comparison with the aid input into post-Sihanouk Cambodia by the United States. The United States has certainly sought to encourage other nations to help in Cambodia, but as so often in the past, the United States has been primarily concerned to add a multinational coloring to its efforts in East Asia. But there is no escaping the conclusion that it is the United States' effort alone which has sustained Cambodia in 1970-71. It is the willingness of the United States government to provide more than $250 million in assistance to Cambodia during the past year that allows us to answer in the affirmative, the question whether Cambodia's security is more assured now than in the period immediately after the overthrow of the Prince.

It also seems likely, however, that if the provision of $250-$300 million annually from the United States is necessary to maintain a nation of six million persons under presently foreseeable Indochina conditions, then the prospects for continued Cambodian independence are not better now than in the period prior to the overthrow of the Prince. For the United States role in Cambodia appears tightly tied to the immediate requirements of Vietnam, and unless there are reasons for expecting a continued American assistance program in the range of $300 million annually for a significant period, Cambodia has not experienced a long-term boost to its security prospects.

The reason for reaching this conclusion lies also in the nature of the change in its international relations that Cambodia has effected. Cambodia has traded a past situation of Soviet and Chinese endorsement for its neutrality and independence and at least the implied support of the United States for the principle of noninterference in its affairs and the integrity of its borders. These items have in effect been traded for the support largely of the United States alone—particularly its dollar support. China certainly has no interest now in endorsing the present Khmer Republic, nor is it reasonable to assume an early resumption of the Soviet aid program and its implied support. Functionally, therefore, Cambodia has narrowed the foreign policy base among the major powers on which its national independence was long predicated, and it no longer has the latitude and maneuverability so well developed by Sihanouk.

There has been, on the other hand, a widening of Cambodia's Southeast Asia relations, and in this context, the assistance roles of Indonesia and Malaysia could become more important, as could Thailand's. Those are fragile supports, however, and despite the fact that the nearest foreign capital to Kuala Lumpur is Phnom Penh (excepting of course Singapore), we should not make too much of Malaysia's interesting willingness to train Cambodian defense personnel. It has its own deep problems, and involvement in the Indochina conflict is not likely to be one it wants. This consideration pertains as well to Indonesia, where there are definitely divergent views on the advisability of providing meaningful military support to Cambodia. Indonesia has the physical capacity to give such support, especially if third parties—such as the United States, Australia and even Japan are willing to pay the bill.

But this also reflects the extent to which Cambodia's fate has itself increasingly become tied to broader Southeast Asian developments, which is something the Prince avoided. Cambodia, as it were, was plucked from its geographic environment by the Prince's foreign policy, and although inward looking and perhaps encrusted, Cambodia was removed from many of the region's difficulties which were at least as troublesome as stagnation. Now, in contrast, and because of Cambodia's formal involvement in the Indochina conflict, its people have had to experience much violence and destruction, and that is a consequence most people will deplore.

Cambodia's situation raises a broader problem which concerns the basic issue of the frontiers in Asia and Southeast Asia. Under Sihanouk, Cambodia was at least a country of no contest between the major adversaries in Asia, and its fate of no great relevance. But the remarks of Alastair Lamb in his splendid new book, *Asian Frontiers* are appropriate.

Conflicts like the Vietnam war, there can be no doubt, have for the major parties involved a significance very similar to that detected at an earlier period [1947] in Greece. Just as the Western victory in Greece was a crucial stage in the definition of the postwar limits of Soviet influence in the Balkans, so the outcome in Vietnam will produce a definition of the limits of Western influence in mainland Southeast Asia.[49]

Having now witnessed the introduction of Cambodia into the Vietnam conflict, we must ask whether the question at issue in that conflict has changed. As Lamb has put it the issue was, simply, "Will there be two Vietnams or one?"[50] What is worrisome now is whether the concept of frontier in Southeast Asia, which previously focused on Vietnam, must now include Cambodia. If the answer is affirmative, then Indochina events of 1970-71, from the viewpoint of peace and stability in Asia, and domestic tranquility in the United States, have represented a backward step.

Notes

1. Miss Kathryn Young has provided invaluable assistance in collecting and organizing much of the material on which this discussion is based, and her help is gratefully acknowledged.

2. This article was prepared during April 1971, and is based on materials available (in the United States) through no later than March 1971.

3. Bernard K. Gordon, *The Dimensions of Conflict in Southeast Asia* (Englewood Cliffs, N.J.: Prentice-Hall, 1966), p. 61 (emphasis added).

4. The United States Embassy in Phnom Penh reportedly has recommended a 10 percent increase in aid, largely for military assistance. *New York Times*, 16 February 1971.

5. See AID, *U.S. Overseas Loans and Grants* (special report prepared for the House Foreign Affairs Committee), 1970, p. 66.

6. Among other distinctions, Kudryavtsev was cited by the Canadian government as probable head of the espionage ring exposed years ago by Igor Gouzenko, and has served as chief Soviet representative and Ambassador in London, Bonn, Paris, Vietnam, and Havana (at the time of the missile crisis). See B.K. Gordon, "Shadow Over Angkor," *Asian Survey* 9, no. 1 (January 1969).

7. China's aid program is detailed in Alain-Gerard Marsot, "China's Aid to Cambodia," *Pacific Affairs* 43, no. 2 (Summer 1969): 190.

8. In the summer of 1967, the Prince recalled all but one of his diplomats from Peking and charged the Embassy in Phnom Penh with actively soliciting

Maoist support among Chinese residents there. See Peter Poole, "Cambodia's Quest for Survival" (American-Asian Educational Exchange, Inc., 1969), p. 39.

9. Peter Lyon has described the relationship in similar terms—as a "neotributary" link which "required diplomatic and other forms of obeissance from Cambodia to China, without necessarily involving a surrender of local autonomy." Peter Lyon, *War and Peace in Southeast Asia* (London: Oxford University Press, 1969), p. 134.

10. According to Sihanouk, he was told in Moscow, on the way to the airport and the flight to Peking, that "you are deposed." China's initial reserve may also be explained in part by uncertainty regarding Sihanouk's Russian connections.

11. Jonathan Unger, "The Lonely Prince," *Far Eastern Economic Review* (February 13, 1971).

12. For Sihanouk's typical messages, see *Peking Review* (May 29, June 12, and July 10, 1970).

13. Melvin Gurtov, "Sino-Soviet Relations and Southeast Asia: Recent Developments and Future Possibilities," The RAND Corporation, P4370 (May 1970).

14. Reported in the *Far Eastern Economic Review* (March 20, 1971).

15. From Sihanouk's interview with Allesandro Casella, *L'Expresso*, 27 (December 27, 1970).

16. Reported in *Sankei* (Tokyo), 13 November 1970.

17. Reported in the *New York Times*, 28 April 1970.

18. Members of the task force including Counsellor Hogan of the Japanese Foreign Ministry, Tan Sri Ghazali Shafie of Malaysia, now a Cabinet Minister; and Anwar Seni from Indonesia.

19. Diplomatic relations with North Vietnam were not established at Embassy level until June 1967. A commercial and economic agreement was negotiated with Hanoi in November 1958, and Hanoi's representative under that agreement served in a quasidiplomatic status.

20. This lack of involvement was illustrated by a study completed recently by the author. In this study, the measurable intra-Asian transactions of a dozen Asian nations were collated for a three-year period (1967-69), and grouped into four major categories: economic; political; cultural and communications; and military. Several thousands of pieces of data were compiled, and one of the purposes of the study was to rank East Asian nations in terms of the intensity of their involvement with all others in the region (first in each interaction category separately and then as an average across categories). The study shows that as an actor in East Asian affairs, Cambodia under Prince Sihanouk was consistently ranked with Burma and Laos as among the least involved and active of all East Asian nations. Its findings are reported in Bernard K. Gordon (with Kathryn Young), *Asia Defensive Postures (ADPOST): Implications of an Asian Transactions Analysis for Identifying Key States in US Defense Policy*, (2 volumes; McLean, Virginia: Research Analysis Corporation, 1971).

21. From an interview in *Réalités Cambodgiennes*, 12 February 1971, pp. 10-11.

22. I am indebted to one of my graduate students at The American University, Mr. Michael Schneider, for this reconstruction of events, in his seminar

paper, "Indonesian Diplomacy and the Cambodian Crisis" (January 1971). Schneider utilized a wide variety of foreign press sources, including particularly the following: *Bangkok Post*, 27 April 1970; *Pedoman* (Djakarta), 4 April and 6 May 1970 (translating a press account in the Dutch newspaper *Het Vrije Volk*, 22 April 1970); *Far Eastern Economic Review* (October 24, 1970); the *New York Times*, 23 and 24 April 1970; and for the official Indonesian denials, the *Armed Forces Courier*, 11 April 1970, and *Antara*, 26 April, 10 and 19 May 1970.

23. It will be recalled that the initial step in American military assistance to Lon Nol was the shipment of several thousand AK-47s, and the *New York Times* reported that the American *chargé* in Phnom Penh (Lloyd Rives) instructed the Cambodians to ask Indonesia for the ammunition, which was not then available in the United States. *New York Times*, 23 April 1970.

24. *Réalités Cambodgiennes*, 19 February 1971.

25. Reported in the *Far Eastern Economic Review* (July 9, 1970). This followed a visit by Cambodian Army General Srey Saman to Djakarta *after* the May conference.

26. Press reports quote Malik as having said in January that Cambodian non-commissioned officers were being trained in Indonesia. According to this report, Malik stipulated that their numbers were classified information, and shortly after, both governments denied that training was being undertaken in Indonesia. See, e.g., *Asian Almanac*, 6 March 1971.

27. *Réalités Cambodgiennes*, 15 January 1971.

28. Quoted in *The Evening Star* (Washington), 7 December 1970.

29. *New York Times*, 21 March 1971.

30. As reported in the *Far Eastern Economic Review* (13 February 1971).

31. *New York Times*, 5 February 1971.

32. Ibid., 21 March 1971. The same report noted that many Cambodians believe their government "is laggard in compelling Saigon to enforce discipline among its troops. . . ."

33. These and other visits between the two nations have been compiled from the weekly column "*gazette du pays Khmer*," in *Réalités Cambodgiennes*, March 1970-April 1971.

34. These and related agreements were reported in *New York Times*, 28 May 1970, and *Réalités Cambodgiennes*, 20 January 1971.

35. This problem arose because of agreements reached at the Pau Conference of 1950, which provided for Cambodia to have a share (23%) of the customs revenue collected in Saigon for the Associated States of Indochina. This and other understandings were disrupted when South Vietnam devalued the *piastre* in 1953, and as a result, large sums apparently are still held—available to neither party—in Paris.

36. Thailand and Cambodia have signed draft agreements in the fields of trade and payments arrangements, tourism, customs, postal service and transportation, and draft papers on border activities and fisheries. (See *Bangkok Post*, 25 October 1970.) Rail links, broken in 1961, were resumed in October 1970. *Bangkok Post*, 28 October 1970.

37. Ibid., 29 May 1970.

38. Ibid., 14 July 1970. See also Bernard K. Gordon, "U.S. Policies in Southeast Asia," *Current History* 59, no. 352 (December 1970): 324.

39. Reported in *Agence France Presse*, 1 June 1970.

40. *Bangkok Post*, 2 and 3 June 1970.

41. Ibid., 24 July 1970.

42. From an interview with Thanat in the *Christian Science Monitor*, 12 September 1970.

43. Thanat's remarks in London, in connection with the 1971 Southeast Asia Treaty Organization (SEATO) Ministerial Conference, are reported and quoted in the *Washington Post*, 29 April 1971.

44. Prior to his deposition from power, I pointed to the domestic disaffections that weakened the Prince's authority in Phnom Penh and made his removal not altogether unlikely. The same article detailed the long-standing activities of the North Vietnamese forces, since at least 1967, within Cambodia. See Bernard K. Gordon (with Kathryn Young), "Cambodia: Following the Leader?," *Asian Survey* 10, no. 2 (February 1970): 169-176.

45. Clearly divergent policy lines became apparent as early as July 1970, when Saigon proposed a defense pact to include Laos, Thailand, Cambodia and South Vietnam. Apparently, Premier Thanom was prepared to formalize the arrangement. *Agence France Presse*, 15 July 1970. It was also reported that Indonesia and Malaysia had expressed a clear distaste for the idea. Not surprisingly, and perhaps reflecting those views, Foreign Minister Thanat said simply that "this may be necessary in the future." *Bangkok Post*, 14 July 1970. Not surprisingly, no more was heard of the notion at the time, but is not unlikely to surface again.

46. *Réalités Cambodgiennes*, 11 December 1970.

47. Information derived from the following: *Sydney Morning Herald*, 23 June 1970; *Current Notes* (Canberra) 41, no. 9 (September 1970): 489, 450; and ibid., 41, no. 12 (December 1970): 640. It should be pointed out here that New Zealand has separately provided approximately $100,000 in military and related equipment.

48. *Tokyo Shimbun*, 8 December 1970. Data on Japanese assistance figures to Cambodia from *Réalités Cambodgiennes*, 1 January 1971.

49. Alastair Lamb, *Asian Frontiers, Studies in a Continuing Problem* (New York: Frederic A. Praeger, 1967), p. 2.

50. Ibid., p. 3.

11

The Nixon Doctrine and the New Policy Environment

Robert H. Johnson

It is widely agreed that the United States is caught up in a period of very basic transition in foreign policy, in part because of changes in the international environment, in part because of changes in our own perspectives and problems. It is also widely agreed that the appropriate broad direction of foreign policy change is toward relative disengagement. This now-conventional wisdom has been reflected in the Nixon Doctrine and incorporated in the President's two State of the World reports.[1] The key questions for the future are whether policy-makers yet have an adequate understanding of the changes in the environment of policy-making and whether the Nixon Doctrine and related administration policy perspectives respond adequately to the new and evolving situation. In addressing these questions, our focus will be upon East Asia and, ultimately, upon Indochina.

The Nixon Doctrine: Philosophy, Strategy or Tactic?

Is the Nixon Doctrine a philosophy (posture), a basic foreign policy strategy or a set of tactics which have been given a grandiose label? The answer must be that it is a combination of all three. It is a philosophical statement emphasizing reduced engagement for the United States and urging greater self-reliance upon others. It represents, as the second State of the World report acknowledged, a "philosophical attitude" rather than a "detailed design." But it is also a broad strategy dealing with United States responses to various levels of military threat. As a strategy, it seeks to shift primary responsibility for providing military manpower to nations under threat (and their neighbors), while at the same time reaffirming all existing treaty commitments. It therefore leaves a large area of future policy indeterminate.[2]

Finally, the Doctrine rationalizes United States military withdrawal tactics in a fashion that provides wide latitude in responding, on the one hand, to the pressures of United States domestic public opinion and, on the other, to reactions of United States friends and foes. The Administration itself acknowledges this tactical aspect; it also recognizes that the Doctrine only begins the process of United States readjustment in East Asia and that a major restructuring of the international order in that area will be required.[3]

175

Because it combines all of these aspects, the Nixon Doctrine is subject to the danger that it will, in the end, turn out to be that typical American foreign policy product—a policy which oscillates between broad, ambiguous statement of principle on the one hand, and specific, case-oriented actions which bear no clear relationship to principle on the other. Or, to put the matter somewhat differently, there is some danger that the Nixon Doctrine will turn out to be a kit-bag of tactics masquerading as a strategy. The Cambodian and Laos invasions, which were rationalized in terms of the withdrawal—self-reliance principle, suggest the danger quite well.

The tendency to broaden the meaning of the Doctrine to the point of meaninglessness is illustrated by the 1971 State of the World report in which it became *the* organizing perspective for the whole of United States foreign policy. Such diverse subjects as foreign aid, the Strategic Arms Limitations Talks (SALT) and world ecology were placed under the shelter of this large umbrella.[4] Thus, a policy stance for Asia, designed to place the Vietnamization tactic in a wider strategic context, has become a principle undergirding all of American foreign policy.

The central ambiguity of the Nixon Doctrine, however, revolves around the role of United States forces in dealing with local conflicts, including internal conflicts. There is an interesting parallel here between the broad doctrine and its more specific application in the Vietnamization policy. The Doctrine is widely understood in this country and in Asia as implying that it is most unlikely that the United States will again commit its armed forces, especially its ground forces, in Asia.[5] On the other hand, the Administration acknowledges that it cannot wholly rule out such involvement and argues that its objective is to reduce the likelihood or to raise the threshhold at which involvement occurs.[6] Similarly, the Administration's defense of its Vietnamization policy has often left the impression that it is designed to remove all American forces from Vietnam within a relatively short period, while at other times it has been indicated that a substantial residual force will be retained for the indefinite future.

Such ambiguity is, of course, necessary up to a point. The United States government is speaking to both a domestic audience wishing for disengagement and an Asian audience, a part of which is worried about disengagement. Accordingly, the Administration has indicated that the need to maintain public support at home and confidence abroad are the two critical factors determining tactics of implementation of the Doctrine. It is also evident that the Administration is very concerned about Communist reactions to the disengagement process.

The content of the second State of the World report and the atmospherics surrounding its issuance illustrate how the balancing of these considerations can have a significant effect upon the interpretation of the Doctrine. During this period, the President displayed considerable confidence that he had public opinion well in hand with respect to the central problem toward which his doctrine is currently directed—the problem of Indochina. At the same time, the ambiguities of the Doctrine and its implementation were causing politically significant uncertainties among the non-Communist countries of Asia as well as fear in Washington that it was being interpreted by the Communists as evidence of American weakness.[7] Against this background, in which foreign pressures and considerations were temporarily felt more strongly than domestic pressures, the tone of the President's report (and the apparent tone of press backgrounders on the report) was one which emphasized the importance of maintaining United States credibility, of not disengaging too rapidly, and, in general, of maintaining consistency and continuity with the past. The public opinion problem was seen as a danger that the pendulum would swing too far, "sweeping us toward an isolationism which would be as disastrous as excessive zeal."[8]

Adapting the interpretation of doctrine to changing circumstance is obviously necessary and not necessarily damaging, provided that such adjustment is undertaken with a clear and determined sense of ultimate goals and is based upon an adequate understanding of, and acceptance of the implications of, the major changes that have occurred in the environment of policy-making. The question of clarity and determination with respect to goals is not an easy question to analyze—partly because it relates to motivations and partly because it can only be demonstrated over time. The question of the degree to which the changes that have occurred in the environment of policy-making have been reflected in the assumptions underlying the Administration's policies is one which is somewhat more accessible to the outsider.

There are some striking similarities between the Nixon Doctrine and the basic policy posture of the Eisenhower Administration on the same range of issues. Both Administrations came to power on the wave of public discontent generated by our involvement in ground warfare in Asia. Both sought to disengage the United States and to turn over primary responsibility for defense on the ground—but not necessarily in the air or on the sea—to Asians (cf. "let Asians fight Asians" and "Vietnamization"). Both saw military and economic assistance as primary means to this end. And the Eisenhower Administration even anticipated the Nixon (and Johnson) Administration's emphasis upon regional approaches to security and economic development.[9] But the times have changed since Eisenhower and it is to these changes that we now turn.

The New Environment of United States Policy-Making

Both the domestic and the international environments of United States policy-making have changed radically in the past decade, though the basic processes of change began much earlier. The world we confront is partly changed in fact, partly changed in perception. Most of the objective changes are relatively easy to identify and most have been identified in the last State of the World report.

Even so, our understanding of the reasons for these changes and our acceptance of their implications has often been imperfect. Perceptual changes tend to be subtler, more controversial and not so clearly identified.

The Erosion of the Bases of United States
Policy in East Asia: Power and Interest

Explanations of international politics, as of politics more generally, are of two broad types—those based upon interest (generally defined in terms of power) and those based upon psychocultural factors (e.g., values or national style). So also for United States Asia policy.

The most common explanations of United States involvement in Asia run in terms of interest and power. One type of such explanation, currently enjoying a renewed vogue as a result of the work of the Cold War revisionists, emphasizes United States commercial interests in Asia. The "Open Door" policy, interpreted wholly in economic terms, is typically seen as defining the central theme of policy. The more orthodox foreign policy "realists", on the other hand, generally see the United States as concerned primarily with the balance of power and interpret the Open Door policy as a reflection of such a policy emphasis. One variant of this latter theory, popular especially since the Communist takeover of China and the Korean War, argues that the United States has been preoccupied throughout its involvement in East Asia with preventing domination of the area by a single hostile power or group of powers.[10]

That the lure of markets was a factor in United States East Asian policy is unquestionable; that it was the central factor is quite doubtful. This is not the place to deal with the problems of interpretation of evidence on which such economic theories of our Asian policy are based. Suffice it to say that a good deal of the evidence is plausibly subject to other interpretations.

That we have been concerned with the balance of power in East Asia is also evident, though during most of the period since the end of the nineteenth century that concern seems to have derived primarily from the marginal impact of developments in Asia upon the European balance. There have been only two relatively clear-cut situations in which fear of domination of the Asian mainland by a single nation or coalition became a major factor in United States policy and then only because this threat was seen as part of a larger threat to the world balance. These occurred during the period after 1938 when we developed such concerns about Japanese imperialism and in the period since 1950 (especially the decade of the 1950s) when the Sino-Soviet Alliance and the Korean War triggered similar fears of Sino-Soviet dominance.[11] In the second Indochinese war, our employment of the single-nation-domination rationale followed, rather then preceded, our own escalation of the war. It was more rationalization than reason.

In this perspective, as in other important respects, the geopolitical moorings of United States policy are being rapidly undermined. The Sino-Soviet conflict and the revival of Japan have completely eliminated any possibility that a single hostile nation or any foreseeable combination of such nations could dominate East Asia. Only some combination of Chinese and Russian or Chinese and Japanese power and ambitions could pose such a threat and neither combination seems plausible for the foreseeable future. Japan will probably move toward limited rapprochement with Communist China, but significant defense or foreign policy collaboration between the two seems most unlikely. On the contrary, the Sino-Japanese relationship is likely to involve an important competitive element. Against the background of the Sino-Soviet split and the retreat of European power from Asia, it is even clearer that plausibly possible developments in Asia pose no threat to the balance of power in Europe.[12]

In this situation, balance of power theorists have tended to deal in terms of purely hypothetical threats, such as a Communist-dominated Japan.[13] Such a perspective is certainly not in itself wrong, but it can be dangerously misleading if it produces current policy prescriptions based upon the linking of this interest to more immediate actions in, say, Indochina. In addition to the usual difficulties associated with even relatively sophisticated versions of the domino theory, such a perspective suffers from the defect of attempting to link present actions to a very long-range and uncertain threat.

Second, if our conception of the balance of power problem in East Asia has been called into question, so have our assumptions about the threat of Communist China. In part, the diminished sense of threat is a function of the gradually growing awareness among wider publics of what the China specialists have been telling us for a long time about Chinese intentions, and, in part, it is based upon changes in our perceptions of Chinese capabilities. The consensus of China specialists in and out of government with respect to Chinese intentions has been well summarized by Doak Barnett:

China is not committed to broad territorial expansionism. . . . It appears predisposed to keep Chinese military forces within China's boundaries . . . except in cases where it feels Chinese security—or that of a Communist buffer state on its periphery—is seriously threatened. . . . Its primary stress . . . is on defense rather than offense . . . it places a high priority on the desirability of avoiding large-scale war . . . it is strongly predisposed, in general, to low-cost, low-risk policies, and while it encourages and supports revolutionary struggle in other countries . . . it . . . opposes the use of Chinese forces to fight other revolutionaries' battles for them.[14]

Some specialists would go beyond this and argue that Chinese encouragement for revolutionary violence is confined to states in which the " 'imperialist' powers have interposed themselves."[15] If this latter view is correct, the military disengagement of the United States from the Asian mainland should reduce

Chinese support for such violence. In any event, the increased influence within China of the Chinese military, who are presumed to be especially cautious with respect to external adventure, points in the same general direction.

But even if one were unable to accept such interpretations of Chinese intentions, the increasingly evident limitations of Chinese military and nonmilitary capabilities should now produce a more relaxed view of the threat. Border difficulties with the Soviet Union limit China's effective conventional military capabilities. And, as the Chinese themselves recognize, their capacity to generate revolution, or even to provide it influential support, is very limited. They, no less than the Russians and ourselves, have regularly been disappointed in their expectations for influence in countries like Indonesia. The capacity for resistance of even a politically and militarily weak country like Burma to outside pressures has been formidable. The political evolution of these countries has an inner dynamic of its own which is relatively little subject to direct, manipulative intervention by outsiders. (Nonetheless, the diffuse, largely unmanipulatable, impact of a modern society like the United States, produced by the spread of the values and techniques of our liberal technocratic culture, is generally enormous.)

A third, and more basic change that raises fundamental questions about balance of power analysis and much else in Asia and elsewhere in the less developed world is the radically declining value of overseas territory. Many factors have contributed to this development, but most of them can be summarized under the heading of the impact of science and technology on military and civilian needs. Among the more specific factors are the decline of mercantalist economics and the rise of the new economics; the diversification of sources of supply for raw materials and energy through discovery of new sources of supply and through the development of substitutes; the decline in importance of overseas bases; the decline in the importance of war potential; the development of large, long-range tankers and cargo vessels; and the expansion of air transport.[16]

The importance of overseas bases to the maintenance of the United States strategic deterrent has been reduced with changes in weapons technology. The value of bases in deterring, or defending against, conventional military attacks on less developed nations has declined with the reduction in value of the territory of those nations and with the changed perception of the likelihood of such attacks. If, under the Nixon Doctrine, the United States intends to avoid deep involvement in guerrilla wars of the future, the case for an Asian base complex rests primarily upon the very marginal possibility of conventional attacks on nations to which we have existing commitments (which may, however, be revised) or on nations which we might defend for more subjective reasons such as United States reputation, past associations, or the desire for order). While this set of cases cannot be wholly ignored, they provide little determinate basis for policy.

In the 1950s, National Security Council papers justified our interest in most of the less developed areas of the world in terms of the importance of the communications routes which they were athwart or astride. At other times, we saw (and thought that the Chinese must see) Indochinese rice as the solution to China's food problems. Such perspectives are fast losing such limited reality as they may once have possessed. The classic point of supposed strategic importance in Southeast Asia is the Straits of Malacca. But today, despite the heavy use of the straits by the Japanese for the transport of essential petroleum supplies from the Middle East, some Japanese assessments see the straits as considerably less than vital.[17] In fact, the use of very large tankers, which the Japanese are building and which will have difficulty transiting the Straits, will probably make the route around the horn of Africa the more economical. The point is not that loss of the straits would not impose some costs, especially in the short run, but rather that they are far from vital to Japan and that United States interests are, to a significant degree, derivative from our interest in Japan. In addition, of course, it is not easy to envisage the circumstances under which the straits would fall into the hands of a hostile power that would have a substantial incentive to attempt to close them.

One effort to differentiate the countries of East Asia in which the United States has a vital interest concludes that such interests exist in Japan, South Korea, Australia-New Zealand, the Philippines, Thailand, and Taiwan.[18] Two points are striking about this list and the analysis that supports it. One is the omission of the Indochinese states. The other is the fact that, apart from Japan and the Japanese security interest in Korea, our interests are seen as derived wholly from a combination of existing United States security commitments and historical associations rather than from intrinsic economic or strategic importance. Our interests, in other words, derive primarily from *past* perceptions of threat and from *past* associations. In seeking a foundation for our policy there is some danger that we shall cling to the anchors provided by the past rather than confront the fact that, in a deeper sense, the bases of policy have become substantially indeterminate.

If it is evident that the benefits of access to territory in the less developed world have declined, it is even clearer that constraints upon the use of military force in order to maintain such access have risen. These constraints include the impact of nuclear deterrence and the fear of nuclear war upon the use of conventional force; the relative irrelevance of outside military force to the most important aspects of internal war; the new legitimacy of the nation state; the worldwide instantaneous communications system and the existence of the United Nations which have helped enforce the national legitimacy principle; and, not least, the restraints imposed by United States domestic politics.

One consequence of the decline in the value of territory and the constraints on the use of force has been some shift of focus of international politics away from specific efforts to expand or maintain national possessions and toward much broader and vaguer efforts to establish or maintain some conception of world order or otherwise to structure the international environment.[19]

To what extent does the Nixon Administration recognize these changes? In attempting to answer this question, we shall rely primarily upon the evidence provided by the two State of the World reports.[20] The first of these reports contained the most explicit statement on the subject of the threat in Asia.

Our important interests and those of our friends are still threatened by those nations which would exploit change and which proclaim hostility to the United States as one of the fundamental tenets of their policies. We do not assume that these nations will remain forever hostile, and will work toward improved relationships wherever possible. But we will not underestimate any threat to us or our allies, nor lightly base our present policies on untested assumptions about the future.[21]

In the second report, President Nixon conceded that Communist China "proclaimed more often than followed" its doctrines of violence and revolution in its international relations but also implied that it still harbored hegemonial aims in Asia. At the same time, he clearly discounted the possibility of one-nation domination of Asia, whether that nation be Communist China or the United States. He saw the main threat from the Communists not as massive invasion, but as "a subtle mix of military, psychological and political pressures." But he also raised the old bugaboo, familiar from the arguments of the fifties, that Communist China and the USSR might take advantage of their increasing nuclear strength to undertake nonnuclear military actions.[22] The Administration elsewhere has taken a generally unchanged view of Communist China's capabilities for supporting conventional or guerrilla warfare.[23]

On the basis of presently available information, it is difficult to determine the extent to which the planned Presidential visit to Peking reflects a basic policy change grounded in a fundamentally changed view of the threat and role of China in Asia. Of the various possible rationales for the trip, the most plausible is that it represents a logical outgrowth of the effort that began about 1963—and that has been accelerated under the Nixon Administration—to draw China out of its isolation and back into the family of nations. This policy stance has been based from the beginning partly upon a moderated view of the Chinese threat, but also upon the belief that Chinese behavior is potentially dangerous and needs to be influenced through international contact away from revolutionary ambitions and toward a more moderate policy. In arguing for such a strategy before he became President, Nixon made the following statement.

The world cannot be safe until China changes. Thus, our aim, to the extent that we can influence events, should be to induce change. The way to do this is to persuade China that it *must* change: that it cannot satisfy its imperial ambitions, and that its own national interests require a turning away from foreign adventuring and a turning inward toward the solution of its domestic problems.[24]

Such a rationale for increased contact with China is also implied in the second State of the World Report.[25]

At least six other rationales for the visit suggest themselves: (1) a desire to create pressures on the USSR for accommodation on such issues as strategic arms limitation by playing the detente game with Communist China (the Gaullist strategy); (2) a hope that the United States can reach broad strategic understandings with Communist China with respect to the future of Asia which would facilitate United States withdrawal from Indochina (e.g., on neutralization of Southeast Asia); (3) no expectation of such broad understandings, but a clearer reading of Chinese intentions to provide a sounder basis for future United States policy decisions, including troop withdrawals; (4) a hope for a broad spirit of detente ("the spirit of Peking"?) which would facilitate United States withdrawals through its effects on Asian and United States opinion; (5) a goal of placing an impending defeat in the United Nations on the China membership issue in the context of a basic change in the United States-Chinese relationship; and (6) an expectation that the drama of the visit will have broad usefulness in the coming United States Presidential election.

Of these other rationales, only the possible hope for broad strategic understandings would clearly imply a major revision in the view of the Chinese threat, but most of them, and the simple fact of the trip itself, suggest some moderation of past views.

There is less evidence of a change in the Administration's view of the stakes of international politics. It acknowledges that the old game of seeking marginal gains at the expense of a competitor with the objective of altering the balance of power is dangerous in the nuclear age and ought to be played with more self-restraint. However, it also states that continued self-restraint on the part of the United States in its competition with the Soviet Union will require reciprocity from the latter.[26] It is difficult to draw anything from this line of argument except a general sense that marginal gains cannot be ignored and that the contest with the Communists tends to be viewed in zero-sum terms even while there is a longing for more evidence of Communist recognition of the common stake in peace.

If the President recognizes the dangers of unbridled competition, he also evidently rejects the view that we live in a new kind of world in which the constraints upon the use of force can or should limit United States willingness to go to the military support of a small nation in trouble from within or without. Thus, while a Stanley Hoffman may argue that the characteristics of the present international system make of the United States a "Gulliver in the chain gang," President Nixon insisted, at the time of the military action in Cambodia, that the United States, as the world's most powerful nation, must not act like a "pitiful, helpless giant."

Two, quite divergent, overall interpretations of Administration assumptions and strategies are suggested by available evidence. The argument contained in public policy statements quite clearly indicates that the President bases his Doctrine and the policies that flow from it much less upon fundamentally changed hypotheses as to the nature of the stakes or the character of the threat than upon optimistic assumptions as to the growth in strength of non-Communist Asian nations and of Asian regionalism. In discussing the "new Asia" which provides the basis for United States policy under his Doctrine and beyond, he focused, in the second State of the World report, entirely upon these latter changes. What appears to have been revised, on this view, are less the assumptions as to the nature of the stakes or the goals of policy than the means of achieving those goals. In an uncertain, unstable world, it has seemed safer to base present policy upon past perspectives rather than upon what the Administration has called untested assumptions about the future. On this interpretation, the trip to Peking can be seen as a logical extension of past policy toward China based partly upon some moderation of the view of the threat, but partly upon a fear that an isolated China could become a quite serious threat.

But speculation as to the meaning of the ambiguities in present policy toward China and Indochina suggests a quite different interpretation. That is that the Administration has embarked upon a new grand strategy for Asia which may or may not accept the arguments with respect to the stakes offered above, but which bases itself primarily upon a changed attitude toward China. The fundamental purpose of such a strategy might be the achievement of a broad set of understandings with Communist China on a number of different areas which would basically alter the character of international relationships in Asia. Among the possibilities might be an agreement for the neutralization of Southeast Asia (presumably excluding Vietnam).

There are, however, good reasons for taking the Administration at its public word and assuming, for purposes of present analysis, that the first interpretation comes closer to the truth than the second. The second interpretation implies that the Administration does not recognize the basic incompatibilities between present United States and Chinese positions on a number of issues. It also implies a belief that Communist China has a great deal more ability to determine the future of areas like Southeast Asia than is, in fact, the case. Finally, such a view would be based upon the assumption that the United States has a great deal more willingness and ability to implement grand strategic conceptions than it has exhibited in the past, despite the fact that the world has become less, rather than more, malleable to United States will and power and that the problems of achieving domestic consensus are more, rather than less, severe. These kinds of unrealism seem quite unlikely.

The Erosion of the Bases of United States Policy in East Asia: The Sense of Mission

We turn now from changes relating to power and interest to changes relating to the cultural and psychological dimensions of our relationship to Asia. The two realms of explanation are linked, however, in the sense that the changes in both are most fundamentally related to the impact of science and technology. We shall be concerned here with the effect of modernization processes upon the United States, upon Asian countries, and upon the interaction between them. The analysis draws upon and extends an analysis by Akira Iriye.[27]

We can define modernization for present purposes very generally: those processes of change in economy, society, polity and culture that *tend* to be produced by the impact of science and technology on these several spheres. It is widely accepted that one of the key aspects of psychocultural modernization is development of a greatly increased sense of ability to influence and control one's environment. Science provides the understanding and technology the means by which improved influence and control are achieved.

This sense of ability to control and dominate the environment, and its accompanying sense of superiority and optimism, seems especially strongly developed among Americans, perhaps because we have been at the cutting edge of modernizing change and because we largely escaped the experience of traditionality. To use de Tocqueville's characterization, we were "born free." Traditional cultures are not missionary in character because men in traditional society adapt to their environment much more than they seek to change it. But "America," as President Nixon puts it in his current State of the World Message, "has always had a belief in a purpose larger than itself." We have been missionaries, both secular and religious, and nowhere more than in Asia.[28]

In our approach to Asia, we have tended to confuse modernization with Westernization and have tended to believe that the transformation of Asian societies would be a total transformation which would produce societies with values, beliefs, political systems, social structures, and economies basically congruent with our own. Japan was the first Asian nation to modernize and it was the first to raise, then disappoint, our hopes. We came to realize that the economic transformation of Japan would not necessarily be accompanied by a parallel transformation of Japanese values. In view of our expectations, it is not surprising that when Japanese modernization increased Japanese power and produced Japanese imperialism, our reaction, in the period from Presidents Taft to Franklin Roosevelt was less power-political than moralistic.

From the period just before the Chinese revolution of 1911, we began a similar cycle with respect to China, starting on an optimistic note, which lasted through World War II, and ending in a highly moralistic reaction to the Communist takeover of the mainland. The reaction might not have gone beyond the moralistic plane if it had not been for the fusing of the China problem with our conflict with the USSR as a result of their alliance and the Korean War.

In the period since World War II, we have gone through a very similar cycle with respect to most of the new nations of Asia. We approached these nations in the same missionary spirit and with the same kind of assumptions as to the inseparability of economic modernization and other desired kinds of political and cultural change. Because these nations are diverse, our experience has been diverse, but generally, it has been disappointing. However, it has been the war in Vietnam that has raised the gravest doubts. As Neil Sheehan says in his introduction to *The Pentagon Papers*, the Vietnam decision-makers of the 1960s were confident men—"problem-solvers who seem rarely to doubt their ability to prevail."[29] But the outcome of our policies has now caused us to doubt our ability to understand the complex problems of development, at least in a revolutionary context. It has raised serious doubts about our ability, despite our sophisticated military and civilian technology, to order our international environment. And, most basically of all, it has caused us to question seriously the purity and absolute validity of United States purposes in the world.

It would be possible to discount these effects of Vietnam perhaps if it were not for the fact that they receive powerful reenforcement from still deeper processes of change. Science and technology, the primary means through which we have dominated our environment and increased its predictability, have now also become the principal generators of insoluble-seeming problems and new levels of uncertainty. This is most obvious with respect to such problems as the ecological balance of our physical environment. Less obvious uncertainty-producing effects include the way that the process of social and cultural differentiation generated by science and technology have deprived us of our sense of social and cultural wholeness. Paradoxically, man in modern America is reverting to something like the condition of man in traditional societies assailed by forces of which he has little understanding and over which he has little sense of control. Interestingly, too, the reactions embodied in the counterculture of youth bear some significant resemblance to the defenses of traditional man. The loss of sense of mission abroad and the reconsideration of old values is, in brief, simply an aspect of a much wider and deeper phenomenon.[30]

Insofar as it is based upon changes in American attitudes, the Nixon Doctrine appears to be rooted more in an assumption that the American people have grown weary of their international burdens than in a belief that there may have been a more fundamental loss of the sense of optimism and mission.[31]

One other aspect of the cultural basis of our policy toward East Asia deserves mention. That is the fact that our conception of the desired international order throughout has been inspired by, and infused with, our classical liberal values. Whatever else the Open Door policy may have been, it was clearly an expression of the American desire for an open world, characterized by free access to all. When Japanese imperialism threatened the survival of China, our protests related primarily to Japanese violation of principles of peaceful, orderly change.[32] Chester Cooper, searching at the end of his book on the evolution of United States policy toward Vietnam, for the persistent theme in the welter of official rationales for our policy, decided that it has been the archtypical liberal principle of self-determination.[33]

There is a deeper need underlying both the power-interest and psychocultural motivations for our involvement in Asia. That is our need for order.[34] Man is, among other things, an order-seeking animal and nowhere is this more true than in international politics where order is so fragile and the threats to it so omnipresent.[35] Some interesting evidence on this subject, as it applies to Asian policy, is provided by William Whitworth's interviews with Eugene V. Rostow, former Under Secretary of State.[36] In answering questions about fundamental United States objectives in Asia, Rostow made all of the usual arguments based upon balance of power, more particular United States interests, and United States values and he made them very well. But when pressed to the wall on the rationale for various actions, he fell back upon the need to act because of uncertainty about the consequences of the failure to act. This uncertainty affected policy-makers directly, but it also affected them indirectly because of their fear that the American public could not live with the uncertainties produced by possible Communist successes, even though such successes did not affect vital national interests. The need to maintain order was the ultimate need.

The balance of power is the classical way of maintaining order in international politics while the United States' projection of its liberal values abroad is implicitly or explicitly based upon an effort to create a different kind of world order. That order is the ultimate name of the balance of power game is reflected in the fact that, as Whitworth pointed out to Rostow, there is a circularity in our typical argumentation for it. Balance of power is seen as the way to protect our interests, but then our basic interests are defined as maintaining the balance of power.

If this view of our ultimate motivations is correct, then the key question for the future is whether we can learn to live with a great deal of disorder. The Nixon Doctrine is based upon an assumption that Asian countries are demonstrating a considerable capacity to maintain order—both order within their own societies and an international regional order. For the longer term, however, this seems a most doubtful assumption. We turn now to a consideration of it.

The New Bases of United States Policy
in East Asia: Asian Strengths and Limitations

The cornerstone of the Nixon Doctrine in Asia is the view that the "central fact of East Asia today is the remarkable political and economic growth of the area, and the justifiable self-confidence that has resulted from it."[37] Asian states are also said to be more confident of their national identities. That there has been marked economic progress in both East Asia in general and Southeast Asia in particular during the past five years or so is undoubtedly true, though, in general, progress in Southeast Asia has been significantly less and a great deal more uneven than in Japan, South Korea and Taiwan. Moreover, the period 1960-65 was a time of economic doldrums in Southeast Asia and an undetermined amount of the prosperity of that area since is based upon demands generated by the war. As war expenditures decline, this basis for self-reliance will be eroded. Political stability has been achieved in much of East Asia through political demobilization under the auspices of military regimes. The two remaining democratic polities, Malaysia and the Philippines, have been in, or are heading for, serious political troubles.

It is questions relating to the longer term and to political change which, however, raise the most serious doubts about the validity of the Nixon Doctrine assumptions. Contrary to American expectations since our first contacts with Japan, there is little basis for believing that, except possibly in the very long run, economic modernization will be accompanied by equilibrating processes of modernization in other sectors of these societies that will be such as to produce nations which, if not like our own, are at least very compatible with United States objectives. In fact, there is a good deal of evidence suggesting that the middle period in the economic development process is likely to create political disorder and breed major radical political movements.

The disruptive effects of modernizing change, the growth of demands (often based upon primordial rather than modern forms of identity), and such particular problems as population pressure in areas like Java and the Philippines are very likely to place unbearable loads upon social and political systems, leading to breakdowns. The recent conflicts in Pakistan and Ceylon are reminders of future possibilities. (Until quite recently, Pakistan was, of course, one of the prime economic development success stories.) While some have proclaimed the end of the era of radical nationalism, seeing it as the romantic afterglow of the nationalist revolutions, the prospects are that renewed problems of national identity and regime legitimacy will, in conditions of breakdown, produce new radical nationalist regimes. The growth of millenarian movements is a classical form of response to social and cultural stress and who would be so bold as to predict that the societies of East and Southeast Asia will not be subjected to severe stress in the foreseeable future?

A development which receives almost as much emphasis in the rationale for the Nixon Doctrine in Asia as the growth of national political and economic strength is the progress of regionalism. Relative to the past, recent developments in regional cooperation have assuredly been gratifying, but by any absolute standard, they must certainly be seen as very modest. The institutions established, aside from the Asian Development Bank, have been consultative in character. Moreover, as the experience of the Association of Southeast Asian Nations (ASEAN) demonstrates, even consultative arrangements are very vulnerable to political upset by developments within the nations as well as by conflicts between nations.[38] The old argument that there are very severe limitations on the prospects for regional cooperation among states that are not themselves well integrated and institutionalized seems to be borne out by recent experience in East Asia.

It is usual for United States policy makers to hope that economic cooperation in Asia will lead to eventual political and military cooperation. Cooperation in security matters is, presumably, the ultimate payoff of regional cooperation in the context of Nixon Doctrine concerns. But while some informal consultation on security matters has taken place within the ASEAN framework, it seems wildly optimistic to believe that regional cooperation will make a major contribution to dealing with the security problems of East Asia in the foreseeable future.[39] In an article in *Foreign Affairs* before he became President, Nixon argued for the development of indigenous regional defense pacts in Asia as a means of containing aggression. While the pact proposal was unrealistic, Nixon did at least recognize that such regional alliances might not be able to cope with local conflicts. In such cases, he still saw a regional approach as valuable because it would permit presentation of the issue to the United States in clear-cut terms and would provide the United States with automatic allies in responding to the threat.[40] But even if the pact members were able to concert their views in a meaningful sense, as this argument implies, the outcome would be, at best of doubtful utility to the United States. Perhaps the real value of such a hypothetical pact in such situations would be that the inability to achieve agreement on a request to the United States for help could provide a politically useful excuse to the United States for avoiding involvement.

Our emphasis upon regionalism seems inspired in part by our projection of our own federal experience upon the world (not just in Asia) and in part upon our traditional emphasis upon multilateralism in our approach to Asian problems.[41] Particularly when we feel in deep trouble, as in 1954 and in 1965, we see the values of a multilateral and regional approach as a way of sharing responsibility. Between these two periods, however, it was exceedingly difficult for those who were interested in Asian regional cooperation within the United States government to elicit interest in action to support the modest kinds of regional activities that were feasible.[42]

The third pillar of the Nixon Doctrine in Asia is the growing strength and role of Japan. United States government policy papers have for a good many years looked toward the time when Japan might play a larger economic, political, and, eventually, security role in Asia. (During those years, however, many experts on Japan within the United States government have had for a variety of reasons real reservations about prodding Japan toward a security role.) With the development of Japan's increasingly dominant economic role in Southeast Asia, with the undertaking by Japan of some modest political initiatives in the area, and with the gradual strengthening of Japan's self-defense forces, these hopes have at last seemed to find some solid confirmation. But the evidence is quite misleading.[43]

It is clear that Japan still sees its role primarily in economic terms. Its increased activity in support of regional cooperation represents no fundamental departure from long-standing positions and is related primarily to its perceptions of its economic interests. Insofar as it sees itself playing a separate political role, it is as mediator and bridge (the latter *vis-a-vis* Communist China and the West) rather than as a major independent actor. The Japanese evidently feel no substantial sense of military threat, certainly not in Southeast Asia. Perhaps they perceive the strategic importance of the less developed world in much the way that we have suggested that it should be perceived.

While Japan's trade with Southeast Asia has grown substantially in absolute terms, the area's relative importance as a source of supply to Japan has remained generally stable since 1961 (at about 10-11%), while its importance as a market initially declined somewhat (from about 16 to 12% between 1961 and 1964) and has since remained stable. The same general trends also hold for the less developed areas of Asia as a whole. For two Southeast Asian countries—the Philippines and Indonesia—Japan provides a market of very large and relatively increasing importance, while for Thailand, South Vietnam and Malaysia it has been a market of relatively large, but relatively stable, significance. Thus, Japan's relative interest in the area in trade terms, while moderately significant, is hardly overriding and the relationship of economic dependency tends to run from Southeast Asia to Japan rather than the reverse.[44]

Although the second State of the World report is substantially correct in suggesting that the enmities of World War II are dying, it is also true that Asian leaders view their increasing economic dependence upon Japan with some concern. Since Japan's primary foreign policy motivations remain economic, we can anticipate that the Japanese will go to some lengths to avoid actions that will unduly alarm other Asians and thus threaten trade and investment relationships. It has, for example, been suggested that Japan's more active interest in regionalism beginning about 1965 may have been inspired in part by an awareness of growing Southeast Asian economic dependence on Japan and by a desire to avoid its possible political consequences in a politically unstable area.[45] Japan therefore may have seen the virtues of regionalism in terms very parallel to those in which the United States now sees them. Altogether, it is difficult to see the Japanese playing a significantly different role in East Asia in the foreseeable future than they have played in the recent past.

The Nixon Doctrine and the Nixon Conception of an East Asian Order: A Summary Critique

It is evident, then, that three of the pillars of the Nixon Doctrine in Asia are weak reeds indeed. That leaves the fourth—the role of the United States. So we return to the questions with which we began: Does the United States government have an adequately revised view of its environment, a clear sense of its goals and a real determination to pursue those goals while making only modest tactical concessions to contrary foreign pressures? The answer to such questions must be that, while the evidence is unclear, it is far from reassuring for those who see substantial disengagement as essential.

Apart from its recognition that no nation can dominate East Asia, there is little evidence of acceptance by the Administration of a changed view of the threat or of the traditional geopolitical conceptions of the bases for United States interests.[46] Assuming that the Administration does not have deeper purposes which it has not yet revealed, it is not difficult to accept the judgment of Max Frankel that "the principal goals and ambitions of American foreign policy have hardly changed at all" and that "President Nixon has labored to perfect the foreign-affairs concepts of the last two decades against the widespread disenchantment with Vietnam and against the allure of insular doctrines."[47] Fundamental questions about the threat and the stakes have, in fact, tended to be bypassed in favor of an analysis of the future based upon shakily optimistic assumptions about the strength of Asian states, the growth of regional cooperation and the future role of Japan. There is a distinct flavor in much of this of rationalization of domestic political necessity. At the same time, it is not clear that there is full recognition of the deep cultural changes that appear to underlie domestic changes in attitude.

There are several basic dangers in this situation. One is that when our optimistic assumptions as to the strength of non-Communist Asia are called into question, as they certainly will be, traditional United States views as to the threat and the stakes will be activated and the government will once more be tempted toward interventionism. At the same time, the deep-lying sentiments against interventionism will be brought into play. The outcome of this tug-of-war will be very difficult to predict.

This is not an academic, far-in-the-future kind of problem. Even though the North Vietnamese have now apparently adopted a policy of protracted war, at some time in the future when political conditions in South Vietnam seem ripe, they may be strongly tempted to take military actions in Laos or Cambodia (most likely the latter) designed to have a critical effect upon the morale of the South Vietnamese regime and armed forces.[48] The possibility of major military moves in South Vietnam also cannot be ruled out. Depending partly upon the size and character of the residual United States forces in the South, such a development could put the President in the sort of bind we have just described. Any reescalation of the war short of return of United States troops is likely to be irrelevant or dangerous or both. But the return of United States troops to Indochina will be "unthinkable."

A second danger is suggested by the first. In the absence of a basically revised view of the threat and the stakes, and ever nervous about the problem of order, we may do so much backing and filling in the process of disengagement that we shall undermine any remaining political basis in the United States for a continuing minimum involvement in East Asia of the sort suggested below. Finally, the Nixon Doctrine contains within it the danger of repeating an error of the fifties. That was the tendency to overemphasize military assistance at the expense of economic aid out of a desire to reduce direct United States security burdens.[49]

Our basic problem, perhaps, is that we are afraid of letting go. Partly because of our belief that Communism necessarily feeds on disorder, we have been pre-occupied with maintaining order. As we move toward disengagement, we search anxiously for some new principle of order that will not be so dependent upon our presence.

The Nixon schema for the future of East Asia, so far as one can discern it, seeks to combine the decentralization of power with some element of continued hierarchy. It might be characterized as international "guided democracy" or "multipolarity with management." Self-regulation is to be provided by regional cooperation; management, by a combination of the United States and Japan, and, beyond that, by a quadrilateral balance involving Communist China and the USSR as well. While there is something to be said for some version of such a balance, the whole concept of balance may be called into question.[50]

It is extremely questionable whether either Japan or the USSR will play major balancing roles in most of Asia, although the Sino-Soviet border dispute will serve as a potential inhibition on the actions of those two disputants. It is also unclear how such a balance would inhibit intervention in what is generally conceded to be the most likely form of violence in the area—internal conflict. Moreover, the decline in the value of overseas territory raises questions about the meaning of the counters in terms of which the balance of power game has traditionally been played.

An Alternative Model of the Future

While it may be somewhat unfair to critique existing policy at length and then to offer an alternative set of policy prescriptions without specific justifications for each, limitations of space force us to rely upon the general argumentation already offered to support most of our proposals.

East Asia as a Whole

In general, we should relax drastically our preoccupation with order. There will be order in East Asia because men are order-oriented, but there will also be disorder because men are change-oriented. The structure of the future is unlikely to be anything so neat as the patterns suggested by quadrilateral balance or regionalist models. Only some rather vague label like pluralist will fit the variety of interaction that is likely to develop.[51]

This more relaxed posture implies that we shall have to be willing to see Communist regimes come to power in some Asian countries—certainly in Indochina if nowhere else. Under conditions of underdevelopment, almost any Communist revolution that succeeds will, perforce, be strongly nationalist in character because only nationalism provides the cement that will hold the traditionalistic rural masses and the more modern elites together in a single movement. If this is true, then the prospects for Communism do not appear terribly bright in Asia, and, if a Communist movement does succeed, the resulting regime is unlikely to be anyone's satellite.

We should disengage our military forces completely from the Asian mainland with the exception of South Korea and move to an offshore basing strategy. This has been virtually conventional wisdom as a post-Vietnam strategy for the past few years, but we need to begin to implement it. Further, we need to recognize that almost no base is essential. Accordingly, we should avoid paying high political prices to stay in places like the Philippines.

We should now have learned from our past involvement in the internal affairs of other Asian countries how little we know about the politics of these societies and how little we can influence their politics. Meanwhile, such involvement has carried significant political costs. We should, therefore, accompany our reduced military presence in Asia with disengagement from direct efforts to influence Asian politics except as we may impose conditions on our foreign aid related to its purposes.

Japan is the one non-Communist country of East Asia of really substantial political, economic, and strategic interest to the United States. A great deal of our effort in East Asia should be devoted to the continuing cultivation of this relationship. If we are to avoid development of a dangerous "go-it-alone" attitude in Japan, we must, as we have often promised, consult her prior to important Asian policy moves such as the decision of the President to visit Peking. We should not encourage Japan to undertake a major rearmament effort or to assume regional military responsibilities. Such action can only be divisive within Japan and in Asia. Cute ideas for involving the Japanese in such roles—such as the notion of Japanese participation in a postwar security supervisory arrangement in Indochina—should be eschewed. There is no point in getting the Japanese into the same kind of losing game from which we are currently attempting to extricate ourselves. Australia has a parallel, if lesser, interest for the United States.

On the assumption that Japan continues to view South Korea as quite important to its security—important enough, say, so that the Japanese would permit use of its own territory by the United States for bases in the event of a renewed war—we should retain some forces in South Korea indefinitely. The risks seem unlikely to be very high in the foreseeable future.

The Nixon visit to China should become a major step toward genuine acceptance of Communist China as a major state in the area and in the world. Instead of taking another decade or more to make clear through our actions that we accept China as a major world power, (and in the process repeat errors we have made in our relationship to the Soviet Union), we should deal with China now in a way that evidences such acceptance. This means further action to eliminate discriminatory regulations *vis-a-vis* China in trade and other areas; recognition that the United States cannot settle the future of Taiwan, and gradual but steady withdrawal of our forces from Taiwan and the Formosa Straits; revocation of the Congressional Formosa resolution of 1955, but retention for the present of the Mutual Security Treaty; and acceptance of Peking into the United Nations as the representative of China. Our object should not be to lead China by the hand into the world of "civilized" nations nor should it be the mere amelioration of past relationships of hostility. Policy should be based upon genuine acceptance of China as a major state. (A revision of our general policies with respect to recognition and nonrecognition of states could provide a broader policy context which would facilitate changes in our relationship to Communist China.)

In parallel with such changes, we should encourage the nations of East Asia, especially Southeast Asia, to undertake similar normalization and acceptance policies. As we take the lead, they will, in fact, need little encouragement.

It is difficult to add anything to the already widely accepted views on the future of foreign aid. Foreign aid and diplomacy should be our principal instruments of policy in East Asia in the future. Aid for the economic and non-economic modernization of Asian states is important, not because we are likely to be able to use it very effectively in achieving particular United States foreign policy goals, but because it is likely to be important for the United States to be involved in the key processes of change that will be taking place in East Asia. Assuming that there has been a fundamental lessening of our sense of mission, maintaining public support for aid will certainly be difficult.

We should begin thinking now, if we are not already doing so, about what kinds of aid programs may be necessary to take up the economic slack that will be created in Asia with the reduction of United States involvement in Indochina.

We should continue to do everything we can to provide support for the development of regional cooperation in East Asia. At the same time, our expectations need to be much more modest.

The Indochina Peninsula

Present United States policy toward Indochina does not promise a way out of involvement. A policy based wholly upon Vietnamization leaves the central political issues of the war unresolved while South Vietnam's continued need for United States support (in the form of massive military aid, if no other) will mean a continuing substantial United States presence of some sort, and, therefore, continued prospect of United States involvement in future disasters. Whatever one's degree of optimism about the immediate situation in the South, it is difficult to be optimistic about the longer run prospects for non-Communist success. We may leave Vietnam, but the Communists will not quit. Furthermore, as suggested above, there is a strong possibility of serious trouble in Laos and Cambodia where the Communist positions are stronger. Finally, if—as presently appears likely—we seek to maintain the non-Communist position in Indochina after United States troop withdrawals through continued massive bombing, we shall perpetuate indefinitely indiscriminate killing and destruction in the area.[52]

It is unoriginal to suggest it, but some kind of early publicly announced deadline for withdrawal of all United States forces remains the best way out. Such a policy could be combined with diplomacy to provide a negotiated settlement directed toward political accommodation in South Vietnam and toward salvaging something in Laos and Cambodia. But it may be that serious negotiations, which could only put a relatively good face on our exit from South Vietnam, are not within the realm of what any American political leader will find politically tolerable. (Since the South inherited much of the factional diversity of Vietnam, we can anticipate that Hanoi is going to have its hands full attempting to govern a reunified country. This may predispose it to compromise on Laos and Cambodia.)

But, of course, the situation may not evolve this way. Although it seems unlikely, with the help of American military equipment and some continuing American presence, South Vietnam may fight on for some years yet. It is very difficult to know what further stresses an indefinite, but lower-posture, United States military involvement will impose upon the United States and East Asia. But it seems most unlikely that the net results will be beneficent.

Thailand, more than any other Southeast Asian state, obviously needs to establish a new relationship to the Asian communist countries and is certainly inclined to do so. Thai accommodations with Communist China and North Vietnam would almost certainly dissolve our present security commitment to Thailand. But if this does not occur within a reasonable time, we shall need to renegotiate or reinterpret our commitment—consistent with the main thrust of the Nixon Doctrine—to limit future United States unilateral assistance to military materiel. Meanwhile, we must simply accept some deterioration in Thai-United States relations as one of the consequences of disengagement and not rush in with new assurances, or new affirmations of old ones, in an effort to shore up the relationship.

The picture of East Asia that has been set out here is not one that provides a neat structure in which there will be some comfortable niche for the states of Indochina. But, then, neither does the Nixon Administration picture of the future do so. Whatever other role Japan may play, it is most unlikely to become deeply involved in the problems of Indochina. And whatever the utilities of Asian regionalism, it seems equally unlikely that any Asian regional organization will perform significant security functions in the penninsula.

There is some tendency these days to label proposals for more radical disengagement as neoisolationist and no doubt that label will be applied by some to the above views. This tendency is very unfortunate for the effort to polarize the debate between full acceptance of Administration policy and isolationism only blocks out intermediate sorts of possibilities of the kind that need to receive the most serious attention. It is too rigid insistence upon a particular definition of disengagement that is likely, in the end, to produce a genuinely isolationist reaction.

Isolationism is not the issue. The fundamental question for the future of United States policy is whether our relative disengagement is to be made dependent upon the parallel increase in the capacity of Asian states to handle the burdens we have in the past assumed or whether it is to be based upon a fundamental reassessment of the likelihood and the significance of "adverse" political and politicomilitary changes in the area.

Notes

1. *U.S. Foreign Policy for the 1970s: A New Strategy for Peace*, Report to the Congress by Richard Nixon, President of the United States, February 18, 1970 (Washington: Government Printing Office, 1970) and *U.S. Foreign Policy for the 1970s: Building for Peace*, February 25, 1971 (Washington: Government Printing Office, 1971). Hereafter these reports will be referred to as *U.S. Foreign Policy for the 1970s I and II*, respectively.

2. The other aspect of the strategy, which extends the United States nuclear umbrella to allies and other countries vital to United States security, has a purpose opposite to the general self reliance objective of the Nixon Doctrine. Like similar statements by the Johnson Administration, it is presumably designed to reduce the incentives to the development of nuclear weapons by presently nonnuclear powers.

3. *United States Foreign Policy for the 1970s–II*, pp. 92, 97-98.

4. Security assistance (military and related aid) is obviously most clearly related to the Doctrine and is most clearly brought within its rubric, but some effort is made to tie all of economic aid to its purposes. See ibid, pp. 15 and 183-185.

5. On the Asian understanding, see the report by Flora Lewis on an extended trip through Asia: "The Nixon Doctrine," *Atlantic* 226 (November 1970): 6.

6. *United States Foreign Policy for the 1970s–II*, p. 14.

7. On Nixon's confidence, see, for example, his interview with C.L. Sulzberger, *New York Times*, 10 March 1971, p. 14. On nervousness in Asia, see Lewis, "The Nixon Doctrine . . . ."

8. *United States Foreign Policy for the 1970s–II*, pp. 16-17. See also the interpretations of Robert B. Semple, Jr., and Max Frankel, *New York Times*, 26 February 1971, pp. 1, 14.

9. This regional emphasis was reflected in the creation of SEATO and in the establishment of an Asian regional economic development fund within the United States aid program designed to stimulate and support regional economic cooperation in Asia.

10. For the revisionist view, see William Appleman Williams, *The Tragedy of American Diplomacy* (New York: Dell, 1962), especially ch. 1. For balance of power analyses, see Bernard K. Gordon, *Toward Disengagement in Asia: A Strategy for American Foreign Policy* (Englewood Cliffs: Prentice-Hall, 1969), especially chs. 3, 4; and Fred Greene, *U.S. Policy and the Security of Asia* (New York: McGraw-Hill, 1968), especially ch. 2.

11. While we protested Japanese violation of the principles of peaceful change and self-determination in China in the interwar years, we *acted* only when we perceived the Japanese actions to be part of a larger, unified threat to the status quo. See Akira Iriye, *Across the Pacific: An Inner History of American-East Asian Relations* (New York: Harcourt, Brace and World, 1967), chs. 5-8, especially pp. 201-206. The perception of a serious unified threat to Indochina developed just before the attack in Korea, following conclusion of the Sino-Soviet alliance. See Harrison Salisbury, "Image and Reality in Indochina," *Foreign Affairs* 49 (April 1971): 385-386. The Korean War, as often noted, was seen within the United States government against the backdrop of the first Soviet nuclear test and the Communist takeover of the China mainland. It was interpreted as presaging a series of attacks along the boundaries of the so-called Sino-Soviet Bloc. Green deals with the ambiguity of United States purposes in East Asia by arguing that while United States policy has not reflected a conscious "sophisticated balance of power rationale," such as concern over one-power dominance, it was, in fact, motivated by concerns that were broadly of this character. Greene, *U.S. Policy . . .* pp. 35-36.

12. Since Russian-Chinese relations were apparently characterized by a great deal of tension even from the beginning of their alliance in 1950, this aspect of the change is less a change in the actual environment of policy-making than in the United States perception of that environment. A major Sino-Soviet war, could, of course, pose major dangers to world peace and has therefore been consistently recognized as contrary to United States interests.

13. See, for example, Greene, *U.S. Policy. . . .* Greene also includes the avoidance of Communist domination of India in his definition of the primary long-term United States objectives in Asia.

14. A. Doak Barnett, "A Nuclear China and U.S. Arms policy," *Foreign Affairs* 48 (April 1970): 437.

15. David P. Mozingo, "Containment in Asia Reconsidered," *World Politics* 29 (April 1967): 367.

16. A good discussion of a number of these changes is contained in Klaus Knorr, *On the Uses of Military Power in the Nuclear Age* (Princeton: Princeton University Press, 1966), ch. 2.

17. William P. Bundy, "New Tides in Southeast Asia," *Foreign Affairs* 49 (January 1971): 191.

18. Melvin Gurtov, *Southeast Asia Tomorrow: Problems and Prospects for U.S. Policy* (Baltimore: The Johns Hopkins Press, 1970), ch. 3.

19. For discussions of such constraints and their effects, see, in addition to Knorr, *Uses of Military Power . . .* , Stanley Hoffman, *Gulliver's Troubles, or the Setting of American Foreign Policy* (New York: McGraw-Hill, 1968), especially ch. 3.

20. I am, of course, aware of the fact that public statements usually have very serious limitations as bases for foreign-policy analysis. However, it does seem to me that these two reports, and especially the second, represent a quite sophisticated effort to state the basis of United States policy. They are comparable in general character to the "Basic National Security Policies" prepared more or less annually during the Eisenhower Administration. If these reports are often less than clear on the issues being discussed here, their lack of clarity seems no greater than that of other Administration statements and actions.

21. *U.S. Foreign Policy for the 1970s—I*, p. 55.

22. These points are from *U.S. Foreign Policy for the 1970s—II*, pp. 106-107, 92, 94, and 177-178, respectively. Barnett specifically rejects this last view, which is inconsistent with the picture of Chinese intentions which he presents in *Nuclear China . . .* , p. 436.

23. See *Statement of Secretary of Defense Melvin R. Laird before the House Armed Services Committee, March 9, 1971* (Washington: Government Printing Office, 1971), p. 52. Laird acknowledges that the Sino-Soviet border conflict and logistical difficulties limit the Chinese capability for conventional warfare against non-Communist states to one front. China is also said to have a "significant ability to promote and support subversion and insurgency in peripheral areas."

24. Richard M. Nixon, "Asia after Vietnam," *Foreign Affairs* 46 (October 1967): 121 (emphasis in original). See also, *U.S. Foreign Policy for the 1970s—II*, p. 106.

25. *U.S. Foreign Policy for the 1970s—II*, pp. 157-163.

26. Iriye, *Across the Pacific. . . .*

27. For a much fuller, but congruent, exploration of the sources of the missionary impulse in the West, see Theodore Geiger, *The Conflicted Relationship: The West and the Transformation of Asia, Africa, and Latin America* (New York: McGraw-Hill 1967), chs. 1-3.

28. Neil Sheehan, et al., *The Pentagon Papers* (New York: Bantam Books, 1971), p. xiv.

29. I recognize that the argument here necessarily has a speculative element and that the apparent loss of a sense of mission and mastery over their environment may be a phenomenon confined to those especially influenced intellectually by the Vietnam experience—middle-class youth and a part of the foreign-policy elite. Even so, since foreign policy making is a function performed predominantly by a middle-class elite, the development is significant. For generally confirming evidence on the attitudes of youth, see Graham Allison, "Cool It: The Foreign Policy of Young America," *Foreign Policy* (Winter 1970-71): 144-160. It is my guess that many of Mr. Allison's "Axioms of Young Americans" would now be accepted by at least the middle levels (and younger members) of the foreign-policy elite.

30. *United States Foreign Policy for the 1970s—II*, pp. 6-7, 10-11, 16-17.

31. See, for example, the statement of Secretary of State Hull, quoted in Gordon, *Disengagement . . .* , p. 45.

32. Chester L. Cooper, *The Lost Crusade: America in Vietnam* (New York: Dodd, Mead, 1970), pp. 443 ff.

33. On the need for order, generally, see Everett E. Hagen, *On the Theory of Social Change: How Economic Growth Begins* (Homewood: Dorsey Press, 1962), pp. 106-107. Hagen's generalized but useful description of the traditional state of society emphasizes the role of uncertainty in traditional society and describes a number of devices by which men cope with it by creating order. See ibid., ch. 4. In this, as in other respects (suggested elsewhere by Roger Masters), there are interesting parallels between traditional society and international society.

34. William Whitworth, *Naive Questions about Peace and War* (New York: W.W. Norton, 1970), especially pp. 42, 49, and ch. 7.

35. *United States Foreign Policy for the 1970s—II*, p. 93.

36. See the useful report by Barbara F. Pace, Kathryn Young and Kathryn Rafferty (with Bernard K. Gordon), *Regional Cooperation in Southeast Asia: The First Two Years of ASEAN—1967-1969* (McLean, Virginia: Research Analysis Corporation, RAC-R-398-2, 1970). ASEAN's predecessor, ASA, was virtually destroyed by the Malaysia-Philippine dispute over Sabah.

37. For supporting Asian perspectives, see Lewis, "The Nixon Doctrine . . . ,"

38. Richard M. Nixon, "Asia after Vietnam," 114-115.

39. On the latter, see Bernard K. Gordon, "U.S. Defense in the Nuclear Age," *Current History* 57 (August 1969): 100-104.

40. Two commentators on an earlier draft of this paper have suggested that this discussion *may* overemphasize the role of regionalism in Administration thinking. While it is always difficult to separate rhetoric from real views, it is interesting that there was a marked increase in the emphasis upon regionalism between the two State of the World reports. (Compare, for example: "Asian regional cooperation is at its beginning," with "the scope and effectiveness of regionalism in Asia has now reached significant levels.") Perhaps the difference reflects an awareness of a gap between the Nixon Doctrine and Asian reality which was filled by new rhetoric on regionalism.

41. For appraisals of the Japanese role, see Kenneth Hunt, "Japan's Military Policy: A New Era Begins?" *Interplay* 4 (March 1971): 44-48; Akira Onishi, "Japanese Interests in Southeast Asia—A Japanese View," *Asian Survey* 11 (April 1971): 413-421; Kobun Ito, "Japan's Security in the 1970s," ibid. 10 (December 1970): 1031-1036; Matthew M. Gardner, Jr., "Perceptions, Economics and Assumptions Concerning the Japanese Relations with Southeast Asia during the Sato Incumbency" paper delivered at the Annual Meeting of the Association for Asian Studies, Washington, D.C., March 29-31, 1971; Gurtov, *Southeast Asia Tomorrow*, pp. 60-62.

42. The propositions about Southeast Asian trade are based upon the tables in Gardner, *Perceptions . . . .* On the wider area, see Onishi, *Japanese Interests . . .*, p. 414. It is of interest that Onishi sees Japan as moving increasingly away from a Southeast Asian regional approach and toward a global approach to foreign aid.

43. Gardner, *Perceptions . . . .*

44. In this connection, the Administration's view of the past Communist threat is of interest. It argues that the nations of Asia, in the period following

World War II," . . . faced a common menace of thrusting Communist ambition" and were able to survive and progress because of the United States security shield. (*U.S. Foreign Policy for the 1970s—II*, p. 93). In other words, our interposed strength, rather than limited Communist ambitions, explains the earlier survival of non-Communist Asia. The China specialists generally assume a continuity of Chinese Communist purposes and methods and view our earlier fears as exaggerated and based upon misperception.

45. *New York Times*, 24 January 1971, p. 1.

46. The Kellen, Pond and Turley papers in this volume all agree on the likelihood of a Communist strategy of protracted war and a gradualist approach to victory. However, Hanoi has had, at least since 1965, a serious problem as to how it is to achieve final victory. This problem appears likely to lead it, at some time in the future (as in the past) into bolder moves. So long as the Communists remain in a relatively stronger position in Laos and Cambodia than in South Vietnam, it also seems likely that they will use their strength there to put pressures on South Vietnam (as Gurtov suggests in his paper).

47. There has, in fact, been a reversal of the trend toward reduced levels of security assistance under the Nixon Administration. See Earl C. Ravenal, "The State of Nixon's World (2): The Political-Military Gap," *Foreign Policy* (Summer 1971): 32.

48. For a sophisticated version of such a model, see A. Doak Barnett, "The New Multipolar Balance in East Asia: Implications for United States Policy," *The Annals* 390 (July 1970): 73-86. Some of the policy ideas in this chapter are drawn from Barnett's discussion.

49. Badgley, taking a somewhat similar view, has suggested the label "Byzantine." See John H. Badgley, "The American Territorial Presence in Asia," *The Annals* 390 (July 1970): 38-47.

50. For a further development of the argument briefly stated here, see my article, "Vietnamization: Can It Work?", *Foreign Affairs* 48 (July 1970): 629-647.

12 The Impact of the Indochina Involvement on American Political Institutions

MacAlister Brown

The 1960s have been nominated by Chester Cooper, as the Decade of Vietnam.[1] This designation may catch on with American historians as well as weary and reflective Southeast Asia veterans. Since it relegates Vietnam to the past, and implies a new theme for the 1970s, it has a practical attraction. As to competing symbols for the 1960s, the self-assertion of Black America, the race to the moon, or the flowering culture of Youth, these movements maintain their momentum, while the war in Vietnam may none too soon become a distinct episode in our history. Its impact on our national life has been sharp and probably lasting.

This essay will attempt to weigh the impact of the war in Indochina on our political institutions, both constitutional and administrative, and their public environment. It is not intended to suggest what the impact should have been, or what lessons should be learned from Vietnam. Rather we start with the question whether the prolonged involvement in Indochina has exerted as profound an effect on our system as the great events of previous epochs, the Great Depression, World War II, or the Cold War. Has anything as lasting as the New Deal Coalition at the polling booth, or the governmental internal security apparatus of the 1950s arisen out of the frustration and dismay of Vietnam?

The involvement of the United States with Indochina is not a thing of the past decade alone, though the intensity of the relationship skyrocketed during this period. The time frame for measuring the impact of Indochina on our political institutions can reach back as far as our initial military assistance to the French in May 1950, or more significantly to the French cry for help at Dienbienphu in April 1954. Critical issues arose then concerning legitimate procedures for involving the nation in war, the availability and appropriate use of military power (including atomic bombs), and our capacity to exercise political influence in emerging nations. The choices made by the Eisenhower Administration in 1954 set the stage for hundreds of critical choices in the 1960s, which have affected our political institutions.

To attribute significant impact to the American involvement in Indochina, this essay will apply several ground rules. The Indochina-related change or stress in our institutions must be inconceivable if the United States involvement had never occurred. In other words, if the United States had not fallen in behind the departing French in 1954 (or later), the impacts we shall identify could not have taken place. This is obviously a stringent limitation on our possible findings, which will rest upon somewhat headlong historical speculation. While this may depart from the preferred method of modern political scientists, there can be no controlled experiment in accounting for the change in our political institutions. Before and after observations and best guesses as to what would have happened if the designated variable (in this case the post-1954 involvement with Indochina) had not appeared will have to suffice. To remove almost two decades of diplomatic and military involvement from our political life leaves tremendous room for other relationships of equivalent nature to have developed. We shall assume, however, that any United States involvements which might have developed elsewhere in the world would not have been wholly equivalent to that which did arise in Indochina. The impacts which we associate with Indochina should stand as the outcome of that particular overseas involvement. They should not reflect secular trends which would have appeared even if Ngo Dinh Diem and John Foster Dulles had never entered public life and John F. Kennedy had never visited Dallas. They should not be the artifacts of a particular President or political leader unrelated to the unique problems which Indochina presented to him. The further question of whether changes in our institutions were prevented from happening by the Indochina engagement is a speculative problem of even greater dimension, which we cannot hope to solve. However, the question of the *lasting* impact versus the *temporary* impact, that is, effects on our institutions which will lose their hold as the United States recedes from the region, is not too formidable to permit a modest effort at prediction. The purpose of the exercise in any case is reflection in the interest of suggesting areas for definitive assessment upon the conclusion of the Indochina affair.

The Executive Branch

With the memory of the 1968 Presidential election still discomfiting us and speculation about Richard Nixon's prospect for reelection growing topical, a linkage between Indochina and the Presidency is easy to assert. Lyndon Johnson believed that Vietnam cost him 20 points in the public opinion polls and, though his wife's memoirs tend to confuse the issue, it seems clear that without Vietnam, President Johnson would have seen no need to remove himself as a Presidential candidate in 1968. Even though later scholarly analysis of the polls has attributed to the Vietnam War no independent additional impact on Johnson's decline in popularity, it is Johnson's perception of the matter that counts for our purposes.[2] Harry Truman also decided not to seek another term in office in the midst of an unpopular war, but his initial memorandum to himself on the subject antedated the war itself. Richard Nixon now faces the prospect of a challenge to his renomination, similar to Johnson's in that it will arise out of the Congress and express itself in the earliest state primary elections. Without projecting the parallel any further, one must ask whether this intraparty challenge to incumbent Presidents is significantly new and whether it is war-related.

Customarily incumbent Presidents have been able to use their office as a presumptive claim on renomination and deter all but the most determined or alienated party cohorts from challenging their return.[3] Since 1952, the Twenty-second Amendment has limited the President to one such renomination, and state primary election campaigns have achieved heightened significance through national television coverage. The party primary challengers to Johnson in 1968 and Nixon in 1972, have presented the war in Indochina as their fundamental issue, with a special moral fervor. The New Hampshire primary voters who actually supported the Presidential challenger in 1968, however, were responding negatively to a variety of issues concerning the man in the White House, and will doubtless do the same in 1972.[4] Nonetheless, the Indochina War has served as a catalyst to ambitious political personalities who seem to feel strongly about the war policies of their own party leader. With the President's presumptive claim to renomination clearly diminished by the primaries of 1968, and possibly 1972, there is reason to foresee this intraparty challenge continuing with a regularity that did not exist before the Indochina War provoked its effective use. This apparent insecurity of our national party leadership may reflect a deeper realignment process overtaking the party system. Yet that phenomenon itself, if it exists, is partially related to the existence of the war. Whether or not American party politics resume the traditional path of two parties contending over the center ground, the phenomenal decline of Lyndon Johnson's electoral prospects between 1964 and 1968 has demonstrated a fragility in Presidential mandates arising to a large degree out of foreign relations, which was partially obscured by Harry Truman's not wanting renomination in 1952.[5] This threat to Presidential second terms, is quite unlike the nemesis which overtook Herbert Hoover and William Howard Taft. It has been underscored by the Indochina War, and presidential aspirants will henceforth give this issue area the very special attention it deserves.

The war has probably affected another aspect of our Presidential elections beside the political security of incumbents. We saw in 1968 a shredding of the conventional civility accorded our President in the public pursuance of his ceremonial and partisan duties. One can only speculate whether the threshold has been lowered to a new level of abuse of the President's person, which Lyndon Johnson spared himself by abandoning the quest but which future Presidents might nonetheless have to suffer. The siege of a President in his White House can be lifted by helicopter and by carefully selected friendly audiences prepared to hear uplifting messages. Yet, the physical threat to the dignity, not to mention the safety, of the Presidency, which the radical antiwar movement posed to Lyndon Johnson in 1968 may be regarded by extreme political activists of the future as a proven instrument for ending Presidencies.[6] If young people are ready to resort to such intimidating tactics, it may reflect changes in their social values with regard to authority and seniority quite apart from the purely political element of their socialization, but the passions generated by the prolonged and bloody war in Vietnam have stimulated and reinforced this change in values.

The public relations efforts which four successive Presidents have devoted to explaining their Indochina policies to a steadily more attentive public have grown more ventive and consuming. As the burdens for the taxpayer and fighting man have grown heavier, so have the selling techniques, and the public doubts and skepticism. If President Kennedy's finest speeches, at American and Yale Universities, were devoted to international affairs and economics, President Nixon has almost nothing to choose among but a series of televised protective reactions on the Vietnam question. The overriding salience of the war issue has also affected the relationship between the Presidents, and possibly their successors, and the press. Lyndon Johnson, to be sure, broke immediately with his predecessor's pattern of rather regular bimonthly televised performances before the press corps, because he shrewdly saw his talents more effectively applied to impromptu encounters in a variety of more intimate settings.[7] The perverse turn of fortunes he experienced with the war, however, combined with his ingrained conviction that the press would never give him, a Texan, a fair break, made any return to regularly scheduled general encounters with the journalists quite out of the question. Johnson's penchant for springing surprises and his many months of groping for good news and withholding real news from Vietnam and other trouble spots developed a public uncertainty which the press labeled "the credibility gap," thereby intensifying the tension.[8]

President Nixon, relieved by Johnson of the periodic general press conference tradition, has groped for his own best medium. Again, the threat of disagreeable questions about a clearly unpopular war (as well as a famed unwillingness to "be kicked around again" by the press) have encouraged him to minimize the formal conferences and find more intimate and favorable settings.[9] These have veered from old-fashioned press conferences to televised chats with a few correspondents or the hostess of the Today Show. The electronic media invite a variety of formats for the President to convey information and advocacy to the nation, which resourceful Presidents were bound to try out, just as their opponents have captured television time with articulation devices of their own. The unpopularity and dragging quality of the Indochina War issue, however, have reinforced the use of Presidentially staged presentations to the public at the expense of encounters shaped by the press. This precedent if sustainable after the War, would seriously alter the manner in which the press can function as a democratic device within our political system.[10]

Another striking feature of the Indochina involvement has been the close White House guidance over operations as the war expanded. In part, this Presidential control over military action reflected the restless, domineering nature of Lyndon Johnson, but it reflected his situation as well, and implicitly assimilated the lessons learned by Harry Truman in dealing with his theater commanders in a limited war in Asia. President Johnson's grudging conclusion in February 1965 that he must selectively but punitively bomb the North to save the South spurred the enthusiasm of Air Force planners for their vocation and seemed to require the White House as an air command post, which carefully designated targets and missions in weekly packages. The gradual narrowing of vision, the rigidification of thought, which overtook this informal, secretive and personalized system of civilian control has been deplored by journalists and peripheral participants.[11] It has not apparently prompted Lyndon Johnson's successor however to reduce the involvement of the President and his national security staff in military operations.

The burgeoning growth of the National Security Council Staff under Henry Kissinger, and the prominence of the McGeorge Bundy and Walt Rostow operations during the Kennedy and Johnson periods have reflected to some degree the force of personalities, both in the White House basement and on the seventh floor of the State Department. Yet, the Indochina intervention served to reinforce this administrative innovation of the post-Eisenhower years, the creation in the White House of an influential national security adviser to the President himself. The competing perspectives of the diplomatic, military, and intelligence bureaucracies were continually juxtaposed in conducting a limited war in tandem with an unpopular, incapable client regime before a dismayed or hostile world audience. Walking such a tightrope, the President needed an additional voice and an organizing hand to clarify and resolve conflicting biases of his military and political bureaucracies. With the National Security Council Staff growing to more than one hundred persons under Kissinger, a reaction may be brewing which will reduce the scope of influence and the unaccountability of the Special Assistant in the future. The staff is not a product of the war *per se*, but Congressional resentment of it is an outgrowth of investigations into executive secrecy about Indochina operations.[12]

Led by the Senate Committee on Foreign Relations, a strong reaction has also set in to the flimsy legal basis upon which our Presidents committed the nation to so costly a military venture. The reassertion of the Senate in this confusing constitutional struggle is a topic to be dealt with in its own right, but the net impact on the Presidency can be estimated here. Under Secretary of State Nicholas Katzenbach asserted before the Fulbright Committee in 1967 that the Protocol to the Southeast Asia Treaty extending its scope to the "free territory under the jurisdiction of the State of Vietnam," together with the Tonkin Gulf Resolution approving Presidential determinations to assist Vietnam, constituted a "functional declaration of war." This seemed to be a high water mark in interpretation of the Constitution in favor of the Chief Executive. The Tonkin Resolution has since been not only renounced by its Senate sponsor, J.W. Fulbright, but repealed by the Senate altogether (July 10, 1970). Senators Mansfield and Mathias are gunning to wipe out all such enabling resolutions which Presidents have received from the Congress since Korea for authorizing military aid or action in the Formosa Straits, the Middle East and Cuba. The second thoughts which arose out of the suddenness and confusion of the Tonkin Gulf affair were sharpened by the almost taunting use to which the Resolution was put by the President many months and thousands of casualties later. Even before the Pentagon Papers revealed the Administration's private thoughts about public and Congressional relations, the well of Congressional trust had been poisoned by President Johnson's dramatic stage management and rhetorical legalisms. The "blank check" resolution authorizing discretionary Presidential use of force so neatly used by President Eisenhower, will not be passable in the Senate for some time to come. President Nixon has already prepared himself for the situation by asserting no need for such resolutions in achieving his purposes.

Here is a case of the political style of one President nullifying a particular device for modernizing the war-making clause of an 18th century constitution. It need not necessarily have happened. The further ramification of the issue, however, is the Senate's National Commitments Resolution of June 25, 1969 which Senator Javits has hailed as a "watershed in the American Experience";[13] even though the Executive Branch has expressed no similar enthusiasm. This resolution affirms the sense of the Senate that "a national commitment by the United States results only from affirmative action taken by the Executive and Legislative branches of the United States Government by means of a treaty, statute, or concurrent resolution of both Houses of Congress specifically providing for such commitment." Pursuing the matter through investigative hearings, the Senate Foreign Relations Committee pried loose information concerning nuclear weapons abroad, intelligence activities, and other matters previously locked in Executive Agreements with Asian and nondemocratic governments receiving American military assistance.[14]

Having once divulged this much, the Chief Executive was under pressure to disclose more to the Congress, and perhaps the public, than they had been wont to do in the past, and the unexpected leaking of the *Pentagon Papers* to the press created a situation which virtually forced the Executive Branch to be more forthcoming.[15] Congressional champions of freedom of information have not hesitated to press their momentary advantage. This probably long-term diminution of Executive discretion (or expansion of the public's right to know) is not simply a reaction to the penchant for secrecy of President Johnson. It seems probable that the issue would have arisen regardless of presidential personalities once the nation had been committed incrementally to such a costly, ill-defined venture as the war in Indochina and begun to worry about why it had happened.

Congress

As the Indochina venture has been drained of patriotic immunity to public criticism, the Congress has asserted a more independent role in the enterprise. Traditionally such Congressional reassertions have occurred in the aftermath of wartime enhancements of the Presidency, as Woodrow Wilson learned to his sorrow. Harry Truman, despite the election of an opposition Congress in 1946 and the overriding of his vetoes in key domestic legislation, was able to cultivate Senator Vandenberg and sound the alarm over British bankruptcy and the Greek and Turkish jeopardy, thereby maintaining Presidential initiative in fighting his Cold War with Communism. Presidents after Indochina may find their leeway in overseas affairs even more restricted by the Congress than Harry Truman's would have been without the threat of civil wars and Communist Parties in Western Europe. Not only has the U.S.S.R. settled down and the international system become more complex since the 1940s, but also important precedents have been established during the Congressional agonizing over the withdrawal from Vietnam.

In the final moments of the 92nd Congress (Dec. 22, 1970), the two houses of Congress agreed in the Foreign Assistance Act on prohibiting the introduction of United States combat troops or the provision of military advisers to Cambodia and requiring full disclosure regarding other aid activities there. This legislation was a logical extension of the Senate's Cooper-Church Amendment to the Foreign Military Sales Act of 1968 which had sought in June to bar the retention of U.S. forces in Cambodia. The House would not agree at that time to tie the President's hand in military operations. Six months later, as its aged Speaker McCormick, steeped in World War II and Cold War perspectives, stood on the threshold of retirement, the House began to catch up with the Senate. It passed a joint resolution admonishing the President "whenever possible" to consult with Congress before involving American forces in armed conflict, and acceded to the Senate version of the Defense Appropriations Act which sought to make illegal the introduction of American ground forces into Cambodia or Laos.

The spate of bills and resolution designed to control the President's use of military forces which the shock of the Cambodia incursion produced, has been followed by more deliberate efforts by the appropriate committees in both houses to scrutinize and redefine the Constitutional responsibilities for initiating and waging war.[16] The Senate even went so far in June 1971 as to pass an amendment to the draft extension bill which would declare United States policy to be the withdrawal of all military forces within nine months of its passage provided all prisoners of war were released by Hanoi. Although the tide of such efforts may crest and recede without legally restraining the President, just as the Bricker Amendment to restrict Executive Agreements fell just short of Senate adoption in 1954, the notice will be served that military operations abroad will not automatically receive the benefit of the legislative doubt in the future. A significant precedent has been established in using the defense appropriations process to legislate limitations on the disposition of military forces during an actual military campaign.

A potent use has been made in the Senate of the televised hearing process to focus public attention on the Executive rationale for his policies, and on learned criticisms by outsiders. The dogged performances of Secretary Rusk and Mc-Namara before the Fulbright Committee and the frequent invitations to Secretaries Rogers and Laird to testify are measures of the strain arising in the bipartisan modalities of Congressional advice and consent when foreign military interventions bog down short of Executive promises. In 1951, General MacArthur's letter to Republican Minority Leader Joe Martin challenging Administration policy in Korea did not evoke the sustained critique within the Congress or its appropriate committees that the Senate has witnessed with respect to Indochina since 1966. To be sure, the issue is curiously reversed. In 1951, the Congressional critics wanted more military power to be used, in 1966, they pressed for less. In 1951, the testimony of the Chiefs of Staff and their military Secretary of Defense held wide respect, in 1966, the military men were overshadowed by the uningratiating Rusk and McNamara. In 1951, the Chairman of the Senate Foreign Relations Committee remained loyal to the President's policies, even though the internal security committees rampaged through the attic of recent Far Eastern policy in search of spies and scapegoats. In 1966, some members of the Foreign Relations Committee were written off by the White House.

Another important difference between these wartime relationships is the larger staff available today to gather information independently for the foreign affairs committees. The publication of Staff Reports for the use of the Senate Committee on Foreign Relations has served to arm the attentive public with official documents from the legislative branch which challenge Executive policy quite independent of Executive testimony.[17] The build-up of committee staff, reflects a need felt throughout the Congress in seeking to retain a grasp on the immensity of Government operations. The dispatch of investigators abroad, however, and prompt publication of their findings and opinions is a new dimension in the struggle between the two branches of government for control over American foreign policy. The more decorous procedure of issuing reports by individual Senators, which Senator Mike Mansfield first used with respect to Indochina in 1955, or publishing reports following committee hearings, might still be in vogue but for the frustrations and surprises of the Indochina War and the deep distrust of Executive testimony which they have deposited. As Senator Javits put it, "Senators today are inclined to cast a jaundiced eye on Presidential assessments, and, unfortunately, even on assertions of fact."[18]

The fabric of bipartisanship so carefully woven by Secretary of State Dean Acheson and Senator Arthur Vandenberg for coping with the Cold War has been stretched and torn but not wholly rent. President Johnson's sternest critics arose within his own party, swelling the band of two Democratic Senators who voted against the Tonkin Gulf Resolution of August 1964. The opposition party did not threaten to deny him legislative support for his diplomatic or military moves so much as the doves and presidential aspirants in his own camp. President Nixon chose a shrewd veteran of the legislative halls as his Secretary of Defense and a likeable, low-keyed lawyer for his Secretary of State. These men have won a minimal forebearance from the Democrats for their policy of gradual withdrawal from Indochina, even though the United States Senate today is much richer in budding Presidents than it was in the days of Acheson and Vandenberg or John Foster Dulles and Walter George. The Secretaries' efforts have been hampered, it seems, by the lesser grasp that they had over the shaping and ultimate deciding of policies such as the incursion into Cambodia or the prison camp rescue mission. Unlike the fateful consultation between the Eisenhower Administration and the leadership of Congress over whether to rescue the French at Dienbienphu, the Nixon Administration avoided taking the Democrats into their confidence before the sweep into Cambodia in 1970. Despite the shock and anger this breach of bipartisan conventions produced, the Administration was able half a year later to win a moratorium on hostile Congressional criticism during its allied Laotian incursion. The failure of this mission to live up to the promise of its secret Senate briefing, however, burst the bonds of bipartisan self-restraint with a new round of committee hearings aimed at pushing the Administration to accelerate its indefinite, unsteady course of withdrawal. Bipartisanship, and the courtesies and devices by which it has been nurtured, has not been obliterated by the Indochina War, but many Senators now consider the war an exception to the rule, and such redefinitions can become habitual.

The strenuous opposition to the Antiballistic Missile (ABM), the Supersonic Transport (SST), and the proposed B-1 supersonic bomber fall somewhat outside the critical zone of bipartisan tradition, but they provide a warning that the President cannot count on the unquestioning support of his own or the opposition party for major spending programs related to defense or national prestige. The enormous financial burden and pernicious economic effects of the precipitous Vietnam military build-up ordered by President Johnson have contributed to the Congressional readiness to resist the Executive in previously sacrosanct areas of expenditure.

The Executive Bureaucracy

In addition to affecting the relationships of the Presidency and Congress, the Indochina involvement has left its mark upon the many agencies and personnel of the Executive Branch, particularly the national security elements. One of the most fruitful byproducts of the period has been the forced acquaintance of Americans with Southeast Asia. Thanks to a tradition of relative indifference toward the area during western colonialism, and the debilitating purge of State Department Far East experts spurred by Senator Joseph McCarthy in the 1950s, the government assumed responsibility in Indochina with precious little knowledge at the time of the Geneva Conference of 1954.[19] The fateful consequences of this inadequacy during the Eisenhower administration has been pointed out many times, but even eleven years later, as we moved into full-scale military operations, the number of true Vietnam experts in this country "could be counted on one's fingers."[20] Our deep involvement in not only military defense but also economic and political development of South Vietnam, with limited efforts in Laos and Cambodia, has created a civil corps of Indochina veterans, but effective use of them has been hampered by the rapid turnover rate of military and even State Department personnel in the theatre. The disenchantment and hostility toward our policies in Indochina which swelled up after 1965 within the academic community may have turned some younger scholars away from serving in the area, but it also stimulated a good deal of semischolarly writing about Indochina.[21] Even though military, administrative, and social science research experience in the field has developed a knowledgeable cadre of Vietnam hands during the 1960s, these persons are often torn or sensitized by their past involvement in the policy controversies, operations and predictions in the area. If the United States will not lack for experienced people in dealing with these countries in the future, it may find it hard to decide, nonetheless, whose advice may claim proven or even probable reliability.

The national peace movement, beginning with the teach-ins organized on university campuses in early 1966, polarized faculties and students, and professional academic associations alike. The Committee of Concerned Asian Scholars, organized in 1968, united social scientists of many disciplines who had jostled and disturbed their own Associations but generally failed to politicize them to the point of passing condemnatory resolutions on the government's Vietnam policy. The deep animosity and the scholarly training of thousands of professors and students who felt they must condemn their government produced a parade of radical commentary and journalism which has undermined the linkages between the government and universities. The resort to bomb attacks on prominent Centers of International Studies by extreme elements in the antiwar and young radical movement will probably decline with the casualty lists. The political residue of the radical challenge, however, will be a widespread unwillingness of faculties and scholarly groups to formalize relationships with government agencies or their semiautonomous research organizations. The sensitivity to being branded as a CIA cohort or the chosen instrument of the Department of Defense will prevail not only on the campus of Michigan State or Southern Illinois University, but also within the minds of individual scholars who might otherwise have been useful consultants to government and among the officers of foreign area study groups which heretofore have accepted government funds to support their work. These inhibitions to joining the national security enterprise in any indirect fashion may provide a more discerning outside criticism and evaluation of government policies. Yet it may also deprive the government of acute inside consultation and contractual services and haunt the reputations of scholars who have been "compromised" by Vietnam service prior to 1968.

Another reaction to the Indochina failures of the bureaucracies is emerging in the writings of both outside critics and former insiders. The acclaim which Robert McNamara initially won for cost-benefit analysis at the Pentagon has been dissipated by the bitterly contested, unreliable TFX aircraft and by the tragic use of quantitative indicators to publicly pronounce the "light at the end of the tunnel" or the "turning of the corner" in the warfare and "pacification" in Vietnam. Under mounting criticism of the war at home, McNamara's department was driven ever harder to provide systematic measurements of progress. The techniques of systems analysis were geared to providing a flood of statistics "on priority programs in key provinces, graphs, slides and charts, regression curves. Numbers! There was a number mill in every military and AID installation in Vietnam . . . Sometimes the numbers were plucked out of the air, sometimes the numbers were not accurate. Sometimes they were accurate but not relevant. Sometimes they were relevant but misinterpreted.[22] Even though the Pentagon Papers now document the extent to which the chief spokesmen for systems analysis accurately gauged the failure of the bombing policy, dropped their earlier advocacy of sustained reprisals, and played a part in turning President Johnson around, the future claims of noncareer officials may be treated less deferentially within the government.[23] Estimates of political viability of regimes and the capacity and tenacity of hostile forces will be made with more recognition of the unquantifiable elements, and the judgment of the career intelligence community may be given greater respect by political appointees.

This caution may make for better decisions, but what is not so salutary is the public skepticism of government numbers, surveys, and predictions which the dismal catalogue of "progress reports" on Vietnam has helped to reinforce. This impact has been compounded by the hyperbole which has characteristically intruded into Presidential addresses on Vietnam. In striking contrast, one can read in the Pentagon Papers the understated dehumanizing jargon of the military planners. Neither style of expression will reassure the informed public of the future.

A more sweeping challenge to the government's approach to the outside world is found in the indictment of "national security managers" expounded by writers such as Richard J. Barnet and utilized in part by "establishment" liberals.[24] Even though many participants in the Adlai Stevenson Institute's conference on Vietnam in 1968 considered Barnet's analysis extravagant or erroneous, it speaks the viewpoint that will be held by aggressive elements of the coming generation of potential civil servants. The "interventionist thrust" of postwar American foreign policy can be accounted for in their view by the exaggerated definitions of threat, the confrontation model of world politics, imposed upon the nation by the "national security bureaucracy." A military mold has encased our foreign policy. With young revisionist historians challenging the conventional view of the Cold War, as might be expected this long after the event, the dolorous results of the Indochina intervention are undermining the operational code of the Cold War generation bureaucrats who conducted it. The generalized discredit the revisionists have cast upon the foreign affairs bureaucracies may prompt some sophisticated members of the Vietnam generation to move into government where they might reorient the structure, but many others will be inclined to seek the company of nongovernmental or domestic reform agencies instead.[25] The impact on recruitment to the national security services may very well be significant. A State Department Task force on recruitment found in 1970 many college students less interested in Foreign Service career possibilities than in asking questions about the efficacy of the State Department and our Southeast Asia policy. The applicants as a whole are frequently not of as high quality as they once were and often the most promising candidates fail to accept appointments or resign early. The applications from the best colleges and schools of international studies have declined.[26]

The post mortems of the Indochina failure are hard upon us, spurred by the writing of memoirs and a bonanza of documents. Public recriminations may yet take a turn to the right, if the popularly held objective of an independent non-Communist South Vietnam is not achieved. Whether viewed from the right or the left, however, the Indochina episode has left our foreign and military affairs departments ready for new doctrines to replace the tatters of their operating assumptions of the 1960s. A Kennedy stalwart of the Defense Department, Adam Yarmolinsky, has plainly questioned the "flexible response" posture which he once considered such an improvement over the "massive retaliation" doctrine of the Eisenhower Administration. In an article for *Foreign Affairs*, he wrote, "Theories of limited war and programs to widen the President's range of choice made military solutions to our foreign problems more available and even more attractive."[27] The Green Berets and exotic training schools for counter-insurgency techniques may be viewed as dangerous by encouraging intervention in an era when that term has taken on a negative connotation as evocative as appeasement in the 1940s. "No more Vietnams" will ring as an alarm through the halls of government for some time, just as the post-Korean "Never Again Club" prompted U.S. Army staff officers to counsel, unsuccessfully, against land warfare in Asia.[28] President Eisenhower's simile of the falling row of dominos will be not only old-fashioned but unconvincing to boot. Many critics of our Vietnam policy have already challenged it. They have also argued that a great power can afford to withdraw from a mistaken foreign undertaking. The Congress has sounded its warning about secret executive agreements with foreign governments. If that were not enough, the agonies of two Administrations in selling their Indochina policies to the public has certainly demonstrated the pitfalls of deceptive dramatization of American involvements and objectives abroad.

The atrocity incidents and antiwarfare journalism gradually reaching the public consciousness may force an examination of the cryptoracism implicit in many American policies in Indochina, from the forced relocations to saturation bombing and free fire zones, or the use of Meo and Montagnard mercenary forces.[29]

The sham and connivance involved in managing a miniwar in Laos via the Central Intelligence Agency is coming under closer scrutiny as the fighting ebbs in South Vietnam, and the public tolerance of such subterfuges may be effectively reduced. A public mood of introversion, mixed with bitterness over such prolonged and pointless losses, will call for new sets of operating assumptions in the national security apparatus to replace the weary rationale of the European Cold War so rudely applied in Asia. The generally favorable response to President Nixon's readiness to visit Red China suggests that minds are open to such a shift.

Of all the government services the military have probably suffered the most notable effects from Indochina. To be sure they have practiced their vocation under combat conditions for a longer period than any previous war afforded them. They have tested weapons and tactics at the subnuclear level against a determined foe. Yet, they may have reason to wonder whether this will prepare them for any comparable engagement in this generation. Furthermore, the prestige and credibility of their chief spokesmen which was so high following World War II, and even during the dismissal of General MacArthur in 1951, has been severely wounded by the record of false promises of victory and grim insistence on pursuing an unpopular war. The failure of aerial bombing once again to achieve victory, the rejected recommendation of General Westmoreland to invest another two hundred thousand troops in the contest following the Tet offensive, and the sickening weight of armament and explosive so lavishly expended in this corner of Asia to such little tangible gain for the United States, raise frightening challenges to the competence and vision of the military profession. Doubtless the senior officers who helped plan and fight the war will raise counter challenges of their own,[30] just as the field commanders who were not allowed to win the Korean War vented their spleen on political influences and civilian leaders for some years after the Armistice. The post-Korea Army had grown to accept the doctrine of limited war by the time the Vietnam situation beckoned—the debate was largely settled by the Congressional investigation following General MacArthur's dismissal—but it will be more difficult this time for the military services to take stock and reorder their thinking. The prolonged and partially successful effort at counterinsurgency and creation of a self-sustaining foreign military force will leave a confusing record for assessment.

The fall of the military elite from its former high repute is paralleled by alarming avoidance of military service by draft eligibles. The readiness of young men to flee abroad, construct a conscientious objection, accept imprisonment, connive at draft exemptions, or resign commissions from the military academies is a reflection primarily of the particular war which faced them. An attack upon the territory of the United States or a war to defend our capacity to exist as a great power would not produce such antiwar behavior. Pending such a catastrophe, the military services, probably operating without a draft, will face a recruitment problem which televised commercials about the Army wanting to "join You" will not entirely rectify. The Reserve Officer Training Program will be dead at many university campuses, and veteran officers may retire in bitterness over the punishment of officers implicated in the My Lai and perhaps other incidents. The recriminations over atrocities committed in Vietnam may swell before subsiding, and it may etch into the minds of potential service academy appointees an image of a dangerous profession scarcely offering honor or renown.

The restoration of morale and discipline within the more narrowly recruited postwar military services will be a major undertaking due to Indochina. The easy access to drugs in the alleys of Vietnam has not in itself produced their widespread use among armed forces stationed there. The drug craving has also flourished at home, fed in turn by returning Asia veterans. The tensions and disorientation of American military service in Vietnam, the death and maiming suffered in behalf of a strange and even sullen people, are nonetheless a major cause of the phenomenon. Once this proximate cause is removed, with the exit from Vietnam, the services will probably be able to restrict serious drug abuse, estimated in 1970 as between 10 and 20% among G.I.s in Vietnam.[31] The scars left upon the veterans of Vietnam will remain for the nation and the Veterans Administration to handle. More than 300,000 wounded servicemen, not to mention the psychologically disturbed, will keep that organization going for decades to come.

The traditional authority of officers over their men has been loosening with the growth of humane standards in our society, but the Indochina War has weakened the command relationship within the services and military morale has eroded to the point of threatening operational effectiveness. Flogging or execution of deserters are well removed from our military practice, but the current procedure of separating new men in the field from those who have already refused to fight is a sign of fundamental weakness in an Army. The wearing of uniforms may be scorned without diminishing fighting capacities, but it becomes serious when maintenance of equipment is neglected. If weapons in garrisons must be turned in and locked up, the situation is serious. The "fragging" of officers or NCO's in revenge or resentment of their authority claimed 39 lives in 1969, and the 209 incidents in 1970 was double the previous year.[32] The alienation and license suggested by these figures are a threat to military effectiveness which an end of combat or a different sort of war will doubtless rectify. Indeed, some U.S. Army planners favor the withdrawal of all ground forces from Vietnam in order to safeguard the Army's capability and reputation. The military services will have to proceed cautiously in trying to reoccupy the terrain of traditional military manners and discipline following the departure of their unwilling and unruly drafted manpower.

The Political Public

The state of the public mind during the Indochina War has been difficult enough to understand without trying to project it beyond the end of hostilities. Relatively high levels of information about the war were found by opinion surveys well before the 1968 election campaigns. The vivid presence of the battlefields on television in the homes of newswatchers has been a unique feature of this war. Passive support for the President in his handling of the situation was strong, as it customarily is in foreign policy matters, but a readiness to negotiate and an opposition to the prosecution of the war were also found in significant proportions well before the election.[33] The distribution of opinion among members of Congress in 1966 represented rather accurately the mood of the people, but in September 1970 a majority of the public favored withdrawing troops by the end of 1971, while the Senate rejected such a plan by 55 to 39. In June 1971, the Senate passed the Mansfield amendment calling for a nine-month withdrawal deadline, but the House of Representatives failed to support the specific time limit. Partisan loyalty to the President helps account for this lag behind public opinion.[34] Six citywide referenda during 1966-68 on the question of withdrawal from Vietnam, and public opinion polls, show that the lower the income, education and occupational status, the greater the tendency to favor withdrawal.[35] It is also apparent that Blacks have been more hostile to the war than non-Blacks and would remain hostile to future diversions of attention from their demands at home. Also, women have shown greater disapproval of the war than men.

None of this is particularly surprising, but it may have some consequences for the American political system. The persisting permissive mood toward Presidential leadership in foreign policy and the "rally round the flag" upsurge of approval of the President following his involvement in dramatic international events have shown unprecedented weakness in the final stages of the Indochina War. The allied incursion into Laos in February 1971 was followed by a *decrease* in public approval of the President in the next month's Gallup poll.[36] The stealthy nature of the Administration's public announcement of the venture may have dissociated the event from the President himself sufficiently to account for this unexpected lack of uplift. On the other hand, the independent press and the peace movement may have achieved such influence as to counteract the long-prevailing presumption in favor of presidential foreign affairs leadership. Such a phenomenon would be of major significance were it to continue, but the likelihood of prolonged disapproval of presidential leadership in Indochina is somewhat limited by the coming elections. Nonetheless, the striking disparity between public preferences with regard to a withdrawal timetable and the probable achievement will push many of the generation just entering politics to view our institutions as impossibly unresponsive.

The new voters entering the political system in 1972 will be younger than ever before, thanks in part to the war itself, which has dramatized the claims of eighteen year olds to a voice in their nation's policy making. They will enter with a mood of skepticism of official pronouncements and distrust of old dogmas which few political generations have experienced. And though their distrust of officialdom has been shared by leading Senators and television networks, their own "impudence" will be a political issue in the minds of older generations. The confrontation mode of politics which the civil rights movement stimulated in the early sixties has been carried further with grim imagination by the peace movement into new chapters in political articulation. The youthful imagination of the antiwar groups has developed mass convergence on Washington or political convention sites, student strikes, teach-ins, local referenda or international issues, symbolic seizure of buildings, obstruction of government recruiters and military induction, relentless harassment of progovernment speakers, guerrilla theater, and a host of other devices for expressing their political views. The response of television news teams, law and order forces, and public opinion will help to sift out the political effectiveness of all these new devices. Already, "martyrs" have emerged from the conspiracy trials with which the Justice Department has responded to key leaders of the movement. A sufficient sense of efficacy has probably been retained by the rank-and-file activists, however, to keep them from turning to more violent modes of protest.[37] As the war becomes a less immediate issue, all but the most ideological protesters will probably be coopted into normal electoral form of politics, but they will be joining a political system whose prevailing assumptions about the range of United States responsibilities abroad have been notably affected by the arguments expressed by the peace movement.

Conclusion

The Indochina involvement of the United States has left its mark on the political security and the operating processes of the Presidency, and on its relationships with the Congress in the overlapping spheres of national security policy-making. It has challenged and shifted the perspectives of the bureaucracies which manage these policies and possibly affected their recruitment. It has activated a young generation of political participants, whose claims and outlooks have made headway in the public mind. While these impacts may not add up to the political earthquake that the Great Depression caused in party realignment and philosophical reevaluation, they equal in intensity and significance the turbulence of old versus new perspectives on our responsibilities in the outside world which the much larger event, World War II, precipitated two decades ago.

Notes

1. Chester Cooper, *The Lost Crusade: America in Vietnam* (New York: Dodd, Mead and Co., 1970).

2. John E. Mueller, "Presidential Popularity from Truman to Johnson," *American Political Science Review* 44 (March 1970): 18-34.

3. The most notable party primary challengers to incumbent Presidents

have been Senator Hiram Johnson in 1924, Vice President John N. Garner in 1936, Senator William Knowland in 1956, and Governor George Wallace in 1964. President Richard Nixon's dramatic trip to Peking toward the end of his first term may retrieve the presumption in his favor in a rather unprecedented way.

4. Philip E. Converse, et al., "Continuity and Change in American Politics: Parties and Issues in the 1968 Election," *American Political Science Review* 43 (December 1969): 1083-1105; Mueller argues that a connection between presidential popularity and an ongoing war cannot be simply made, because survey questions may stimulate a response to the President rather than to the war. Cf. "Trends in Popular Support for the Wars in Korea and Vietnam," *American Political Science Review* 65 (June 1971): 370.

5. For the view that an era of new party loyalties is in the offing, see Walter Dean Burnham, *Critical Elections and the Mainsprings of American Politics* (New York: W.W. Norton, 1970); and Frederick G. Dutton, *Changing Sources of Power: American Politics in the 1970s* (New York: McGraw-Hill, 1971). For a conventional interpretation of the 1968 election, see Converse et al., "Continuity. . . ."

6. Theodore H. White alludes to the abuse experienced by Johnson, more vicious than any modern President has had to live with, and the intense worry of his Secret Service based on actual evidence of planned degradations of the President. *The Making of the President 1968* (New York: Atheneum, 1969), pp. 103-04.

7. Elmer E. Cornwell, *Presidential Leadership of Public Opinion* (Bloomington: Indiana University Press, 1965), pp. 201-03, contrasts L.B.J.'s techniques with those of his predecessors.

8. Eric F. Goldman, *The Tragedy of Lyndon Johnson* (New York: A.A. Knopf, 1969), ch. 15, describes Johnson's manipulative responses to being beset by criticism over Vietnam. More recently, the New York Times, *The Pentagon Papers* (New York: Basic Books, 1971), chs. 6-7, has documented the devious manner in which the public was to be handled as the United States military involvement escalated.

9. TRB, *New Republic* (April 27, 1971). At least one editorial complained that President Nixon has met with the press corps only 17 times in 28 months, less than once every two months.

10. Moynihan, in his critique of the Press' handling of the Presidency, acknowledges that "in the most essential encounters between the President and the press, the advantage is with the former." He also concludes that the relationship between the two have grown so troubled most immediately because of the war in Vietnam, which involved "a massive deception of the American people by their government." Daniel P. Moynihan, "The Presidency and the Press," *Commentary* (March 1971).

11. Cooper, *Lost Crusade*, pp. 421-425; *The Pentagon Papers*, ch. 7; and Townsend Hoopes, *The Limits of Intervention* (New York: D. McKay Co., 1969), pp. 6-7. In spite of the concentration of control on such tactical matters at the White House, Cooper notes with regret that no one person, no "Mr. Vietnam," was ever designated to ensure a comprehensive grasp and coordination within the government.

12. Speech by Senator Symington, U.S. Congressional Record 117, no. 2 (2 March 1971), criticizes Kissinger and describes his apparatus. A fuller historical view is given in Robert H. Johnson, "The National Security Council: The Relevance of its Past to its Future," *Orbis* 13, no. 3 (Fall 1969). Senator Fulbright's resentment of the White House "superbureau" that is "shielded from Congress" is reported in the *New York Times*, 28 July 1971, p. 8.

13. Jacob K. Javits, "Congress in Foreign Relations," *Foreign Affairs* 48 (January 1970): 234.

14. U.S., Congress, Senate, Committee on Foreign Relations, *Security Agreements and Commitments Abroad*, 91st Cong., 2d sess., 21 December 1970.

15. The supportive reaction of the Supreme Court, the Congress, and the press to the publication of the secret Pentagon study of the Vietnam War seems to have pushed the Executive Branch into more rapid declassification of information and strengthened the hand of opponents of governmental secrecy. Since the Court decision, the Congress has received for the first time a breakdown of current military assistance grants by countries and an acknowledgment of CIA expenditures in Laos.

16. *Congressional Quarterly Weekly Report* 29, no. 7 (12 February 1971), lists the bills and resolutions to end the Indochina War and curb the war powers of the President which were introduced in the 92nd Congress. Subsequent hearings conducted by the Senate Foreign Relations Committee seem to be developing strong support for legislation setting a time limit on presidential dispatch of armed forces without specific Congressional authorization.

17. A notable example of this device is the series of Staff Reports entitled *Cambodia: May 1970*, and *Cambodia: December 1970*, written by two staff members and issued as Committee Prints. U.S., Senate, Committee on Foreign Relations, 91st Cong., 2d sess. More recently (August 3, 1971), the same staff issued a report on Laos in which the CIA publicly affirmed its military role for the first time.

18. Javits, *Congress . . .* , p. 227.

19. Cooper, *Lost Crusade . . .* , pp. 16-18. A year after World War II, the United States had but one consul and two vice consuls in the area. *No More Vietnams?: The War and the Future of American Foreign Policy*, Richard M. Pfeffer, ed., (New York: Harper & Row, 1968), p. 204.

20. A somewhat special example, Noam Chomsky, whose training was in linguistics, turned himself into a prolific writer-journalist on Indochina.

21. N. Chomsky, *At War With Asia* (New York: Pantheon Books, 1969).

22. Stanley Hoffmann indicts this phenomenon, the shorthand translation of hard facts into statistics, which we tried to use "in ignorance of the context" and with "excessive self-confidence." See, *No More Vietnams?*, p. 134; and Cooper, *Lost Crusade*, p. 422.

23. See *Pentagon Papers*, pp. 389, 516-517 for the changing viewpoint of John T. McNaughton, Assistant Secretary of Defense for International Security Affairs.

24. Richard J. Barnet, *Intervention and Revolution* (New York: World Publishing Co., 1968). See also A.M. Schlesinger's critique of Barnet's thesis in Pfeffer, *No More Vietnams?*, pp. 83-85. John K. Galbraith points to the problem

of "bureaucratic momentum" in his article, "The Plain Lessons of a Bad Decade," *Foreign Policy* (Winter 1970-71).

25. In 1971, applications by college graduates for civil service jobs were up 65 percent over the previous year, but many of these will draw the line at entering the Department of Defense. For summary impressions of the new generation, see Graham Allison, "Cool it: The Foreign Policy of Young America," *Foreign Policy* (Winter 1970-71): 144-160; and James A. Johnson, "The Coming Generation of Isolationists," *Foreign Affairs* (October 1970): 136-146.

26. *Diplomacy for the 1970s: A Program of Management for the Department of State*, Department of State Publication 8551 (Washington, D.C.: Government Printing Office, December 1970), pp. 268-269.

27. Adam Yarmolinsky, "The Military Establishment (or How Political Problems Become Military Problems)," *Foreign Policy* (Winter 1970-71).

28. Joseph Kraft, *Profiles in Power* (New York: The New American Library, 1966), ch. 14.

29. James C. Thomson, Jr. has discussed this issue as an "unprovable factor" in "How Could Vietnam Happen?" in *Who We Are: An Atlantic Chronicle of the United States in Vietnam 1966-1969*, edited by R. Manning and M. Janeway (Boston: Little Brown and Co., 1969). President Nixon's "pampering" of convicted Lieutenant Calley suggests how unprepared the United States public is to acknowledge the racist violence of its war.

30. Some civilian strategists (such as Albert Wohlstetter) have taken up the argument originally made by the Joint Chiefs of Staff in 1964 that the escalation of force applied to North Vietnam was so gradual that its coercive impact was dissipated by the enemy's opportunity to adjust to each step up the ladder. See *Pentagon Papers*, pp. 330, 354-355, 368-370.

31. Committee of Concerned Asian Scholars, *The Indochina Story* (New York: Bantam Books, 1970), p. 109. The Secretary of the Army testified to 10 to 15 percent hard drug addiction in the Army in Vietnam in May 1971. The following month the Army testing and amnesty program for heroin addiction seemed to cut down on its use in Vietnam.

32. Fred Gardner, "War and G.I. Morale," *New York Times*, 18 November 1970, 21 April 1971. "Fragging" refers to assaults with fragmentation grenades, often rolled under a tent flap.

33. Sidney Verba et al., "Public Opinion and the War in Vietnam," *American Political Science Review* (June 1967); and William R. Caspary, "The Mood Theory: A Study of Public Opinion and Foreign Policy," ibid. (June 1970).

34. September 1970, the month of the vote on the Hatfield-McGovern plan, a Gallup poll showed 55 percent favoring withdrawal by the end of 1971. In January 1971, 72 percent favored withdrawal before the end of the year, but in June the Senate defeated (42-55) a Hatfield plan to cut off funds for Vietnam at the year's end.

35. Harlon Hahn, "Correlates of Public Sentiments about War: Local Referenda on the Vietnam Issue," *American Political Science Review* (December 1970). This finding contrasts with that of Verba et al., *Opinion. . .*, who found no consistent relationship in polling data between social status and opinions on this issue.

36. *Gallup Opinion Index* (March 1971): 1, 10. Public approval of President Nixon's "handling of his job" declined from 56 to 50 percent during the month in which the Laos operation began and Americans by a 2-to-1 ratio thought the invasion would lengthen rather than shorten the war.

37. A short analysis of the antiwar protest in relation to other forms of protest is found in Jerome H. Skolnick, *The Politics of Protest* (New York: Clarion Book, 1969), a task force report to the National Commission on the Causes and Prevention of Violence. See also Arnold H. Miller, "Perceptions and Recommendations of Activists in the Vietnam Protest Movement," *Polity* (Spring 1971).

About the Contributors

David E. Brown: Analyst in Bureau of Intelligence and Research, Department of State, June 1970 to present. Fellow, John F. Kennedy School of Government, Harvard University, 1969-1970. Foreign Service Officer in South Vietnam, Department of State, 1965-1969.

MacAlister Brown: Associate Professor of Political Science, Williams College. Fulbright Lecturer in Public Administration, Nepal, 1968-69, and Budget Examiner, International Division, U.S. Bureau of the Budget, 1963-64. Contributor to *Asian Survey, Journal of Central European Affairs, Western Political Quarterly, Midwest Journal of Political Science* and *Nepal Review.*

Arthur Dommen: Bureau Chief for the *Los Angeles Times*, with extensive residence and research in East Asia. Author of *Conflict in Laos: The Politics of Neutralization* (Praeger, 1964; revised edition, summer 1971), and articles in *Asian Survey* and *Current History.*

Allan E. Goodman: Assistant Professor of Government and International Relations, Clark University. Author of *Politics in War: The Bases of Political Community in South Vietnam* (forthcoming), and studies on political development and internal politics of South Vietnam in *Asian Survey, Orbis, Economic Development and Cultural Change, Yale Review*, and *Pacific Affairs.*

Bernard K. Gordon: Chairman, Department of Political Science, University of New Hampshire. Formerly Southeast Asia Project Chairman, Research Analysis Corporation. Adjunct Professor, George Washington University, and Lecturer in Asian Studies at the School of Advanced International Studies, Johns Hopkins University. Author of *Toward Disengagement in Asia: A Strategy for American Foreign Policy* (Prentice-Hall, 1969), and *The Dimensions of Conflict in Southeast Asia* (Prentice-Hall, 1966), as well as numerous articles in scholarly journals.

Melvin Gurtov: Associate Professor of Political Science, University of California, Riverside. Staff member, Social Science Department, The RAND Corporation, from 1966-1971. Author of *The First Vietnam Crisis: Chinese Communist Strategy and United States Involvement, 1953-54* (Columbia University Press, 1967), *Southeast Asia Tomorrow: Problems and Prospects for U.S. Policy* (Johns Hopkins Press, 1970), *China and Southeast Asia—The Politics of Survival: A Study of Foreign Policy Interaction* (Lexington Books, D.C. Heath and Company, 1971), and *The Cultural Revolution in China*, with T. Robinson and others (University of California Press, 1971). Also contributed to several books on North Vietnam and China and to such publications as *Current History, China Quarterly, Pacific Affairs* and *Problems of Communism.*

Robert H. Johnson: Harvey Picker Professor of International Relations, Colgate University. Served on National Security Council staff from 1951-1962 and as member of Policy Planning Council, Department of State, specializing in the Far East, from 1962-1966. Author of "Vietnamization: Can It Work?" *Foreign Affairs*, July 1970, and articles on international relations in *World Politics, Orbis*, and *Journal of Conflict Resolution*.

Konrad Kellen: Staff member, Social Science Department, The RAND Corporation, since 1965. Author of studies on North Vietnamese and Viet Cong forces and also on NATO's political climate and tactical nuclear warfare. Served seven years as Chief of Radio Free Europe's Information Department and four years as Chief of the Broadcast Review Staff. Consultant to the Ford Foundation's Office of Policy and Planning. Has contributed to a variety of journals such as The *Reporter, The New Leader, Yale Review* and is author of a biography of Khrushchev (Praeger, 1961).

Donald Lancaster: Visiting Research Professor, Southeast Asian Studies Program, Cornell University. Member of Prince Sihanouk's staff for almost a decade, until 1969. Author of *The Emancipation of French Indochina* (Oxford University Press, 1961).

Milton Osborne: Associate Professor of History, Monash University (Australia) and Visiting Associate Professor, Cornell University. Australian Foreign Service Officer in Phnom Penh from 1959 to 1961, and a frequent researcher there during the 1960s. Author of *The French Presence in Cochinchina and Cambodia: Rule and Response (1859-1905)* (Cornell University Press, 1969), *Region of Revolt: Focus on Southeast Asia* (Pergamon Press, 1970; to be republished by Penguin Books, 1971). Contributor to such publications as *International Affairs, Journal of Asian Studies, Encyclopaedia Britannica,* and *Australian Outlook*.

Elizabeth Pond: Staff correspondent for *The Christian Science Monitor* in Tokyo. *Monitor* correspondent in Saigon in 1967 and 1969. Alicia Patterson Fellow in Saigon in 1969-1970. Winner of the Dumont Award for excellence in international journalism for 1968 coverage of Czechoslovakia.

William Turley: Assistant Professor of Government, Southern Illinois University, and Associate of the Center for Vietnamese Studies. Conducting research on civil-military relations in North Vietnam. Contributor to *Asian Survey*.

Joseph J. Zasloff: Professor of Political Science, University of Pittsburgh. Smith Mundt Professor of Political Science, University of Saigon, Vietnam, 1959-60. Co-author of *North Vietnam and the Pathet Lao: Partners in the Struggle of Laos* (Harvard University Press, 1970). Author of numerous Rand studies, and articles in such journals as *Asian Survey, Pacific Affairs* and *Commentary*.

Index